The Com...

Letting
Property

The Complete Guide to
Letting Property

7th edition

LIZ HODGKINSON

KOGAN
PAGE

Author's note

For simplicity and clarity, I have throughout referred to landlords as 'he' and tenants as 'she'. Although obviously landlords can be either male or female, all laws on the subject relate to 'landlord and tenant' and not 'landlady and tenant'. Also, the term 'landlady' has other connotations. Use of the female pronoun to distinguish 'tenant' is simply to avoid using 'he/she' or any other such clumsy nomenclature in the main text, where I have referred to tenant in the singular. No sexism is intended in either case.

Publisher's note

Every possible effort has been made to ensure that the information contained in this book is accurate at the time of going to press, and the publisher and author cannot accept responsibility for any errors or omissions, however caused. No responsibility for loss or damage occasioned to any person acting, or refraining from action, as a result of the material in this publication can be accepted by the editor, the publisher or the author.

First published 2000
Second edition 2002
Third edition 2003
Fourth edition 2004
Fifth edition 2005
Sixth edition 2006
Seventh edition 2008

120 Pentonville Road
London N1 9JN
United Kingdom
www.koganpage.com

© Liz Hodgkinson, 2000, 2002, 2003, 2004, 2005, 2006, 2008

The right of Liz Hodgkinson to be identified as the author of this work has been asserted by her in accordance with the Copyright, Designs and Patents Act 1988.

British Library Cataloguing in Publication Data

A CIP record for this book is available from the British Library.

ISBN   978 0 7494 5220 9

Typeset by Saxon Graphics Ltd, Derby
Printed and bound in Great Britain by Thanet Press Ltd, Margate

Having the correct Landlords Insurance

Buying a buy-to-let property as an investment is the start of a journey. To make that journey easier one of the most important steps is to make sure that you have the right landlords insurance in place. If you own a buy-to-let property you might be surprised to know that a conventional home insurance policy is unlikely to be adequate for your purposes.

You could probably get an ordinary insurer to provide cover on a private dwelling let furnished or unfurnished, but it is probably better to go for a specialist cover which will include some aspects that you may not even have thought of. An ordinary household insurance would be limited and could exclude some of the most important "add-ons" which a landlord's insurance policy would include.

When searching for the best landlords insurance, you should make sure the policy includes cover for the following....

Loss of rent

Most household insurance is likely to include cover for the cost of alternative accommodation for the insured, but a formal landlord insurance policy will put this on a commercial footing. This will mean that you can continue to receive rent during the time that the premises are uninhabitable as the result of an insured event like a fire or flood.

You will also be able to claim for the additional costs associated with providing alternative accommodation for tenants, and for storing furniture for up to a year. This is providing that the cost does not exceed about a third of the sum insured on the building (the limit is different for commercial property or the commercial part of a multi-use building). This cover is available even if it is not your building that is affected, but you and your tenants are denied access as the result of damage to adjoining premises.

Liability

A property owners' policy will include full employers' and public liability cover but, unlike domestic insurance, it also covers legal representations at any hearings associated with Health and Safety legislation.

Wrongful arrest

An area that many business people may not consider – particularly in respect of property ownership – is the potential liability for wrongful arrest. If you detain someone on suspicion of theft or damaging your property, for example, you could be sued for malicious arrest or prosecution. Cover should protect you against costs and awards up to at least £25,000.

Automatic cover for additional premises

One of the potential problems associated with building a property portfolio is that you could make a quick purchase without remembering to arrange the necessary insurance. Property owners' insurance policies will usually include a provision that, provided you let the insurance company know within 90 days (and pay any required additional premium) they will include any new properties you buy, up to a set limit (perhaps £500,000) automatically.

They will usually automatically increase the sum insured to cover the value of any improvements you make to the property (again giving you 90 days to tell them about it) up to 10% of the value of the premises as a whole (usually subject to a maximum value of £500,000).

Some words of warning

It is important to be aware that some terms and conditions are less generous than a standard domestic insurance policy. In particular, the level of excess may well be higher under a Property Owners' policy.

In addition, the position if you fail to insure your property sufficiently to cover the cost of rebuilding can be far more onerous. This can result in "average" – that is a proportionate reduction in the amount of any claim to reflect the degree of underinsurance – being applied to each property individually. So if you have five shops in your portfolio and one is underinsured, then even if the overall sum insured is adequate to cover a loss, average would apply if that property were to be damaged.

Fortunately for those in the buy-to-let market, this does not normally apply to private dwellings, where there is no element of commercial occupancy.

If you are building a property portfolio, or have already done so, why not ask Alan Boswell Group for details of Landlords Property Owners' insurance? Contact Alan Boswell Group's landlord insurance experts on **01603 216399**, alternatively visit **www.alanboswell.com/landlords** for further information.

Market your Property to millions and find Tenants fast.

 **Discount Letting**

Tenant Find Service Only £59

36+ Million views from partner sites

No fees passed on to the Tenant

Your Property Shown on the
UK's Leading Property Portals

Full Management Service Only 6%

Call **020 8697 0984**   www.discountletting.co.uk

Whether your property is part of the Full Management Service or our
Tenant Find Service, every landlords rental property is presented in the
same way to millions of potential tenants across a vast internet resource.

Contents

Stronger together

With a long-established and reliable service, HomeLet has the strength to reinforce your property investment.

Through our network of professional letting agents we've been offering first rate support to the letting industry for almost two decades.

Ask your letting agent about HomeLet's range of insurance, referencing and Rent Guarantee solutions or call us on 0845 117 6000 or visit homelet.co.uk

HomeLet™

TAKING THE RISK OUT OF PROPERTY RENTAL

The strength to reinforce your property investment

As a property investor, you'll know there are potential pitfalls around every corner. That's why it's vital you choose the right partner to help manage your investment – one who can give you the right advice and help you choose the right tenant.

By selecting an authorised HomeLet letting agent you will have access to market-leading referencing solutions together with insurance policies which guarantee your rental income should the worst happen, giving you real peace of mind.

HomeLet is the UK's largest tenant referencing and insurance provider for the lettings industry and offers landlords a wide range of products through its network of almost 5,500 letting agents across the UK, meaning you can access a full range of products from letting agents in almost every high street.

The UK has seen a massive increase in the number of property investors in recent years, particularly in the buy-to-let market. However in the current financial climate it is more important than ever to protect your income, whoever your tenants are.

HomeLet works in partnership with its network of professional letting agents to offer you a wide range of tenant referencing products, enabling you to make a truly informed decision when selecting a tenant. And as experts in their field, in 2007 alone HomeLet completed approximately 350,000 tenant references.

The services HomeLet can offer include checking the tenants' credit worthiness; ensuring there is no history of past defaults; obtaining references from their previous landlord or managing agent; and contacting their employers to check their salary will cover the rent.

Taking the risk out of renting to overseas tenants

The UK has seen a significant increase in the number of migrant workers. According to a recent ARLA (Association of Residential Lettings Agents) review, the number of buy-to-let investors reporting a significant impact on the rental market due to immigration has increased by nearly 10% since 2006. In response to this, HomeLet can also offer a fast and reliable International referencing and Rent Guarantee service, which means you can make an informed decision about a prospective tenant's suitability whatever their nationality.

Rental income guaranteed

Even with the most thorough background checks any tenant can fall on hard times. In fact, most rent defaults occur because a tenant's circumstances change – owing to redundancy, the breakdown of a relationship or long-term sickness – rather than a refusal to pay the rent. As a landlord you may be sympathetic, but you still need to pay your mortgage.

HomeLet's Rent Guarantee and Legal Expenses policies can include rental payments for up to 12 months, with 50% of the rent paid for up to three months after vacant possession has been obtained whilst you find a new tenant. It also includes full legal cover for eviction costs and cover can be obtained for any breach of tenancy.

In the last two years alone HomeLet have paid over £4 million in rent guarantee claims. This is money many landlords simply can't afford to lose.

Protect yourself against the unexpected

In addition to HomeLet's extensive range of referencing and Rent Guarantee products, your letting agent can also offer an outstanding range of specialist buildings and contents insurance products designed specifically for investment property owners and tenants.

The range of products includes a Comprehensive Buildings insurance policy which not only protects you against all the things you would normally expect, but which is also there to help with all the things you don't expect, such as loss of income and re-letting costs, protecting you, your tenants and employees, cover whilst your property is empty, changes in tenants and the rebuilding of your property following loss or damage.

Making your portfolio easier to manage

And for those landlords with a portfolio of investment properties, HomeLet provide an insurance policy so that all your properties* can be covered by one single policy; this allows you not only to save significantly on individual policies, but also to have just one payment and one renewal date.

For additional peace of mind, all HomeLet policies can also include accidental damage cover, and for those who don't want any unexpected surprises there is a nil excess option which means you won't have to pay a penny if you make a claim.

Alongside your buildings insurance HomeLet can also offer a range of contents policies, whether you let your property furnished or unfurnished, plus an invaluable 24/7 Emergency Assistance Service, so if your tenant has an emergency at any time of the day of the night, it won't be you they disturb.

In-house claims service

Furthermore, in the event that you do need to make a claim HomeLet has an in-house Legal and Claims department which means they process all of the claims themselves and provide a much faster and more efficient service than many of their competitors.

So, if you're considering becoming a landlord, don't go it alone. HomeLet have a national network of letting agents who, working together, can help you to avoid many of the pitfalls of being a landlord and maximise the returns from your investment property.

Ask your letting agent about HomeLet's range of insurance, referencing and Rent Guarantee solutions.

* Up to a maximum of 10 properties

About this book

When the first edition of this book was published in 2000, Buy-to-Let was still a gentle little cottage industry, very much in its infancy. In just a few short years, it has matured to become both highly professional and highly competitive. The big boys with big money and clever marketing campaigns have moved in, and the term Buy-to-Let has entered the language.

Buy-to-Let continues to grow fast, with up to half of all newbuild apartments and houses now being sold to Buy-to-Let investors. During the first half of 2007, 172,000 new Buy-to-Let mortgages were created, making the growth far stronger than in the general mortgage market.

In 2002, Buy-to-Let mortgages accounted for just three per cent of the total mortgage market; by 2007, this had crept up to 10 per cent.

To give an idea of how quickly this sector continues to grow, there are now more than a million Buy-to-Let mortgages outstanding, with a total value of over £108 billion.

And remember – we are talking here just about those investors who have taken out mortgages, as there are no reliable figures available for cash buyers. But very many Buy-to-Let investors do pay cash – so the total value of the current UK market could easily be twice that accounted for in the mortgage figures.

So popular has Buy-to-Let become that nowadays almost everybody who purchases a property also asks themselves: should I go for a Buy-to-Let as well?

Buying property to rent out is commonly seen as a safe alternative investment to stocks and shares and pension schemes. In fact, the received wisdom from almost every quarter is that with bricks and mortar, you just can't lose. All the fast-proliferating companies offering mortgages, property investor courses, Buy-to-Let packages and so on make it sound so easy. But of course the advice and services offered by these companies, although no doubt excellent in many cases, are not impartial. They all want your business and your money. And that is why this book is more essential than ever before, for both the novice and the experienced property investor. As the market expands, so do the traps for the unwary.

But at the same time as the rental market keeps growing – and some experts predict that by 2020, over 20 per cent of properties in the United Kingdom will be rented rather than owned – the government is stepping in and interfering ever more in landlord and tenant matters.

The Housing Act 2004 has implemented a whole host of new regulations, many of which are difficult for both new and experienced landlords to understand fully. And yet there are severe penalties for infringing all of these new laws, which are still, at the time of writing, unfolding.

These new laws, which cover health and safety issues, the thorny question of tenants' deposits, overcrowding, licensing and energy efficiency, all mean that the business of being a landlord is becoming ever more bogged down in rules and regulations.

There is much more to know about the apparently simple matter of renting out properties to others than in the old days, and all will be explained in this new edition.

On the other hand, the publicity that these new laws have attracted has made ever more people consider being landlords or – as we are now grandly called – Buy-to-Let investors.

To my mind, property is the most exciting and rewarding investment you can make. When you get it right, it is also relatively low risk, in spite of the large sums of money involved. The trick is to get it right.

This fully updated new edition of *The Complete Guide to Letting Property* shows you how to make a success of buying to let, and how to enjoy the many pleasures of being a modern property investor and landlord.

The National voice for landlords

SUPPORT | ADVICE | TRAINING | REPRESENTATION

SUPPORTING & ADVISING LOCAL LANDLORDS

The National Federation of Residential Landlords (NFRL) is a large professional landlords' organisation representing thousands of landlords across the UK, dedicated to protecting and representing the interests of private landlords.

We have been protecting and advising landlords for over 30 years, guiding our landlord members through any new legislation and working to provide them with a valuable knowledge base to assist them in developing and advancing their rental business.

One of our most valued services for members is our professional 'Helpline Service' giving FREE advice to members though our experienced helpline staff, landlords, solicitors and tax advisors. This is an extremely useful and immediate service which helps landlords through difficulties they are having with either understanding the implications of any new legislation or providing a way to discuss dealing with problem tenants. Our skilled advisors are able to give direct advice and also guide landlords to where they can access further information sources, often pointing them to our website, where we have a full range of comprehensive information, guidance notes, forms, tenancy agreements & notices all available for free downloading.

We now also provide a range of training courses at a discounted rate for members on topics from Local Housing Allowance, Possessions to Inventories and also more general courses like the 'Survival Guide to being a Landlord'. These courses offer more detailed advice on topics that are of special interest to both members and other interested landlords.

Our magazine *Successful Renting* is a quarterly publication, packed full of useful information and tips for landlords – with plenty of good practical advice, basic business information, updates on financial, tax and law matters and, of course, updates on what is happening in the NFRL with the latest on member benefits, training courses and events.

We also organise branch meetings in various regions throughout the country, but primarily in London and the South of England. These meetings are where local landlords can gather, listen to presentations on topics of interest and of course network. This forms a key ingredient in the success of our organisation with local landlords finding it incredibly useful getting together and discussing important issues face to face, with other landlords, in this type of environment.

We also offer our members a range of discounts from discounted buildings & contents insurance, full tenant referencing service at a discount, a competitive rental guarantee service and now Energy Performance Certificates for residential lettings, as well as an increasing number of member benefits.

We actively represent our landlords when we feel it necessary to do so, and very much value the support that a growing membership base provides us. We are able to represent landlords locally at local government level through our active branch network of Chairs and their committees. We have a representative from the NFRL on all major government policy steering groups, to be a voice for our members, and to have the opportunity to inform, shape policy and, more critically, respond to issues on a national government level.

We are very proud to have our own national conference, which we have held with great success for the past 10 years. Here we invite key individuals from our industry to speak – again to inform our members and keep them up to date with industry matters.

Every member is important to us, and as a member you really do have access to a wealth of information, advice and support to help you to succeed as a landlord in today's competitive, changing and challenging market.

We hope that you would like to join us and take advantage of our membership. If you would like to become a member you can join through our website **www.nfrl.co.uk** or by calling us on **01273 423295**.

We are giving all readers of the *Complete Guide to Letting Property* a joining offer of 15 months NFRL membership for the price of 12 months. Just quote this reference CGLP3FM01 to be able to enjoy your readers offer and start benefiting from our valuable landlords support and advice service.

NFRL
National Federation of
Residential Landlords

Introduction

A (very) short history of rented property

From medieval times until the end of the First World War, around 90 per cent of property in the United Kingdom was rented. Buying your own place did not become widespread until the 1920s, when the growth of friendly societies and building societies enabled ordinary people to borrow money to buy their own, usually extremely modest, homes. This development meant that large numbers of people could finally escape the clutches of greedy, grasping landlords.

The growth of social housing at the same time shrank the private rented sector even more. Old-style renting was given its final death-blow by a series of Rent Acts which protected tenants from eviction and rent increases.

Because rents for protected tenants were so low – as little as £6 a week as late as the 1980s – and could not be increased, what little remained of the private rented sector was, by the end of the 1980s, the utmost in undesirability. Nobody wanted to be a landlord when tenants could not be evicted, and nobody wanted to rent if they could possibly afford to buy.

Then in 1989 a new Housing Act introduced the concept of the Assured Shorthold Tenancy. This was a legally binding contract intended to make the private rented sector fairer for both landlords and tenants, and bring more rented properties onto the market. The new contract gave existing and prospective landlords powers to evict unsatisfactory tenants and also to charge market rents. As a result, the private rented sector began to rise from the ashes, and renting gradually lost its former stigma.

The other factor to revolutionize rental properties in the United Kingdom was the introduction of the Buy-to-Let scheme in 1996. This made it possible to obtain a mortgage especially devised for the investment landlord. Previously, lenders did not allow you to rent out a mortgaged property, and money for investment properties had to be borrowed at punitive rates.

The Buy-to-Let scheme has been so phenomenally successful that ever more people are now taking the plunge and deciding to become investment landlords. As a result, rented accommodation has become both extremely smart and highly desirable. Because there are now so many lovely properties available, renting is becoming chic again and in some situations can be a smarter option than buying.

Over the past few years, the lettings industry has become mature, sophisticated and mainstream. At the same time, the industry remains unregulated, although whether that is a plus or a minus depends on your particular politics and outlook.

What we can say is that the private rented sector is expanding all the time, with up to half of all new units in apartment blocks now being bought by investors to rent out. Ever more people are deciding to become property investors and landlords, as other investments begin to look increasingly shaky and uncertain.

I believe that it is exciting and challenging to be a landlord in today's dynamic, ever-changing rented market. There are many options available, many ways to be a property investor. You can decide to rent out just one property, or get the bug and build up a property portfolio. You can let out rooms in your own house, become a social landlord, rent out holiday apartments or properties abroad. You can rent out a caravan or mobile home, or take in paying guests. You can use up some spare cash or savings to buy your investment, or you can purchase with a Buy-to-Let mortgage. And if being a modern landlord is not an automatic licence to print money, it is certainly possible to do very nicely out of the business of renting property to others.

But is the lettings game for you? Read on and find out.

1 Is letting for you?

As we have seen in the Introduction, the era of the private, small-time landlord is with us once again and we are back to the days when it is possible to make a useful income from renting out properties to tenants.

But is letting property really as simple and foolproof as it is often made out to be? In one sense of the word, yes. Anybody at all, provided they have the money or are able to borrow it, can buy an investment property and then rent it out, or attempt to. You do not need any particular training or qualifications and, these days, not even the ready money. So long as you have enough for the deposit and can satisfy the income requirements of lenders, you can now get a specialized mortgage for the purpose of buying an investment property.

So far, so good. But precisely because so many small investors are now entering the private rented sector, the market is becoming ever more competitive, streamlined and professional. Tenants can now pick and choose, and in the lettings game, as with any other type of commercial enterprise, the bungling amateur risks making a loss rather than a profit.

Where property is concerned, you are talking about very large sums of money indeed. Even the most modest investment property will cost at least £65,000. If you are considering signing up for a Buy-to-Let mortgage, you can put another £60,000 on top of that for the interest repayments on your loan.

By contrast, you can buy a car or a computer for £1,000 or less and still pick up a reasonable artwork for a few hundred pounds. If you make a loss on these, it is hardly a major financial setback. But if you buy the wrong property at the wrong price at the wrong time and in the wrong place, you can end up with very considerable losses indeed.

Lettings expert Jason Cliffe, of the Johnson Wood lettings agency, said: 'We are always prepared to give advice to potential landlords but very often, they don't listen to a word we say. Then they wonder why they can't let the property they may have bought and refurbished at enormous expense.

'There's some folklore', he added, 'which says that any old property can be rented out to somebody. If that was ever true, it's certainly not the case now. Not only do you have to buy the right property, but you have to be the right kind of person to be a landlord. As we have learnt from our own experience as letting agents, not everybody has, or can acquire, the qualities needed.'

What it takes to be a landlord

So what are these qualities? Over a number of years of being a landlord myself, talking to other landlords, and spending many hours gleaning wisdom from letting agents, I would say that in order to be successful at the lettings game, you need to possess the following attributes:

- First and foremost, you must absolutely love property, and have a real 'feel' for it.

- You must be businesslike and efficient.

- You should possess people and management skills.

- You should have a problem-solving turn of mind.

- It helps to have an extrovert, rather than introvert, type of personality.

We'll take each of these points in turn and explain why each is essential for success in the modern, highly professional and competitive lettings market.

You must have a 'feel' for property

One of the first rules of financial success is: when thinking of something that might make you money, choose something in which you already have a natural interest. Why? Because if you are already interested you will, almost without realizing it, have developed and built up a considerable level of expertise. If not, you will constantly be at the mercy of those who have, and they will be able to run rings round you.

To take a personal example, it would never do for me to invest in the computer world, simply because computers bore me to death. Although I know there are vast fortunes to be made, as people like Bill Gates and Clive Sinclair have conclusively proved, I cannot readily understand these machines. I have to use computers, but for me they are a necessary evil. I would never willingly attend a computer exhibition, and shudder each time I pass a computer shop. Therefore, for me to invest in computers would be like swimming in shark-infested seas. I would not even begin to know the difference between a bargain and overpriced rubbish.

Similarly, I am not remotely interested in cars. Again, I have to use them, but in the four years that I have owned my present vehicle, I have never once opened either the bonnet or the instruction manual. It has simply never occurred to me to do either. Yet a car-mad friend actually drools over car engines, and slavers over car magazines, hardly able to wait until the new ones come out. Not surprisingly, this friend has been successfully dealing in cars as a sideline for many years, and always drives something a little bit special, a little bit different. This same friend, though, has always made disastrous deals on property.

I'm not interested in antiques either, another area where it is possible for the canny to make a killing. I hate antiques fairs and am never tempted to browse in antique shops. Again, a friend who finds antique and junk shops irresistible has made some very useful sums from buying and selling junk-shop finds.

Because of my total lack of interest in these three commodities, it would be financial suicide for me to invest money in any of them with a view to increasing my capital.

Stocks and shares are another area in which I have no natural interest, so I leave those well alone as well.

When it comes to property, this is a different matter altogether. Ever since I was a small child, I have been fascinated by houses and homes. I used to love my doll's house and was always rearranging furniture and fittings in it. (If you think about it, buying investment properties is only an adult extension of organizing your doll's house.) I also used to love designing and decorating my bedroom and my student bedsit, seeing how nice I could make them on nil resources.

As an adult, I welcome the challenge of turning a horrible tip into a wonderful living space, and wherever I go I embarrass my companions by peering into people's windows to glimpse their choice of interior design and to get ideas from them. Also, whenever I pass an estate agent's window, wherever I happen to be, I automatically glance at the prices and properties on offer, much as my antique-loving friend cannot see an antique shop anywhere in the world without going inside. An exciting weekend for me would be one spent viewing potential properties, always asking the important questions: could I live in this myself? If not, why not?

I am also a sucker for property and interiors magazines and always have a huge stack of them in my home. I find those endless, widely derided house makeover shows on television compulsive viewing as well.

I have also been quite successful at buying and selling my own homes. All have sold at a considerable profit, and most were in terrible condition when purchased. But because I could see their potential, I was willing to take the plunge. It is a mistake, however, to imagine that because house prices generally rise, you can never make a loss. I have also been very successful at buying properties to let, even though I knew nothing whatever when I began.

But not everybody can spot a good location, or assess a good price. Nor does everybody have good taste in decoration. Some people have an unerring instinct for the naff, the gimcrack and the plain ugly. So if, on looking back at your personal property purchases, you have tended to make a loss, then maybe investing in rental flats is not for you.

Although big-time investment landlords are extremely hard-headed financiers who, very often, do not ever see the rental properties they purchase, most people are simply not like that, and any investment has a degree of emotion tied up in it. In order to become a successful landlord on a small scale – and the vast majority of private landlords own four or less properties – it helps if you have already had extensive, and successful, experience of buying, selling and refurbishing homes. If, by contrast, you have lived in the same house for several decades and have hardly touched it in all that time, becoming an investment landlord may not be the best choice for you. In my own case, when I had a little bit of spare money to invest, putting it into property seemed a sensible choice.

A love of homes and interiors is an essential consideration as, these days at least, the market is constantly changing and has to be carefully watched all the time. If you have already got your hand in, then you will be in a better position to make the fast decisions that may be needed in a constantly fluctuating market.

For example, a particular property may let extremely well for a year or two, then you cannot seem to find tenants for love nor money. Why? It may be that a large organization, employing many hundreds of people looking for temporary accommodation, has just closed down. It may be that more people in the area are now buying rather than renting. It could be that just too many rental properties have come on the market for the number of tenants available. When something like this happens, it may be wise to sell your property and use the money to buy another one in a better area for renting. In one sense, investment property has to be considered almost as a share certificate, rather than a once in a lifetime, permanent purchase. You must always be prepared to buy or sell.

Looking good

It will be difficult to keep your eye on a changing market unless you have a natural interest in the matter. If you have good taste and enjoy harmonious surroundings, you also put yourself ahead in today's market. Present-day tenants tend to be extremely fussy and turn their noses up at rental properties that are decorated in the wrong colours and have the wrong curtains or carpets for their particular taste. All lettings agencies report that, even nowadays, when so much advice is readily on offer, properties that gladden the heart are pitifully few and far between.

'So many landlords simply have no idea', said Catherine Cockroft, Lettings Director at the upmarket London agency Aylesford. 'I often view properties which landlords tell me have only just been refurbished, and my heart sinks when I discover that there is a different carpet in every room, gaudy colours on the walls and unmatching sofas and chairs. I know that my tenants simply won't take such a place, however new the furnishings and however expensive the refurbishment programme.'

A vitally important question to ask when considering embarking on investment properties is: am I reasonably competent at DIY? Although you do not have to be a professional-standard painter and decorator yourself, it certainly helps if you have some knowledge of building and decorating. Again, if you have refurbished many of your own homes in the past, you will have already built up valuable expertise. Unless you are aware of short-cuts and cheap but effective ways around property problems, you risk spending a fortune on refurbishment, money that you cannot hope to recoup in rents for many years.

One investment property I bought had a bathroom that, although new and smart, screamed bad taste. It had shiny black and gold tiles, a black vinyl floor and cheap orange pine bath panel, cupboards and units. The whole thing was a mess and I knew that the chic, smart type of tenant I was interested in attracting would not go for it. What to do? It would have cost well into four figures to retile the walls and replace the flooring, so instead I put up a pair of exotically printed black, orange and red curtains, painted all the nasty cheap pine eggshell black, and put in black towels and a black bathmat. The result was that my hideous bathroom looked like a designer statement, as if it was all intended, and I ended up spending around £100 instead of several thousand pounds. My tenants, I'm glad to say, loved it!

Another flat I bought had a hideous bathroom suite which, as well as being old and stained, was a livid pink. The bathroom also had pink tiles, a sticky pink nylon carpet and pink walls. A pink rose-patterned blind was at the window. With such a bathroom, the flat was quite unlettable, but again, installing a new one would cost thousands. In this case, I cleaned the stained bath by filling it with bleach and leaving it overnight, and painted the walls aqua. The skirting board was painted a navy blue that exactly matched the cheap cord navy carpet I put down, and a smart navy-blue Roman blind with rope-effect edging went at the window. I put in dark blue and pink towels, and painted the cupboards navy and white. The finished bathroom had a 1930s ocean liner effect (a few large posters of liners also went up) and looked smart and clean. This refurbishment cost less than £300.

A few years later, however, these cheaply toshed properties had to be given a proper facelift – brand new kitchen, brand new bathroom, new flooring and new curtains or blinds. Walls had to be replastered as well, at great expense.

Rental properties are much like any other product in that they may give perfectly good service for a number of years, after which the full works are required.

All properties, whether rented or owned, require regular maintenance and updating, and this is where bricks and mortar investments differ radically from, say, stocks and shares.

If you rent out property to others, you have to be prepared for this eventuality, and not be so cash-strapped that you cannot afford to carry out necessary improvements, renovations and replacements.

Appliances such as cookers, fridges, washing machines and showers will also need replacing from time to time, and all these cost.

Tim Hyatt, Lettings Director of Knight Frank, advises: 'Never overstretch yourself so that you cannot afford to carry out improvements, as then your investment will suffer.' Tim could have added that also, these days no reputable agent will take on a tired and dated property. And if you have a mortgage, you will almost certainly be required to use an agent according to the terms of the mortgage. If you decide to rent it out privately, you will probably find somebody prepared to take it. But letting agents will not consider properties that do not meet the standards that their tenants expect.

Sometimes you can posh up cheaply and sometimes you can't – and the trick is to know when a 'nip and tuck' will do and when the property needs an extreme makeover.

Eventually, all properties will need an extreme makeover, depending on how long you keep them in your portfolio.

In the cases where the refurbishment cost a matter of a few hundred, I did it myself, but when I had to replace an entire bathroom, I used professionals. Clearly, the more you can do yourself, the quicker your property will come into profit, but at the same time the place should not look botched and amateurish, and I would not advise messing around with plumbing and electrical items yourself. These highly skilled and potentially dangerous jobs always need experts.

Today's discerning tenants appreciate clean, trendy designer furniture and, to get this look, it will save you a lot of money if you can face going to Ikea, or similar furniture warehouses, and assembling flatpack furniture yourself. When equipping an investment property, you have to know by some kind of sixth sense where you have to spend and where you can safely economize. I know that a cheap Ikea coffee table, costing perhaps £50, does the job just as well as an expensive antique or hardwood one. But I also know, or at least have learnt, that you simply cannot get away with providing tenants with an exhausted, clapped-out sofa. Although sofas and chairs do not have to be top of the range, they do have to look new and be comfortable.

Tables, kitchen chairs – in fact anything that can be painted or covered – can be cheap and cheerful, but the bed, if one is provided, should be smart and newly bought, not salvaged from a junk shop or car boot sale.

When embarking on investment properties you have to know by instinct whether a bleak-looking flat can become a dream home by the simple addition of a large green plant in the corner, or by rearrangement of the furniture. Arnaud Cheung, Director of Short Lets for Hamptons International, said: 'In one flat we viewed, the place looked totally different with some magazines on the coffee table and a big vase of fresh flowers at the window. These little touches can make all the difference between a property being instantly lettable and being on our books for a longer period. Even something apparently minor, such as the landlord providing a Tenant's File, containing instructions, guarantees, useful phone numbers, local restaurants and so on, can ensure that a property is instantly let, as it shows that the landlord cares.

'But so many landlords', he added, 'just never think of things like that. You can't just be after the money, but have to give that little bit over and above the basic minimum to be successful.'

You must be businesslike and efficient

In the lettings business, it is essential to be able to move quickly, and to be able to have all the important paperwork readily to hand. (And don't be under any false impression: landlord and tenant transactions generate far more paperwork than you would have ever thought possible.) As a landlord, you will be responsible for preparing the inventory, for checking the tenancy agreement or contract, for repairs and for informing the utilities companies of incoming and outgoing tenants. If you have a leasehold flat, you may also have to deal with managing agents, Residents' Associations, freeholders, service charges and levies. There will, in addition, be tax and accountancy matters to deal with, solicitors, local boroughs, and possibly County Courts if things go wrong. And each one produces its own mountain of paperwork.

So, if you feel you have the property interest and expertise to become a successful landlord, you now also need to know whether you are efficient and organized enough. Answer the following questions to discover your efficiency rating:

1. When receiving potentially stressful or tedious mail, such as bank and credit card statements, tax returns and so on, do you open and deal with them at once, or put them unopened in a drawer where they risk being forgotten?

2. Do you have an efficient filing system for your domestic bills and important documents, so that you can instantly retrieve them?
3. When there are boring jobs around the house that need attention, such as a leaking tap, a patch of damp or faulty wiring, can you shut your mind to them, or do you deal with the problems at once?
4. Do you follow up telephone calls, enquiries and so on right away or leave them for days on end?
5. Do you keep your accounts tidily and efficiently, or are they always in a terrible mess?
6. Do you find that domestic administration, such as paying gas, electricity and telephone bills, comes easily to you or gets on top of you? For landlords, this kind of stuff multiplies a millionfold, and the more properties you have, the more you will have to handle this kind of detail.
7. Are you always losing things like keys and important telephone numbers, or are they always to hand?

If you can answer a confident 'yes' to all of these questions, then you are halfway towards being a successful landlord. You really do have to be orderly. Letting property is not for the dizzy, chaotic person. In my own case, such efficiency did not come easily or naturally, but I soon learnt the hard way and now have separate, easily accessible colour-coded files for each of my properties and spare sets of keys where I can find them when needed. You would not believe the number of times that tenants lose their keys and can't get into their property. Often the lettings agency does not keep a spare set, and even when it does, tenants tend to lock themselves out at midnight or three in the morning, rather than when agencies might be open.

Apart from making life easier, efficiency and a good business sense will recommend you to lettings agencies. All have their 'white' and 'black' lists, and if you are blacklisted, you may discover they are unwilling to deal with you. Also, those people who are known to be good landlords tend to attract better, higher-paying tenants.

You should possess people and management skills

If you are, or ever have been, on the receiving end of glossy brochures from lettings agencies, you will notice that they all stress one thing above all else, and that is that 'we are in the business of people, rather than property'.

Because as a landlord you are involved in providing that most essential service of all – a roof over somebody's head – you cannot leave out the personal element. If you are a pleasant person to deal with, if you have an instinctive under-standing of what a tenant might need, and possess enough empathy to put yourself in the position of a tenant, then you will race ahead in this business.

People working as estate agents and lettings agents learn to be pleasant, however they might be feeling, and they are also, in the main, in professions where a smart appearance is still considered essential. A tenant who is about to hand over an extremely large sum of money to a landlord (and to a tenant, all sums paid in rent are enormous) will be happier when dealing with a sociable, easy kind of personality than somebody who is difficult, defensive or bullying. The landlord–tenant relationship has always been a particularly difficult one to handle, which is why there are so many laws and Acts of Parliament on the matter. Landlords have a reputation for always complaining about their tenants, and tenants have an equal reputation for complaining about their landlords. In fact, it is almost a *sine qua non* of being a tenant that you complain endlessly about the landlord. Where money changes hands on such a personal matter as a home, there is always plenty of scope for misunderstanding, argu-ments and threatening behaviour.

All professional agencies know that the relationship between tenant and landlord is a tricky one to get absolutely right, and their business is to put some crucial distance between the two. But however great the distance, there is always a possibility that you will have direct contact with your tenant.

The skill lies in being neither too friendly nor too cold. All lettings agencies are adamant that the great majority of problems arise when the landlord and tenant become too friendly. 'The friendlier at the start, the more acrimonious at the finish,' pointed out Jennifer Reigate, a professional inventory clerk. 'My heart always sinks when I hear either a landlord or a tenant say they get on famously with each other, as I know that is going to create problems later.'

Letting property is both intensely personal and a business run for profit. The secret is to be pleasant but not over-friendly, and to have as little to do with the tenant as possible once the formalities have been completed. It is not a good idea to appear ruthless, in the mistaken impression that you are being professional, and it is certainly a grave mistake to treat the tenant as a close personal friend.

The best way to look at the relationship is that of slight professional acquaintances, or neighbours. There is nothing wrong with exchanging a few friendly words with your tenant if you happen to pass her in the street, but it is not a good idea to invite her in to dinner. There should not be any scope for either side to take advantage.

How do you know whether you have the requisite people skills? If you are in a management position at work, where you have to handle many disparate individuals, or if you have kept many friends over a long period of time, then you most probably do possess people skills, although you may not be aware of it. It is an advantage to be of an equable, optimistic turn of mind, as there are many ups and downs in this game.

Relationships established in this business can become very close for a short time, and in this they can be compared to relationships with people you meet on holiday, where you can be extremely friendly, even intimate, for a week or two, and then they walk out of your lives for ever.

Arnaud Cheung took a physics degree at London University and originally had no intention of becoming an estate agent. But now he says: 'After graduating, I realized I was not a natural physicist, and much preferred dealing with people.' His instinct was correct, as three years after joining his first agency, he became a director.

As an absentee landlord, you will, with any luck, not have to have all that much to do with your tenant. But you will still have to deal with agencies, officials, inventory clerks and so on – and in a business where there is so much margin for error, so much to go wrong, those possessing people skills will find the whole thing so much less daunting.

If you are considering letting rooms in your own home, or renting out a flat or bedsit in your house, then you will inevitably have much more contact with your tenants. Not all of these may be people you would naturally choose as friends, and the more you can remain pleasant but detached, like the best hotel managers, the better for everybody concerned.

It is essential to have a fairly tolerant turn of mind, to be even-tempered and have an ability to remain calm. Those forever on a 'short fuse' may like to consider some other way of making money.

You should have a problem-solving turn of mind

Again, you will probably already know from previous experience whether a problem-solving turn of mind is among your attributes. If, when a problem arises – on any matter at all – your mind immediately turns to possible solutions rather than getting into an automatic panic, then you will already possess this skill.

Problems are endemic to the lettings business, and unforeseen circumstances may arise all the time. The lettings agency may go out of business, your tenant may refuse to pay rent or sublet to somebody else. You may find that your immaculate investment flat is overrun with cats and dogs when you specifically stated 'No pets'. The shower may flood the downstairs flat, and you find yourself being sued for the damage. You may have void periods when you cannot let the place. The washing machine may flood the flat. Neighbours downstairs may complain about noisy parties held by your tenants. If you have a leasehold flat, the freeholder may change and you could find yourself with a massive bill for your share of painting the outside.

All the things that can happen in your own property can also happen with an investment property. These are equally subject to all the ills that bricks and mortar are heir to – and then some, because with investment property, you always have to look at the difficulty from another person's point of view as well as your own.

However skilful lettings and managing agencies may be, at the end of the day the property remains yours and you have ultimate responsibility for it. It's your investment, not theirs, and it's up to you to look after it. Others, such as tenants, agents and the like, can just walk away from it if they want to. You can't; at least not until you sell it and move on.

There are many complicated landlord and tenant laws, and you may be unsure of your rights when a dispute crops up. Would you know how to solve these or other problems instantly, or how to get accurate help or advice?

As a landlord, you must be efficient in finding a way round all the problems that are likely to arise. It must be said, though, that practice makes perfect and although as a rookie landlord you may initially panic when nasty problems develop, you soon gain expertise in dealing with them.

It helps to have an extrovert type of personality

As a landlord, you will be dealing with a large number of different types of people with whom you must develop an instant relationship. You will often find yourself ringing up and contacting complete strangers.

You may have to cope with pushy lettings agencies, wayward tenants, brusque managing agents. The more sociable and outgoing you are, and the pleasanter you can remain, the easier you will find these transactions.

Again, when assessing your own suitability as a landlord, look back to your own life and experience. Do you prefer, like an Anita Brookner hero or heroine, to live on your own in a hermetically sealed flat, rarely admitting visitors? Or are you always giving parties, putting people up overnight, ringing up friends and chatting to strangers?

The chattier and more sociable you are by nature, the easier you will find it to be a landlord, as most of the people you are dealing with will be, and will remain, comparative strangers. You may become extremely friendly with a particular letting agent, for instance, and establish a very good relationship, only to find that the next time you need to find a tenant, that person has moved on and a stranger is at the desk. The lettings world is ephemeral, fast-changing and nothing stays the same for very long, including personnel. You will constantly find yourself dealing with a new set of people. Even if you are lucky enough to have a wonderful tenant who stays three years, eventually she will move on and a stranger will take her place.

Nowadays, very long-term tenants are usually only found in the public sector. The trend in the private sector is towards ever shorter rentals, with some lasting only a few weeks. In some ways, the introduction of the Assured Shorthold Tenancy has encouraged this, but also we are following the United States, where people tend to rent an apartment for an extremely short time.

So don't expect any kind of permanency. On the whole, the shyer and more introverted people are, the more they prefer things to be as permanent as possible. As a landlord, you will be buying into an extremely dynamic, very people-oriented business rather than something slow and steady.

At the same time, patience is a virtue as property investment is seen as medium to long term, rather than something where there are instant enormous returns.

It must be said that by no means all landlords have the wonderful qualities outlined in this chapter – which may be why there is so much strife between landlords and tenants generally. But unless you possess most of the attributes outlined, you are likely to find investing in rental properties a hugely stressful business. It's not an automatic way to riches, and emphatically not a licence to print money.

As one former landlord told me: 'I had an investment flat for a time, but found it just too much hassle: keeping inventories, interviewing tenants, making tax returns, trying not to have void periods.' This person sold his investment flat and was relieved to go back to having a savings account at his bank. The returns are far lower, but he reckons, having tried the business of letting, that it's worth it not to have to deal with tenants and their problems.

The point about Buy-to-Let is that it is an active, not a passive, investment, and as such, requires ongoing work and effort. In finance-speak, you can influence your asset's performance, and you can do this by: keeping a close eye on the market by finding out what today's tenants want, and where they want to be; making sure you get a reputation as a 'good' landlord – word about bad landlords gets around more quickly than you might imagine – and by making sure that all your rental properties are kept in immaculate, up-to-date condition.

Although there are no guarantees, good properties are rarely empty for any length of time. In more than 14 years of being a landlord, I have never had a property un-let for even an hour, and in some cases, the same tenants have stayed seven, eight, nine years. In fact, the main reason my properties eventually needed major works was because the same tenants had been there so long, the properties did not get any kind of improvement for ages. It is difficult to carry out renovations, as opposed to essential maintenance, when there are tenants in situ.

But the effort and expense of putting in a new kitchen and bathroom once in a decade is worth 10 years of completely hassle-free letting.

So the secret of success is to make sure your properties offer that little bit extra, and are always 'club class' – at least when tenancies change.

If you are still keen, the next important question is: what kind of property should you buy?

2 Finding the right property

Supposing you have decided that you want to buy an investment property and, before taking the plunge, you go into a nearby lettings agency for advice. This is a good idea anyway as agencies will be able to give you all kinds of useful preliminary information on the most popular streets, average rents and so on.

It is no longer sensible to buy a property and then just hope to be able to rent it out. The days when potential tenants queued round the block hours in advance whenever there was the slightest suggestion that a flat might be vacant are well and truly over. In many parts of the country there is enormous oversupply, with the result that many perfectly good flats, offered at reasonable rents, are remaining empty. Today's tenants have many properties to choose from, and there is little point in adding to a large pool of unlettable apartments.

Indeed, some agencies have closed their books to new instructions because they have so many properties they cannot rent out for love or money. So more than ever, it is imperative to seek advice from a number of agencies in the locality you are considering, before ever making an offer. Get to know the most popular streets, the type of preferred housing and the typical rents achieved. Then, if you are satisfied that there is a market from which you can make money, start looking.

Because Buy-to-Let is now so intensely competitive, ever more investors are looking at properties many miles, or many hundreds of miles, away from their own homes. If you are investing in Buy-to-Let in an unknown area, research becomes ever more important. Although many companies are offering

Buy-to-Let packages over the internet, there is no substitute for tramping round the streets and getting to know an area. Otherwise, for all you know, the house next door to the one you are considering buying may be boarded up, or contain squatters, 10 rottweilers or neighbours from hell.

In my experience, there are few things more exciting than house-hunting, whether this is for your own home or an investment property. And when making an offer on an investment property, you need to be a hundred times more hard-headed than when seeking a roof over your own head.

If you are new to Buy-to-Let, make sure you pick up plenty of ADVICE before taking the plunge, and suss out the market thoroughly. This is the main secret of success, and one of the best tips is to pretend to be a tenant. In this guise, view a wide variety of properties to get an idea of what is most popular in any particular area, what are the realistic achievable rents, and what the properties look like. Landlords and tenants are often given very different figures on rentals. Letting agencies commonly inflate the figures for the landlord and deflate them for the tenant, in order to try to please both sides.

For instance, one landlord was told she could get £450 a week for a two-bedroom flat she was considering buying; when she viewed a similar property as a potential tenant, she was told she could have it for £320 a week – a big difference.

I often pretend to be a tenant, and snoop round properties to see what is on offer at particular rents, and what condition the places are in when advertised to let. I also go round newbuild properties, where many units are bought to let, to assess the standard, the finish, the décor, the quality of the kitchen and bathroom units, door handles and so on, to make sure I keep a close eye on the market. Then I ask myself: can I do as well? Can I do better? Can I offer something a bit more special than this – or will it cost more than I would ever get back?

Also ask any seasoned Buy-to-Let friends, colleagues and contacts about their own experience. This way, you will gradually build up expertise before you make a serious mistake by buying completely the wrong type of property for your target market.

When considering buying a property to let, make sure you take advice ONLY from dedicated lettings agencies, rather than agencies that also sell properties. Sales agents have a habit of pushing properties to investment buyers when these properties have nothing whatever to recommend them. Beware when you see the words 'investment opportunity' in a sales agent's window. These words are very often estate agent-speak for 'absolutely ghastly with nothing to recommend it'. Also beware of taking investment advice from agents selling newbuild or offplan developments; if you are an absolute beginner and novice at the lettings game, never take advice on rental properties from those who have something to sell you – it can't be trusted.

Every single agency will tell you exactly the same thing, which is that by far the easiest properties to let are studios and one-bedroom flats. The bigger and grander the flat or house, the more difficult it can be to let.

'We often get potential landlords coming into our offices, telling us they want to buy the biggest property they can, so as to get the highest rent,' said Arnaud Cheung. 'And our advice is always the same: instead of buying one big property, why not buy two or three small ones for the same amount? Around 60 per cent of requests in lettings departments are for studios, one- and two-bed flats.'

The reason for this is that nowadays the person most likely to want to rent rather than buy is a single professional person, usually between the ages of 25 and 35, who has a busy lifestyle and who does not, for the time being, want the hassle or permanency of buying. These are people who have outgrown student and shared accommodation, have usually repaid their student loan, and are looking for a place where they can be on their own.

These days, people paying premium rents prefer to live on their own rather than to share, if they can possibly afford it. Even those in relationships very often prefer to have their own pad – and demand for single-person apartments is increasing all the time. Conversely, demand for three-bed-plus flats and houses is diminishing, except for the family market, and this does not exist in every area. And the fewer tenants you have in the one apartment, the less risk there is of trouble and strife therein. The more tenants crowded into one space, the greater the potential for damage, unpaid rent and illegal subletting.

Apart from being easier to let, maintain, and decorate and furnish, small flats usually give, pound for pound, a better return on the initial investment than, say, a five-bedroomed house with a massive garden. Year after year, the quarterly Review from the Association of Residential Letting Agents (ARLA) gives consistently higher percentage yields for flats than houses – and this applies across the United Kingdom, including Scotland. You may be lucky enough to land a fantastic long-staying tenant right away for your big house, but you might also find yourself with lengthy void periods. In a well-chosen location, however, a studio or one-bed is unlikely to remain empty for long. Even in a highly competitive market there is still, report agents, a serious shortage of this type of property, and still more tenants than suitable properties available.

The two main considerations to bear in mind when looking for a suitable investment property are:

1. Could I, at a pinch, live in it myself?
2. Location, location, location, or the three Ls.

Could I live in it myself?

The standard advice when buying property is to put location first, but my feeling is that with investment properties, the principal factors to be taken into account are different from those applying to your own home. And the gut reaction as to whether you could live in it yourself is actually more important, initially, than the location.

You might reasonably point out that since you are highly unlikely ever to live in the place yourself, why should you worry about whether you could bear to live in it? The answer to that is: if you couldn't live in it, why should you expect somebody else to want to? Not only that, but you might find yourself *having* to live in it. Here is a personal example.

In 1996, I bought a one-bed ex-council flat in west London to rent out. It let very successfully over the years and provided a nice little income for me. Then, in 2004, my circumstances changed dramatically. I sold my London house and moved to the coast, but I needed a crash pad for the days I was working in London.

What better than to requisition my little flat for my own use? As soon as the last tenants gave notice, I moved into it myself. And it's very nice indeed. If, though, I had bought a horrible place I could never live in myself, I would not have had this option of turning an investment property into my own home. So I am glad I did the place out nicely, with expensive curtains and colour-coordinated furniture and fittings, as it needed no work at all when I wanted it for myself.

After a couple of years, my circumstances changed yet again and I decided to rent out the London flat. Because it was in such good condition, it was taken the same day it went on the market.

You never know what twists and turns fate may have in store!

But more than that, if you are looking for something that you could inhabit yourself, you are much more likely to make a sensible buy and a sound investment. Although of course there is less emotion tied up in an investment property than in your own home, there is still some. Very few people are completely rational when making up their mind about properties – and potential tenants are the most irrational people of all.

The kind of thing that is likely to put you off will most probably put a potential tenant off as well. I once viewed an ex-council flat that appeared to be a wonderful bargain and was in an ideal location for letting. But once I saw it, I knew I could never market it with any confidence, because it was completely clad, floor to ceiling, in wood. Even the agents selling the property referred to it as 'the sauna' and although they tried to persuade me that it would be 'fantastic for letting', I knew that it would be hard for me even to set foot inside the place, let alone rent it out. Whatever sort of tenant could I hope to attract when I hated the interior so much myself? Yet if you like the place, those being asked to pay rent will most probably like it as well.

I would never consider buying a studio flat that is so small that it would only take a single bed, as I would expect, however theoretically, that I might like somebody to share my bed, at least on occasion. Single beds are for children – or prisoners or hospital patients.

When looking for an investment one-bedroom flat, I always go for those with eat-in kitchens wherever possible. Because I personally like eat-in kitchens and would never buy a property to live in where I had to cart my food to another room, I expect that any tenants would have the same turn of mind. They might not – but you've got to go on something, and I have found that personal preference works every time.

Assuming you have decided to go for a studio or one-bed flat, there are still very many decisions to be made, each with its own advantages or disadvantages. It makes sense to view a number of potential properties in your price range before you decide to take the plunge, and not to exclude any because of unfounded prejudices. Don't, for instance, automatically turn your nose up at the prospect of buying an ex-council flat as a rental investment. You may, as I do, generally prefer character properties to purpose-built and ex-council flats. They are more aesthetic, more upmarket and more appealing. For me, when I started considering becoming a landlord, my overwhelming preference for Victorian and Georgian properties was so ingrained that at first I refused to look at anything else. I have to have something beautiful, I told myself, even as an investment. Yet as I looked, I soon discovered that the best studios and one-beds were often to be found in 1930s, '50s or '60s blocks, where the studios were purposely designed, rather than being converted from small rooms in the attic or basement.

If you are thinking of buying an investment property in a large town or city – where the biggest rental markets are to be found – you will usually have a choice of:

- conversion;
- mansion block;
- purpose-built block;
- ex-local authority block;

- newbuild or offplan developments;
- a freehold house.

All of these, apart from the house, will be leasehold properties. If looking for a studio or one-bed, you are unlikely to be able to purchase a freehold house, although one-bed starter homes do exist. Sometimes, though, the leases are 999 years, so in effect are little different from freeholds. Average leases will be 125 years.

Conversion

'Conversion' is the name given to properties where a previous single-occupancy house has been converted into flats. A conversion will most likely be a Victorian or Georgian terrace, but it may also be a 1930s or later property built as a house and subsequently divided into flats.

The advantages of a conversion are that rooms are likely to be grand, or at least interesting, and may retain attractive period features such as large windows, ornate ceilings, working fireplaces and cornices. Service charges on conversions (which the landlord has to pay) are usually fairly low, as there is unlikely to be a lift or resident porter, both of which push up maintenance costs.

Disadvantages of conversions are that partition walls are often very thin and noise comes through from other flats. Kitchens and bathrooms are usually very tiny, and the common parts are often extremely dingy. These properties are also usually more expensive to buy than flats in purpose-built blocks, as you pay a premium for the 'character' that you may not be able to realize in extra rent. Generally speaking, conversions do not fetch higher rents than more utilitarian properties. It's the *space*, not the wonderful fireplaces or high ceilings, that tenants are prepared to pay for.

Another disadvantage of conversions is that if the place is very old there may be damp penetration, flaking plasterwork and a battered front door. As all refurbishment to old buildings is expensive, remedial work is often not carried out by the free-holder, as it should be. In addition, if the building is listed, it can be difficult to get planning permission for improvements. Planning permission takes time, and if you undertake repairs without obtaining the requisite listed building permission, you risk having to undo all your good work.

Very many smaller conversions, such as those with three or four separate units, may be self-managed rather than employing professional managing agents, and as well as the leasehold, you may also be purchasing a share of the freehold. This has its pros and cons. Generally speaking, although not always, professionally managed blocks are better maintained than self-managed blocks. It is also common to get much bickering and rivalry where there is self-management and, as an absentee landlord, you may not be willing to play much part in management.

You should also bear in mind that very many conversions, particularly those carried out during the 1960s and '70s, when planning regulations were less strict, are very badly done indeed. So, if looking for a property in which to invest your money, don't set your heart on a conversion and believe that you must have a character property at all costs. Also, maintenance is expensive in old properties.

Mansion block

Mansion blocks are those imposing edifices, usually Edwardian, that are common in central London and other big cities.

The advantages of these, as with conversions, are that you get high ceilings, period features and, very often, well-proportioned rooms. As these apartments were purpose-built, you are unlikely to get thin partition walls, as may be the case with conversions. Flats in mansion blocks are usually expensive and, as they are considered desirable residences, the blocks themselves are usually well maintained, with impressive common parts and, very often, a resident porter. There will almost always be a lift. The blocks are very secure and services such as rubbish collection and cleaning of common parts are standard. Very often, gardens and flower beds, if any, are meticulously looked after.

Mansion blocks were originally designed to be upmarket residences and, as such, frequently have features that add to their luxurious feel, such as mirrors in the hall, deep-pile carpets and expensive thick wallpaper in the common parts. *You as a landlord will be paying for all these!* However, studios and one-beds in mansion blocks are usually cheaper than those in conversions, for one very good reason: the service and maintenance charges are often extremely high, and you may not be able to recoup this in extra rent. In many mansion blocks, heating and hot water are supplied via a central system and included in the service charge. You may not be able to pass the cost of these on to your tenant.

Also, as mansion blocks were built to be grand, small units such as studios and one-beds are often found in the worst positions, such as the lower ground floor where there is very little natural light, making them rather dark and gloomy. Kitchens may be poky and bathrooms old-fashioned. Also, as many mansion blocks are now getting old, renovation programmes, always added to your service charge, can run into several thousands extra. Again, you are unlikely to be able to recoup this on rent, although it must be said that mansion block flats usually resell at a profit.

Purpose-built block

The term 'purpose-built' usually refers to blocks constructed from the 1950s onwards, and these almost always have a square, utilitarian, immediate post-war look.

The advantages of buying into a purpose-built block (PB) are that all the flats inside are designed to be studios, one-beds or whatever, and are not cut-downs from larger spaces. Properties in these blocks tend to be cheaper than in mansion blocks, and service charges are correspondingly lower as well, as there is not the same standard to maintain.

In a block of any size there will almost always be a lift, and there may be a resident porter as well. As with mansion blocks, PBs are almost always professionally managed, although in recent years there has been a tendency for the block to be managed by a voluntary Residents' Association formed of owners. In most cases, non-resident landlords are not allowed to become part of the management team, as the property is not their main home.

Flats in PBs are usually cheaper than in mansion blocks and, depending on the whim of the architect at the time, may or may not be well designed. Much 1950s and '60s domestic architecture has not stood the test of time, and many PBs suffer from internal problems not easily addressed, such as all the reinforced concrete central to the construction of the building going rusty. Other disadvantages to PBs may include flimsy walls, low ceilings and metal windows that have rusted up and refuse to open.

These blocks are not as pretty as conversions, or as imposing as mansion blocks, but they do have a 'modern' look and the flats are usually smart, clean and easy to maintain. PBs are extremely popular with tenants, and flats in these buildings, provided the location is right, usually let extremely well.

Ex-local authority block

Another option is to go for a flat in an ex-local authority block. At the time of writing these are the cheapest of all, but they are rapidly catching up with PBs and mansion blocks in purchase price.

For a long time there was a serious stigma attached to local authority properties, especially as in a block of any size the majority of residents would be renting from the council. However, the Right-to-Buy scheme, introduced in the 1980s by Margaret Thatcher, has had the effect of making many former council properties almost as desirable as any other, as owners have often made considerable efforts to improve the appearance of the block, with window boxes, hanging baskets, well-kept gardens and clean communal areas.

The advantages of ex-local authority flats are these: they are around 10 per cent cheaper to buy than other similar investment properties, and as the freeholder is usually the local authority, service charges are often very low as well. But although 'interim' service charges may seem low, leaseholders can suddenly be hit with huge, unexpected bills for repairs and renovation. This is because, unlike private landlords, local authorities are not allowed to charge for works in advance or build up sinking funds. So, although annual service charges may be £300 a year or less, you can find yourself receiving a heart-stopping bill for £5,000 or so for works, wiping out all your profit and more.

The kind of 'works' that may suddenly cost thousands include:

● new windows;

● new roof;

● repointing;

● new lift;

● repainting the outside.

These bills can arrive years after the works have taken place and immediately wipe out any profit on your investment. If considering buying an ex-local authority property, discover whether any major works are likely to be undertaken in the foreseeable future. In particular, find out whether the building is designated to have major works to comply with the 2010 Decent Homes programme. This information should be available to all new leaseholders.

You will not, of course, inherit unpaid debts from previous leaseholders as all outstanding charges have to be paid in full before any ex-local authority property can be sold – but you can suddenly find yourself with a big bill not long after you have bought.

You also need to discover the length of the lease before buying as, although new local authority leases are always 125 years when newly granted, as they run down, they can be worth ever less. Local authorities are also not always the free-holders; sometimes they are the Head Leaseholders instead.

All this information should be available in the Home Information Pack when you buy, together with a copy of the lease. Make sure you read and understand it before buying, as local authority leases can be very different from those in the private sector.

In law, local authorities must circulate all leaseholders in advance for quotes for works, and also inform them which contractors have been chosen. But you may not have much – or any – choice as to whether these works will take place. In the private sector, leaseholders have much more power than in the public sector.

These are some of the reasons why ex-local authority properties are often considerably cheaper than others to buy. As with most 'bargains', there is a sting in the tail.

Then there are several different types of former council flats. The best ones, both from an investment and a rental point of view, are the 'infill' apartments in existing streets. In many Victorian and Edwardian streets, for instance, there will be a small council development, usually built soon after the Second World War, when bomb damage destroyed many houses, or in the 1970s at the end of an existing row. These properties are often very similar in price to the other homes in the street, even though they do not, strictly speaking, fit in with the rest of the architecture.

Infill ex-council properties are always the most expensive, as they are not on an estate.

If buying on an estate, go for an ex-local authority property on a small, rather than a large, estate. Although you can often pick up what seem like incredible bargains on large estates, a lot of tenants are nervous about living in such areas, added to which they may be a long way from transport links, shops, restaurants and other services. Tenants are also put off if there are a lot of children or gangs of teenagers hanging around – particularly the latter and particularly if they are all wearing hoodies.

As a general rule, if an estate looks grim, dirty, neglected or in any way offputting when you go to view a property, leave it alone, however much of a 'bargain' the property appears to be.

Ex-council flats are very often extremely well designed, with large kitchens and spacious living rooms, bedrooms and bathrooms. Many have small balconies, and some may have private gardens as well. They are often well equipped with built-in cupboards and wardrobes, and the block is often very secure, with magnetic keys issued only to owners and residents.

In a small block where every resident is an owner, as is increasingly the case, the common parts are usually clean and well maintained, although basic. You are unlikely to find carpets or expensive wallpaper there. Another advantage is that if you buy into a block consisting only of one-bed flats, there are unlikely to be hordes of children rushing around. These blocks are also often in excellent locations. Penthouse flats in high-rise blocks (now becoming desirable again after being derided for years) often have fantastic views, and can represent a real bargain, although you may not be able to get a mortgage on properties higher than the sixth or seventh floor, which could make the property difficult to resell.

If you are interested in an apartment in a high rise – and these can often appear to be incredible bargains – have a long hard look at the lease before signing up, as these are often extremely short and it may be difficult to extend it. Whenever buying to rent out, make sure you have an 'exit strategy' and that the place is resaleable.

Although it may be possible to extend the lease, this can be a very expensive and long drawn-out process and add considerably to your costs.

The disadvantage of ex-council flats is that from the outside they always look 'local authority' and are usually built to a very basic design indeed. They are emphatically not pretty, and have no frills or designer touches. Their appearance does not gladden the heart, and if you feel that under no circumstances could you ever bear to live in one yourself, you may be better off avoiding this option. But there are council blocks and council blocks. I could not bring myself to buy a property in a council block that looked forbidding and bleak, where there were graffiti scrawled on the walls and where I could hear children screaming. A small, low-rise block where everybody is an owner-occupier, though, may be a different matter.

When purchasing a leasehold property for the purposes of subletting, you must discover whether this is allowed (see page 55). Some leases specify that tenants must stay for a minimum of one year; others discourage the idea completely.

Blocks of flats that have a preponderance of middle-class, middle-aged owner-occupiers may not look kindly on transient populations of people holding noisy parties, coming in at three in the morning and otherwise disrupting their peace and quiet. Although every owner in a block of flats has a duty not to cause a nuisance, if you are an absentee landlord you may not be aware of the nuisance your tenants might be creating.

Newbuild

Over the past few years, very many brand new blocks have been erected in city centres, and flats in these buildings have been eagerly snapped up by Buy-to-Let investors. It's easy to see why: they are obviously in good locations, they are state-of-the-art, with power showers, granite worktops, wooden floors and all the latest design features. Because they are new, they don't need any refurbishment. In addition, many have gyms and leisure centres, which attract young tenants. They also frequently have underground parking – a huge bonus in city centres, where parking can be an utter nightmare. Very many mansion and purpose-built blocks have no parking facilities whatever. Because they are so appealing, newbuild properties bang in the middle of city centres would appear to rent out very easily indeed.

But beware! Very many flats in new developments are block-bought by large investors at a discount. Individual purchasers may have to buy at a higher price, which means they will have to ask a higher rent for an identical property. As many as 50 per cent of the flats may be bought as investments, which means that very many new absolutely identical flats will be flooding the market at the same time.

It is also the case that the percentage rental yield on newbuild properties will be significantly lower than on any of the other types of property mentioned because they are more expensive to buy and because tenants often have a large choice of properties all entering the market at the same time. In fact, rental yields tend to be *very low indeed* in newbuilds.

If interested in a newbuild property, do not be seduced by marketing packages, promises of high yields and finance deals.

In general, the more highly marketed a property, the more expensive it is to buy and maintain, and you may not be able to recoup this in rent.

Any development with extensive leisure facilities, restaurants, 24-hour porterage and underground parking will have a high annual service charge, which you as the landlord will have to pay. Buying newbuild can work, but extreme caution needs to be exercised. It is also a good idea, if interested in newbuild, to look at 10-year-old developments built by the same company, to see how well the condition has held up, and whether the properties have significantly increased in value.

When investing in Buy-to-Let, it is always sensible to try to work out exactly what your costs are, so that you can also work out whether the deal leaves you with a profit. Newbuild properties are notorious for fixing very low service charges initially, to get buyers interested and then, after a year or two, hiking them up to unprecedented and unexpected levels.

Although few, if any, developers will give a guarantee not to increase service charges beyond a certain amount, try to get some idea of likely increases. One problem is that freeholds are often sold on after completion of the development, and the new freeholders almost always increase service charges significantly.

Newbuild developments also often offer guaranteed rents for a period of time, usually set at around 6 per cent for a year, maybe two years. This does not mean that the property is actually rented out at this amount, or indeed that it is rented out at all. Again, you need to get some feedback from local letting agents of likely rentals, before you buy.

Buying offplan

Ever more Buy-to-Let investors are now buying offplan. This can seem a very good idea, as you can often buy before the first spade has begun to dig the first hole, and the earliest buyers are offered the biggest discounts.

Buying offplan can seem like an incredible opportunity and it is often touted as such. But as with everything in life, there are pros and cons. If you buy early enough in the procedure, you may be staking your claim to a property many months, or even years, before its completion. Such a purchase will be heavily hyped, with huge discounts and stratospheric profits being promised by developers and property investment clubs.

The earlier you put down your deposit, the greater the discount you are offered. As a very early buyer you will be offered a discount of, typically, between 5 per cent and 20 per cent on the finished product, and this could be two or three years away. If you buy more than one property you can usually negotiate an even bigger discount.

After putting down an initial deposit of eg 10 per cent, you will buy the rest in prearranged stages. The other advantage of buying early is that you get the pick of the properties, as the choicest ones, not surprisingly, always go first.

Buying offplan also enables you to flip – that is, sell on the property as soon as it is finished. Flipping allows you to take advantage of capital growth without completing the purchase or applying for a mortgage. You also avoid paying stamp duty as the eventual lease will be in the final purchaser's name.

Increasingly, offplan developments are being aimed specifically at the Buy-to-Let investor, so what are the risks and the rewards?

Stephen Ludlow, of LudlowThompson estate agents, says: 'Buying offplan can work if the market is rising and there is sustained capital growth. But at times of high interest rates and a tightening up of the market, you could be left with something worth less on completion than when you bought it.

'And whether you plan to sell straight away or rent out the property, you could find yourself in competition with 50 other identical properties all coming onto the market at the same time. When the sales market goes quiet, you may find selling difficult, and it is impossible to predict any property market two or three years in advance.

'Also, you may not be able to achieve the promised high rents when you come to let.'

For these reasons, Ludlow believes that buying offplan can be a high-risk strategy. New developments are heavily and cleverly marketed and employ glossy, smiling sales teams who may be far better at selling than you are at resisting. Another factor is that offplan properties often start to lose value in the months after completion, rather like a new car loses value as it is driven out of the showroom.

Unlike the car, your property should start to increase in value over time, although Land Registry figures indicate that newbuilds rise at a slower rate than older properties.

Many, many new or novice investors are tempted to buy offplan, but the fact is that anything can happen to the property market between putting down that first deposit and being handed the keys. So although it can work, and has worked for many people, buying offplan can be risky – particularly if there is no slack in your budget.

It is increasingly the case that many first-time Buy-to-Let investors buy offplan or newbuild, as these can seem the most attractive purchases – particularly when you are seduced by a very cleverly designed showhome. The secret, as always, is to number-crunch very carefully before taking the plunge and NEVER sign up before you have gone home, considered the prospect in the cool light of day without persuasive sales teams around you, and undertaken close research into the likely tenant pool, and what such tenants would be able to pay.

Don't forget that offplan and newbuild properties have not been tried and tested on the open market, which means that the prices asked are at most an educated guess. There is evidence that the value of newbuild apartments often goes down in the year or two after completion – because the developer has asked an inflated price in the first place.

Caution: expensive investment seminars often try to persuade you to buy an offplan or newbuild apartment at a supposed discount and tell you not to worry about the deposit, as you can borrow this on your credit card. But never, ever be so overstretched that you are paying out more on mortgages and servicing loans than you can possibly get back in rent. And never, ever depend on a rising market to turn your investment into profit.

When operating as a Buy-to-Let investor, you must always look at your rental yield NOW – not what you might get on resale at some undefined time in the future. It is the yield that should be uppermost in your mind, and you must always be certain that you can get this yield.

Other considerations

Before purchasing, discover whether the property comes with a share of the freehold, and whether there are outside managing agents or the block is self-managed. If you own a share of the freehold and there is no outside freeholder, you are less likely to be clobbered by sudden high levies for repainting the exterior, for example.

It is also essential for absentee landlords to discover whether the block is portered, and who holds spare sets of keys. Where there are porters, make good friends with them, as you will almost certainly need their services before very long. Many porters are also quite good at doing odd jobs for which it may be difficult to find a contractor.

Whenever you buy a leasehold property, or indeed any Buy-to-Let property, make sure there is an exit strategy – in other words, you must be able to sell on, if necessary. Do not ever get stuck with an unsaleable property, because it seems very cheap to buy. It will always be suspiciously cheap for a reason.

Many people, for instance, got caught out by timeshare properties when they realized they could not sell their week at any price. In some cases, they could not even give it away.

Although there are never any guarantees that you will make a profit on resale of a Buy-to-Let, never ever buy something you will never be able to sell, unless the rental yield is so very high that capital growth becomes irrelevant.

Also check that you are actually allowed to sublet, if the property is leasehold. Some freeholders or Residents' Associations do not allow subletting. There may also be a charge for subletting – typically £100 for each new tenant in the property.

Condition

Unless you are buying a newbuild, which is, or should be, in perfect order, what kind of condition should you go for? I would advise going for a property that needs some, but not a great deal of work. If you buy a complete wreck, the budget for renovation will probably run away with you, and often end up costing more than buying new in the first place. Properties that need cosmetic or superficial renovation often sell at cheaper prices than those newly refurbished – and with Buy-to-Let, you need to do everything you can to maximize profit.

Also, do not forget that you are not allowed to claim refurbishment costs against tax while the place is unoccupied. Rental income is treated as unearned – that is, investment – income, even though it can be jolly hard work. Another point is that if the place needs a lot of work, there could be a long gap between acquiring the property and having it ready to let. Properties that need major alterations or building work should be avoided, unless you have a handy team of extremely cheap builders always on tap, or you are a builder yourself.

It is mainly a matter of getting your eye in. Look at a number of places and work out how much it would cost and how long it would take to make the place clean, neat, tidy and safe. Jon Wright, who became a property investor on retiring as an accountant, says: 'Cheap properties should not be wrecks. You can never do these up yourself profitably unless you are a builder, so you should go for those which only need cosmetic improvement.'

Other options

Another type of investment property is now becoming available, and this is the inner-city block converted from a former warehouse, bank, fire station or other commercial building. These properties often make very attractive living spaces and, as they are central, tend to let extremely easily. In central areas of London, these blocks are often entirely bought by investment landlords who never even see the properties, but buy them long before completion. But as these landlords are usually big-time investors from Hong Kong, Singapore or similar, these properties may not be an ideal choice for the timid first-time investor.

The other problem with these properties is that as there may not be anything in the street to compare as to price, you may not know whether you are buying a bargain or not. I myself would not have the confidence to buy into one of these blocks, as I would feel too daunted by the big business and high finance going on all around me. But they may be worth looking into, if they are going up in an area you already know well.

These properties are trendy, 'cool', designed to a high standard, usually with wooden floors, stainless steel kitchens and stone-flagged bathrooms for instance, and they will attract high-powered tenants.

A house

What about buying a house, rather than a flat? Houses are usually freehold, you can often pack in more people than with a flat, and there are no compulsory service and maintenance charges. At first sight, it may seem that a house has many investment advantages over a flat in a block.

The downside of buying a house as an investment is that the percentage yield is almost always much lower than with a flat. Houses are usually more expensive to buy than flats, and the rental yield does not rack up as much as you might expect.

In general terms, unless the rental yield is around 6 per cent, the investment is too risky, as interest repayments on mortgages, renovation costs and void periods can all eat into profit. Also, when renovations are required on apartment blocks, everybody shares in the cost. With houses, you as the owner bear the entire cost.

Houses can be a good bet in areas where there are many families looking for rental accommodation. Otherwise, you would have to accommodate a lot of sharers, and in general terms, the more people who crowd into one house, the greater the potential for wear and tear, somebody not paying the rent, the sharers falling out with each other, or girlfriends and boyfriends being moved in.

The only situation where houses make more sense than flats is where you are buying a house for your student children.

On the other hand, super-investors Fergus and Judith Wilson, the former maths teachers who now own over 700 properties, always buy new two-bedroom freehold houses rather than flats. They have come to believe that these properties offer the best rental investments in the part of Kent where they buy. But, as always, before buying anything, go round to letting agents in your chosen area and ask which properties are most requested, and what is the likely achievable rent.

Don't just go on the say-so of the agent or developer who is trying to sell you the property.

The country market

There is a thriving rental market in the country, where the demand is almost exclusively for large, unfurnished family houses. Very often, these renters are those known as 'in-betweeners', where they are renting for a year or two while looking for their dream country home.

Although the yields are not particularly high on these properties, tenants tend to be reliable, long-stay, stable people who will look after the place, pay their rent on time and all in all, make excellent tenants.

Very often, investors will buy country properties with a view to living there themselves one day, rather than for direct investment. Again, get a feel of the market in the area that interests you by looking obsessively in agents' windows, pretending to be a tenant, working out what your percentage yield is likely to be and the source of the likely tenant pool. It is obviously better to rent a gracious country home to a family, than to an unrelated group of young people. Also, the implications of the Housing Act 2004 may mean that your property will have to be licensed by the local authority as an HMO – House in Multiple Occupation. For more details on this, see page 182.

Very many people rent out their own home, and this constitutes a large section of the country market. The expert advice here is to depersonalize the place as much as you can. The more personal to you, the owner, the harder it is to let.

Very many country homes are let unfurnished, as tenants tend to want to stay in them longer than the average town tenant, and to bring their own stuff into the home.

Jane Russam, country letting expert at Lane Fox, says: 'The country market is fuelled by divorces, young professionals living together for the first time and weekenders, who want a country cottage to rent. This market is quite different from full-time renters, as they want to be within walking distance of a pub, restaurant and village shop.'

There is a real shortage of large five- and six-bedroom houses for rental, but of course these are expensive to buy in the first place.

Buying a house for your student children

Nowadays, many parents may consider buying a house for their student children to live in during their university years. Income on the investment is generated by charging other students to live there, and when the university course is over, the parents can decide either to sell the house, or keep it going as an investment property. For those with enough money to spare, this is worth considering, as it ensures that your student children have a decent roof over their heads, and the money the other student tenants pay gives a little extra income, as well as providing an interesting alternative to having money on deposit. In many parts of the country, especially where house prices are rising fast, this can be an excellent investment.

Buying a house for student children is often the first step on the way to becoming an investment landlord, and many middle-aged people who never previously saw themselves as landlords are now entering the market by this means.

Matthew Munro of Knight Frank said: 'If you buy a house for your student children, you know the offspring are safe and secure, they don't have to worry about a rogue landlord and they won't find themselves out in the street just before finals.

'Those who have chosen to educate their children privately and have spent a great deal of money doing so, can at least expect to break even.' According to Mr Munro, it makes 'frighteningly good sense'. Many parents with almost-adult children will have paid off their mortgage, but of course such a property would also be available on a Buy-to-Let scheme, in cases where the rents would more than cover the mortgage.

One major advantage of investing in this kind of property is that you know in advance who the tenants will be – your daughter or son, and their friends. If the flat or house belongs to mummy or daddy, there is also a greater incentive to look after it.

What is the best kind of property to look for here? Estate agents mainly recommend a classic three-bedroom terrace or semi, especially as the dining room in a three-bed terrace can be converted to a fourth bedroom. Of course returns on the investment depend on area and price paid for the property, but in 2007 a five-bed student house costing £243,000 would yield a total rental income of £15,000 p.a. New houses lend themselves particularly well to this purpose, so long as they are in the right location. New houses being built near stations, universities and colleges are worth considering if you have a student son or daughter.

In order to be popular as a student home, a house must be no more than a mile from the university. Anything further out is likely to prove difficult to fill up with students.

A report commissioned by Direct Line insurance in 2006 found that a total of 83,000 properties had been bought for students by their parents. This number is expected to exceed 100,000 by 2010, as increasingly parents are choosing to buy rather than helping their student children with rent.

Of course the most famous university parents were Tony and Cherie Blair, who bought two flats in Bristol, one intended for their then-student son Euan.

But you do not have to be a parent to buy a student property. The number of students – not just undergraduates but post-graduates and foreign students – is increasing each year and students represent a fast-growing, if somewhat specialized, tenant sector.

The choice is yours, and there is no overwhelming single advantage to any of these types of property. Super-landlord Greg Shackleton, who owns around 50 investment properties in Brighton, always goes for conversions in terrible condition, which he then renovates. His feeling is that conversions are more attractive to premium tenants than flats in PBs, and that the vastly lower service charge is a distinct advantage.

In London, one landlord I know buys up flats in terrible condition in ex-council blocks, then renovates them to a high, modern standard. Although the blocks he buys into are often disgusting in themselves, they are always in prime locations, which brings us on to the second important aspect of successful buying to let – location.

Location, location, location

If you are very new to buying investment properties, you may be unsure of the difference between a good location and a bad one. George Humphreys, of the rental investment department at Hamptons estate agents, said: 'Landlords always think they know what makes a good location, but in our experience few of them do.'

If you have always lived in a leafy middle-class suburb, in a large detached house with a double garage and a lawned garden front and rear, this to you may seem a good location: quiet, sedate, away from traffic and noise and near to good schools, churches and shops. But such a favoured spot may not be so good for transient tenants. On the whole, with very few exceptions, the kind of people looking for rented property want to be very near to public transport, no more than five minutes away from the station or underground, and within walking distance from shops. Most tenants do not have a car, and if they are single people living alone, will not be making an almighty weekly shop at an out-of-town supermarket. They are much more likely to want to pick up their dinner on the way home, or phone for a takeaway.

Most tenants are not interested in gardens or garages, and prize convenience above all. They are not looking for a lovely thatched cottage with roses round the door, but somewhere smart, chic, modern, easy. In some cases, they want to be no more than five minutes away from their place of work, especially if they are working long hours.

When looking for investment properties, it is essential to have potential tenants in mind, rather than just buying somewhere and then hoping that somehow a top-paying tenant will take it. When looking for properties in London, I always make sure that anything I buy is no more than five minutes' walk away from a tube station, and is in Zone 2 at most. Zone 5? Forget it.

Unless, that is, there are excellent bus routes. In many parts of London, the buses, driving along in their dedicated bus lanes, have improved out of all recognition. So if you are considering a property in one of the outer London areas and not near a tube, make sure it is on a good bus route with plenty of night buses. Nowadays, tenants will often consider a property on a fast, regular bus route, as some people do not like using the tube.

The same applies when buying property in any large city or urban area. Most tenants like night life, so make sure they can get home easily and safely at night.

By far the biggest group of London tenants are those working in the City or the West End, and they are looking for living accommodation in a location within easy reach of their work.

My most successful investment flats in central London have been those that are extremely near Central Line underground stations. I have found that high-earning, busy professional people do not object at all to ex-council flats. In fact, if they come from abroad they positively like them, as they remind them of home. The only conditions this type of tenant stipulates are that the flat itself should be spotlessly clean and with everything working as it should.

If you are buying an investment property outside London, the same considerations should apply: the flat should be very close to the shops and other amenities. Anything else is a plus, but properties with shops within easy walking distance will let far more quickly than those that are miles from any convenience of this type. A golden rule for location, wherever you are thinking of buying, is: the property should be no more than five minutes away from main transport links. If it's a good quarter of an hour's walk to the nearest station or bus stop, forget it, as it won't be easy to let. Holiday cottages, of course, come into a completely different category, and we will be discussing these later.

In London's Richmond and Chiswick, there are good links both into and out of London, and the places are attractive in themselves. These areas also have the advantage of being very near Heathrow. Which brings us to another location point: properties that are very near major airports tend to let well, because airports employ many thousands of people, not all of whom want to make a long journey after work – especially if they are shift workers.

Those whose jobs involve frequent flying may also prefer to live near to an airport rather than in a quiet, difficult-to-reach village in the country. One landlord of my acquaintance owned some studio flats in a rather bleak 1960s block very close to Heathrow. They were always let, because the airport was only minutes away, within walking distance.

A town that has many language schools will attract foreigners, many of whom will be rich young people prepared to pay premium rents. Very often, their rents are paid by daddy, who wants to know that his son or daughter is temporarily housed somewhere nice, safe and convenient. I once let a flat to a Japanese student who, quite literally, had a suitcase full of money.

New forms of Buy-to-Let

Nowadays, you do not have to buy a house or flat outright to become a landlord. New schemes are starting whereby you can buy an investment in a boutique hotel, for instance.

Here, you buy a room in a hotel, which is let out by the hotel operator, who guarantees a rental return of a certain percentage, usually 6 per cent. This means the hotel owner will pay you the rental money even if the room is not let. You can also use the hotel room yourself, although obviously the fewer nights you stay, the higher the rental return. Loans of typically 65 per cent of the purchase price can be obtained. You buy a lease of, say, 99 years and the idea is that you purchase a no-hassle holiday Buy-to-Let.

Such schemes are set to grow and are already up and running in several holiday places abroad. But they have not been going long enough to prove themselves, so as yet are high-risk.

There are also several schemes offered by developers whereby you purchase an off-plan apartment as an investment, and the developer offers to rent it out for you at a guaranteed return, again typically 6 per cent. This also means that you will get your 6 per cent whether or not the property is actually rented.

But – beware. Rental returns are only guaranteed for a certain length of time, usually one to three years. After that, you are on your own. Such schemes are heavily marketed with seductive brochures and are made to look almost irresistible. Never buy into them, though, until you have not only worked out all the figures but confronted the worst-case scenario. Also take into account service and maintenance charges. Very often, these are set very low with new schemes and they then rise dramatically after all the units have been sold.

Go for what you know

A question new investors often ask is: should the investment property be very near to my own home? Well, there are considerable advantages to this. By far the greatest number of investment landlords start by buying property in an area they already know well. Big-time investors from the Far East are a different matter, as they frequently buy properties when they are no more than a hole in the ground. But for those of us not in this league, different considerations apply.

It makes sense to buy an investment just round the corner from where you live for a number of reasons. First, if you have lived in a particular area for a long time, you are likely to know the price structure of that location, and whether a particular property represents a bargain or not. I know Hammersmith, west London, very well, and my London investment properties have always been in this borough. I know the shops well, I know the transport links, I am aware of the advantages and disadvantages of living in the area, and I keep a keen eye on prices by obsessively looking in agents' windows. As I am on hand, it is also relatively easy for me to view and snap up a bargain should I come across one. I am not on hand to readily view properties in Shoreditch, for instance, and a property that seems a bargain in an unknown area of London may actually be in an area that has hidden horrors of which I know nothing.

A friend who lives in Putney, south-west London, always buys investment properties in Putney, for much the same reason. Although SW15 is not such an obviously good letting area as W14, he feels more confident buying into an area where he has lived for many years than, say, Hackney, which he does not know at all.

Most people working in the City or in central London would not want to rent a place as far out as Putney, but on the other hand, it is a busy place and there are many people working locally, in banks, schools and offices, who are looking to rent. Although Putney is only 3 miles away from Hammersmith, it represents a completely different kind of rental market. These are all factors that the novice investor should bear in mind when considering any specific purchase.

Greg Shackleton, the super-landlord who has about 50 investment properties, always buys in Brighton, where he lives. He is on hand to view and snap up bargains, he knows precisely whether a particular property is in a good location, and he can quickly call on local agents, builders, handymen and so on.

If you do not know an area at all, it is best to leave it alone, at least until you are in a position to do some research and assess the pros and cons of the place. Very many people who enthusiastically bought investment properties in the Docklands area of London thinking they couldn't lose subsequently found them hard to let. Although they were in one sense central, there were very few facilities, very few good shops and, after work, no 'life' in the area at all. Tenants felt marooned there, and almost as if they were in prison. Most tenants coming to a new area will want to sample at least some of the local life on offer.

Don't forget that the majority of incoming tenants will be strangers to the area and, being mainly young, they like to live in a place where they have access to pubs, cinemas, nightlife, clubs, theatres and other entertainment. They do not, generally speaking, want to be in a sterile ghetto with security gates and nothing but other new developments as far as the eye can see.

I bought a holiday home on the south coast and, once I got to know the area, I also bought an investment property. Before buying, though, I enquired at a number of letting agents as to the extent of the rental market. I learnt that a couple of multi-nationals had recently opened up premises nearby and were employing hundreds of IT and computer workers. Most of these were recent graduates, new to the area, and would be looking for smart, easy-to-maintain rental homes. That decided me. Although rentals were far lower than in London, property prices were correspondingly lower, and so the gross yield was about the same, maybe slightly higher.

The investment property, a small but perfectly formed studio, was soon let to a young man, a recent PhD who had been headhunted at university by an IT firm. He was brand new to the town but as the flat was central, in a pretty seafront location, on major bus routes and near to all the town's amenities, he soon made friends and established a busy social life.

In fact, that property rented out very successfully for 10 years, after which it needed a total makeover. Not only that, but the value of the investment had increased mightily over that time. When I first bought that property, it cost just £3,000. A decade later, and now looking very smart and chic, its sale value had risen to £100,000. So it represented an excellent investment.

What I learned over the years is that many people would rather to have their own self-contained space, however tiny, than share with others. A small studio is affordable by many people, whereas if they went any lower down the rental market, they would have to share a bathroom and maybe a kitchen with strangers. For this reason, it is always worth considering small studio flats in areas where many people want to rent – especially where these are people in their first or second job, or who have outgrown shared accommodation.

Locations that may not lend themselves to an idyllic family life can work extremely well as a letting proposition. For instance, it is very well worth looking at properties over shops. For most of the time that your tenant is in residence, the shop will be closed, and in the evenings and on Sundays, when she is mainly at home, there will be peace and quiet. Also, shops are usually situated in shopping areas.

Just recently the government has been trying to persuade landlords to buy rental properties situated over commercial property, as these often stand empty for a long time. As with any property purchase, there are pros and cons. Detractors argue that the shop beneath the flat may change hands, turn into a noisy video, betting or bike shop, or, alternatively, stand empty for many months and eventually become a dingy charity shop.

On the plus side, residential properties over shops tend to be sold at cheaper prices than other similar properties in the same area. There may be some slight risk in buying a residential property over a shop, as the shopping area may go up or down at any time.

Some councils give grants to investors who want to renovate dilapidated flats over shops, or to turn a derelict or storage area over a shop into a residential property. It's always worth asking the local council whether such grants are available. In 2007 the maximum grant would have been about £10,000, paid once all planning permissions are in place.

A friend bought a rental property in a 1970s block where trains ran very close by. Although this might not be desirable for an old person confined to the home, it was perfect for a tenant who was out all day. The other big plus of this property was that it was close to the station – only two or three minutes away. For tenants who took the place, the proximity of the station more than made up for the noise of the trains.

Buy-to-Let investors can face major problems when they are ready to sell their rental property, as it can mean major disruption for the tenant who may be happily settled, plus often many months of no rent when the property is on the market. Even if a suitable offer is made on day one, it can still take three to four months before a sale is completed, during which time the outgoing landlord has to pick up all bills, such as utilities and council tax as well as continuing to pay the mortgage and service charges if it is a leasehold property.

The reason for this is that housebuyers, estate agents and also solicitors have traditionally insisted on vacant possession before the property goes on the market. But all this is set to change with new schemes whereby investment landlords can buy and sell properties while the tenant remains in situ. This has several advantages in that the tenant does not have to move, the outgoing landlord receives rent right up to the day of completion, and because the tenant remains in place, the new buyer does not have to face the many costs associated with preparing the property for rental.

One such scheme, HomeLet IPEX (Investment Property Exchange), launched a nationwide network in March 2007 which allows buyers and sellers to exchange investment properties online.

How does it work? The IPEX scheme is known as the Readymade Buy-to-Let, and constitutes a one-stop shop whereby the property is valued and put up for sale on the IPEX website. There are also useful links to other homebuying sites. All legal and conveyancing work can be handled by Homelet and there is a 1.5 per cent charge for selling, which is cheaper than many estate agents.

Because the scheme is aimed solely at Buy-to-Let investors who are selling and buying, it is a tailored service not aimed at the general buyer. The big advantage of this scheme for the vendor is that the property is only marketed to other interested Buy-to-Let landlords, so no time is wasted on general marketing. This usually ensures a quicker sale. There are also of course no costs in preparing the property for sale as it remains occupied.

As far as the buyer is concerned there is already proof of rental yield, and this cuts out much of the guesswork and also the stress, as before a property is tenanted you can never be absolutely sure of the achievable rent.

As with buying a car, a complete 'service history' is available, whereby the buyer knows in advance the rental being paid, how rents have increased over the years and whether there have been any worrying void periods. As with the vendor, there are no costs to the buyer in preparing the property for rental, and no costs in advertising it.

For the tenant, there is the inestimable advantage in not having to move out, especially as all the indications are that tenants are now staying in the same properties for longer than ever before – if they are happy with their home, that is.

The IPEX scheme – and others like it – can only grow in future as Buy-to-Let becomes ever more sophisticated and as ever more people want to rent, for various reasons.

There is a still small but rapidly growing tenant market amongst older or retired people who do not want the hassle of ownership any more but who are looking for a safe, secure, long-term rental home.

Another new scheme, RentB4Ubuy, allows investor landlords who are selling their properties to rent to a tenant who basically wants to buy. This is an online service whereby investors who want to sell are put in touch with renters who want to buy. This ensures again that the property is not empty, untenanted and not bringing in income during the time the property is being sold, though the incoming tenant does have to make a commitment to buy.

Keep your eye on the market

Although successful rental properties must be very near to stations and shops, this does not mean to say that every property in such a location will let easily. Before buying, it is essential to establish whether there is a serious rental market in this particular area, and how big this market might be. In some suburban areas, full of young marrieds with families who prefer to buy rather than rent, there may not be much of a market at all. Also, markets may change dramatically. Near where I live in London, two huge premises, each employing literally thousands of young workers, suddenly closed down and established themselves elsewhere. This meant that a vast potential rental market had suddenly vanished.

These are all things that, in the lettings game, have to be watched carefully. Few things stay the same for ever and the essence of success in the investment property market is a willingness to buy and sell as markets change and develop.

Most estate agents maintain that the rental market and the sales market are rarely both good at the same time. If sales are good, rentals are down and if rentals are good, this means that sales are down, usually because of increased interest rates on mortgages. But if you have a smart, clean property in a location where many people are always looking to rent, then the risk is that much less. And remember, whatever the gloom and doom there *always have been* and there *always will be* people looking for homes to rent.

In recent years, the rental market has also been dramatically affected by the huge increase in the numbers of people buying investment properties as an alternative to a pension scheme or other financial investment. As pension schemes and other investments, such as stocks and shares, have taken spectacular tumbles, people are turning to 'safer' bricks and mortar. This has meant that in some areas, the market is saturated with rental properties.

The effect of this saturation is, of course, to force rents down. At the same time, properties are getting ever more expensive to buy. Barry Manners, a director of Chard Letting Agents, says that rents have gone down considerably in many prime London areas, simply because there are so many quality properties for tenants to choose from. This means it is more important than ever to keep an eagle eye on the market, and avoid buying in an area where there is already serious over-supply of rental properties.

Investment pointers

Tim Hyatt, lettings director of Knight Frank, advises: 'First of all, ask yourself what kind of investor you are. Are you thinking of being in Buy-to-Let for the long term, and what kind of risk are you prepared to take?'

Tim believes there are two basic types of investor: those who are looking at the 'dead cert' and those who are looking for trends. 'The first type will go for existing key prime locations and the second type will look at regeneration and the future.

'The way you look at the time frame will affect the way you finance the venture. If you are considering an area which is on the way up but not there yet, you may not get a return on the investment for several years. The longer you can hang in there, the more money you are likely to make, if restaurants, transport links and other amenities are scheduled to come into the area.

'But always, the essential aspect is to do research and also to make sure your financing can weather an unforeseen storm, such as a void period of three months or an unexpected repair bill for a new boiler, new roof or other expensive item.

'A cheap way of sourcing good information,' says Tim, 'is to go to some lettings websites, find a property that you like, then call the agent and find out whether it is still available, and how much rent it is likely to get. That way, you will soon discover which properties in the area that you have earmarked go quickly and which ones hang around.

'The other important aspect is to identify the type of tenant you are going to be attracting and what that tenant most wants.'

Lesley Cooper, a former IT worker who has built up a diverse portfolio of properties in Tunbridge Wells, Newcastle, Hull and Wallsend since becoming a Buy-to-Let investor in 1997, advises: 'Everything points to having lots of small, cheap units rather than big expensive ones.

'I started with studios, as the market overall shows that 90 per cent of tenants pay around £600 a month rent. When you move out of that, you start to reduce your tenant pool. I have bought at auction, and also bought four terraced properties in Gravesend, Kent, a place of incoming regeneration funds.'

In 2001, Lesley left salaried employment to concentrate on Buy-to-Let full-time. She adds: 'I don't think that buying off-plan works, most of the time. You can easily overpay and then be stuck with something you can't either sell or let. Buying off-plan means that everybody wants to let and sell at the same time. For me, it didn't feel right, especially as, although developers offer many incentives such as paying stamp duty and giving rental guarantees, they rarely reduce the actual price. In my view, off-plans are risky.

'My other piece of advice, from experience, is to go for blocks of purpose-built flats rather than conversions. With conversions, you often find that the common parts are dingy and that the freeholder is an amateur who does not really understand how to run a building. This is of course the very opposite of

Greg Shackleton's advice, and illustrates that although there are many shades of opinion, there is no single aspect of Buy-to Let on which all investors and experts agree.

'By and large, bigger blocks of flats are better run, they have a maintenance programme and a sinking fund and they are more attractive to tenants than period conversions with dark, dingy common parts and poor security.'

You also need to ask yourself how long you want to stay in the lettings game. Figures from ARLA (the Association of Residential Letting Agents) suggest that most landlords are thinking in terms of 15 years. More than half of all landlords are investing for a future nest egg, while only 5 per cent are investing for rental income alone.

Or, put another way, most landlords would like to invest for rental income alone, but the percentage yield from rents these days is simply not high enough to allow them to do this. In the past, landlords relied almost totally on rental income, but those days, sadly, seem to be over.

When I first starting investing in property in the mid-1990s, rental yields of between 10 per cent and 13 per cent were common, and not too difficult to achieve. Average yield is now 4.9 per cent, and in order to make the equation work financially, potential capital growth has to be factored in. This means that eventually, most landlords will sell up and cash in.

It may also be that rental income does not even completely cover a Buy-to-Let mortgage. When these mortgages first came in around 1996, the usual ratio was that the rent had to be 130 per cent of the mortgage repayment costs. But many mortgage companies will now lend at a lower ratio than this.

Whether temporarily good or bad, the rental sector will never entirely disappear, and in a sought-after area there are always more tenants than properties. If you are very, very new to the lettings game it might be an idea to wander past a number of lettings agencies and note how busy they are. If the workers inside are chatting to each other and there is nobody in the shop, the rental market, at least in that area, may not be all that good. But if, on the other hand, the premises are crowded with people and everybody looks extremely busy, you are likely to have hit on a location that has more people looking than properties available. It is also a good idea, if you have the brass neck, to pretend to be a tenant and get your eye in by looking at properties on the rental market.

If you are new to the lettings market, it is probably not a good idea to buy a three-bedroom house, with professional sharers in mind. Although there is a demand here, it is much less than for the smaller units. The one exception to this, maybe, is if you are looking to buy accommodation for students to rent.

You may, if you have a lot of money, a lot of nerve, or both, wonder whether to buy a large dilapidated property which you then turn into flats. Such properties can certainly become excellent investments but I would advise leaving them alone until you have got your hand in by first buying studios and one-bed flats. Very often, the budget runs away with you when converting large houses into flats, and it may be a very long time before you see a return on your investment.

Although estate agents always remind clients that buying rental properties should be seen as a medium- to long-term investment, the fact is that by buying a small flat in reasonable condition, you can be receiving income on it within months of purchase. If you buy somewhere extremely dilapidated, it may be years before you come into profit. Also, unless you are a builder or have expertise here, you can find yourself paying through the nose. And if you add on fees for architects, surveyors and so on, you could find yourself with an extremely expensive liability.

The best advice is: start small and build up gradually, if you find it's working. It's easier to extricate yourself from a small studio flat than from a five-bedroom half-converted Victorian pile.

Service charges

Before making an offer on any letting property at all, make sure you are aware of all service and maintenance costs and any possible levies, because you as the landlord are responsible for these. As a general rule, the more lavishly appointed the building, the higher the service charges. It is unlikely that you will be able to recoup these costs in higher rentals.

Facilities that add greatly to service charges, but not to rent, include communal heating and hot water systems, common in older blocks; gyms and leisure centres; porterage; security gates; expensive carpeting and wallpaper in common areas; underground parking, valet parking, restaurants and bars in common parts; swimming pools. Experience has shown that gyms, swimming pools and leisure centres are hardly ever used by tenants, yet the landlord has to foot the bill.

Lifts may not increase rents as such, but it is difficult to rent out a property on the third floor or above which does not have a lift. Moral: only ever buy rental properties on the first or second floor. Avoid the ground floor – some people believe ground floor flats present a security risk – and not everybody likes to be high up, even when there is a lift.

The safer a property appears to be, the easier it is to rent out, so bear security in mind when sourcing potential rental properties.

Penthouses have their attraction, of course, but they usually cost more to buy than other flats in the building, and may not command a significantly higher rent.

As a general rule, ex-local authority blocks and conversions attract the lowest service charges, whilst mansion blocks and designer-led new blocks have the highest charges.

As the leaseholder, not the tenant, is responsible for paying service charges, these must be taken into account not only at the time of purchase, but in the future. Before buying, discover whether any major works are indicated, whether there is a sinking fund and whether ground rent is payable.

The lease is a legally-binding contract between the leaseholder and the freeholder, so make sure you read it carefully before making any offer. Absentee landlords are often the most hated people in a block of flats, so investors should make sure they play their part and act as members of the community.

It is also important to discover whether Buy-to-Let is actually allowed in any particular building, and if there are any rules governing incomers. Some buildings do not allow short-term tenancies; others may not allow holiday lets, or tenancies shorter than one year. Some Residents' Associations like to vet tenants for suitability, before they move in. In any case, you should always let the freeholders or agents know the names of your tenants, and also give a contact telephone number.

As Buy-to-Let increases in popularity and half to three-quarters of any apartment building may now contain sub-tenants, ever more freeholders and managing agents are insisting that renters are given a copy of the lease. Very often a cut-down version will be available which lets renters know about such matters as rubbish disposal, playing music, hanging out washing, parking arrangements and general behaviour while in occupation.

Letting agents are also now commonly asking for a copy of the lease, either in its full or its shortened form, for the benefit of renters.

Before signing any contract, it is vital to obtain three years' accounts from the freeholders or managing agents, and also discover whether there is likely to be any significant building or repair levy in the near future.

Never forget that location remains the number one selling point, closely followed by condition. If the property is not immaculate when you buy it, it should look perfect by the time it's ready to let, at least so far as the kitchen and bathroom are concerned.

3 Working out the numbers

One reason why property can be such an attractive investment, apart from the fact that property is exciting in itself, is that you stand to get two bites of the profit cherry. There is the income you obtain month by month from rentals, and there is also, with any luck, the capital increase on your initial outlay.

For instance, if you buy an investment property for £80,000 and rent it out for £8,000 a year, you don't have to be a mathematical genius to work out that you are making a gross annual return of 10 per cent. This is far higher than you can get by any other relatively safe means. Three years later, that same property may be worth £120,000, meaning that your capital has increased by £40,000. Therefore, in three years, you could have made a whacking £64,000 on an initial investment of £80,000, which is not bad by anyone's standards.

Even though these figures are gross rather than net, this sort of return is still extremely handsome, and not at all unusual in the investment property market. If you take away as much as half for costs and taxes, you have still made a wonderful return on your initial investment.

A friend bought an investment property some years ago for £43,000 and rented it out at £600 a month, the then market rent for that property. Within three years, the value of his flat had shot up to £90,000, more than doubling his initial investment. He would have, therefore, made lots of money *even if the property had remained empty for all that time* – a truth not lost on commercial investors, for whom it may be more profitable to leave a building empty than to rent or lease it out.

However, such large percentage increases cannot be guaranteed or assumed. So, once you have sorted out a good location and have decided, by judicious research, on the type of property you would like to buy, the next thing to do is to sit down and work out all the figures as accurately as possible, down to the last hundred pounds, *before* making any offer.

Cash buyers

We will assume for the moment that you are a cash buyer, as so many people are these days. Once, when I was viewing a potential property, I proudly reminded the estate agent that I was, or would be, a cash buyer. He was unimpressed, saying: 'Everybody is a cash buyer nowadays.' Buy-to-Let schemes, for those who are not cash buyers, will be explained later in this chapter.

Rents and payback times

Let's say the asking price of the type of property you have in mind is £80,000. Before making an offer, it's essential to have a close idea of the kind of rent you are likely to achieve with this kind of property in this particular area. You can do this by asking a number of lettings agencies, or by looking in local newspapers and agents' windows.

You then have to work out, before doing any other kind of arithmetic, the optimum yearly gross rental. Most professional landlords quickly work out the number of years it would take for the property to pay for itself in rental income before deciding whether to go ahead.

Greg Shackleton, in common with many investment landlords, does not expect the kind of properties he buys to increase greatly in capital value. He does not buy with capital increase in mind, so he has to maximize the rental return.

Not long ago, it was possible in many parts of the country to get a 10 per cent gross yield on rentals, but now this is becoming increasingly difficult. However, a yield of 6 per cent or less is too low to cover all costs and eventualities.

If your property is likely to increase substantially in value (this must always be an inspired guess, of course, as nobody knows for sure what will happen in the future) then I would say you could go for a 10-year payback period – but not more. A property costing £80,000 has to be capable of earning back that amount in rent within 10 years, otherwise it is most probably not a wise rental investment.

In any case, the gross annual yield should be at least twice that of any savings or investment account at the bank. As there are very many unforeseen costs and circumstances in the property world, you need to make the investment as risk-free as possible.

When talking about payback times, we are assuming that the property will be fully let at all times, without any voids. And of course you never can assume this. Nor can you be absolutely certain that the high rental you get in one year will be achievable in another year. Many landlords have stories of how a particular property was let at an enormous rent for several years, and then could only be let at a dramatically reduced rent. If you discover you have bought in an oversubscribed area, you may not be able to get the rent you hoped for, or were led to believe you could get.

Any rule of thumb on payback times has to be a guesstimate, because none of us has a crystal ball to see into the future. It has been worked out that a void of just one month represents 8.3 per cent of yearly rental income. Letting is never an exact science, so when working out possible returns and costs, one must be as clear-sighted, not to say pessimistic, as possible.

The most you can hope to do is not to fall into obvious traps. If you are considering buying a property costing £200,000 or more, and you are told that the likely rental is £800 a month, or £10,400 a year, then you are most probably not making a wise investment, as it would take you 20 years, not 10, to get back your investment in rent. This is too long.

If, instead of renting, you invested that £200,000 at 4 per cent, you would be getting £8,000 a year, which is almost as much as from rentals, and without any of the hassle.

Of course, there is always the expectation that property prices will go up, which means your capital will increase. But as a general rule, if the net return is only as good as you can get on a deposit account, it would be better to avoid that particular property. The reason? There are so many hidden costs in letting property that you need a considerable margin for error.

Also, if you bank on property prices rising, you are in effect gambling with your money. Prices may go up, they may stay the same or they may go down; nobody knows for certain. It is probably little better than going to Las Vegas or to bet on a horse to put all your faith on property prices rising faster than inflation.

As a general rule, property rises do beat inflation, but there can be no guarantees of this. Very many property speculators got their fingers badly burnt in the late 1980s and early 1990s when a large amount of residential property went into negative equity.

Greg Shackleton advises: 'Although my properties have substantially increased in value since I started buying to let in 1994, I believe it is a mistake to look for capital appreciation. You must always, always, always look for yield.

'If the UK went into negative equity, which could easily happen, capital appreciation would be wiped out. Unless you go for yield, you are taking a huge gamble. And we are talking about sums of money that are too big to gamble.'

This advice is echoed by Jon Wright, a former accountant who has amassed a diverse portfolio of investment property in Leeds, Brighton and Hove, and north London. He says: 'I soon realized that it is always more important to concentrate on yield than capital growth. The most vital thing is how much rent you can get.'

It is also essential, adds Jon, to work out percentages on everything and to go for as many certainties as possible. 'You should avoid hypothetical figures and any wishful thinking, and always work out how long it will take you to get your money back. It should be no more than 10 to 12 years, at most.

When buying, go on what the place is worth now, not what it might be worth in three or four years' time.'

Jon adds that he likes number-crunching and believes his accountancy background has given him the confidence he needs to proceed in this complicated, high-risk, high-expense world. 'I use accounting methods to evaluate a deal but I also go on my intuition. Never forget this important element. If a property doesn't feel right but you can't exactly put your finger on why, walk away from it.'

Other costs

The cost of purchasing the property, though, is by no means the only cost you have to take into account. If you are buying a leasehold flat, there will also be annual service charges on the property. These are charges for which you as a landlord are responsible. Service and maintenance can vary from as little as £200 a year, for an ex-council property, to £5,000 a year or more for a very smart mansion block.

And the charges can change from year to year. Before exchanging contracts you, or your solicitor, need to obtain from the freeholder or managing agents, accounts for the past three years and an estimation of likely charges in the near future. These charges will have to be deducted from any rent you might obtain, as they are not recoverable from the tenant. If the annual service charge is extremely high, you may not be able to recover this in extra rent.

Much information regarding leasehold properties now has to be contained within the Home Information Pack (HIP). This includes: statements or summaries of service charges for the past 36 months; a summary of works being undertaken or proposed; documentation regarding buildings insurance, any claims for personal injury compensation before marketing began, and the most recent requests for service charge, ground rent and insurance payments.

Wily landlords rarely buy investment properties that have very high service charges, as these can substantially eat into your profits. For instance, I once viewed a potentially very nice one-bedroom seafront flat. The asking price was £59,950 and the property needed at least £5,000 spending on it to make it lettable. An agent advised me that I could get perhaps £400 a month for it in rent. At best, that meant an annual gross yield of around 8 per cent. A possibility, then.

But the service and maintenance charges on the property were £2,400 a year. On an income of £400 a month from the place, I would be paying half that just in service and maintenance charges. I'm no mathematician, but it didn't take even me long to work out that these figures didn't add up to a good investment at all.

Outgoings on the property don't necessarily stop with the annual service charges. There will almost certainly be extra levies from time to time to pay for external redecoration, rewiring, repair of the lift and so on. These could mean extra one-off payments of several thousand pounds; again, money you will be unable to recover in increased rentals. All blocks of flats, even those with low service charges, are liable to these levies.

There will also be annual buildings insurance to pay. Sometimes this is included in the annual service charge, sometimes it is an extra. Again, it is something you must find out about before buying anywhere. Buildings insurance is compulsory, not optional, as without it you will not be covered should any damage occur to your property.

A corporate or celebrity tenant may not mind, within reason, how much rent they pay, as they will value convenience, smartness and a good postcode above financial considerations. But tenants of this type are not available in every area, and if your most likely tenants are office or bank workers, teachers or lecturers on fairly low incomes, rents cannot be sky high.

There will in addition, on leasehold properties, be an annual ground rent to pay. Usually this is not much, maybe £50 or £100 a year, but it all adds up.

Leases

It is important to know the length of lease, as this can affect the property's resale value. If your lease is 90 years or more, there is little to worry about, but if it is getting dangerously near 80 years or less (properties tend to get cheaper as leases shorten, and may therefore be tempting to the investor) you may be better off looking elsewhere. Mortgage providers are not keen to lend on properties where leases are 80 years or less, so you may have trouble reselling the property. Sometimes, though, leases can be extended, although this is always at a price.

If considering buying a property with a short lease, always ask about the possibility of extending the lease, as you may be lucky. A friend took a deep breath and bought an investment flat with a 60-year lease. As he was a cash buyer, he did not have to worry about satisfying a mortgage company. The short lease meant, though, that although the property was very cheap indeed for what it was, the possibility of reselling at a profit was low.

However, a couple of years later, the residents in the block decided to club together and buy the freehold. This meant another outlay of £3,000–£4,000 for my friend, but because the leases were now extended to 125 years, the value of each property in the block doubled overnight. But my friend was not aware of this when he bought; he just had a lucky strike. He was quite prepared to recover, eventually, his initial outlay in rental income, and was not looking for capital growth.

In some specific cases, though, it can be worth considering buying on a very short lease. Interior designer Linda Camp has bought a small London flat cheaply on a very short lease, for the sole purpose of financing her son's school fees. The lease finishes at just about the same time as her son's education and although there will be no value on the property when the lease runs out, she is able to let it at a high rent in the meantime.

Of course, as Linda is a professional designer, she has been able to make the flat look good on a very tight budget.

Leaseholders now have the right to extend their lease, to manage their own property and also to collectively enfranchise; in other words, to buy the freehold between them. All these aspects give leaseholders greater security and increase the value of the property, but they cost money in themselves – again, money that you will not be able to recoup in extra rent, as your tenant will not care whether or not you have extended the lease or enfranchised.

Unless your BTL property is being sold with a share of the freehold, always ask about these issues as they will most probably not be contained within the Home Information Pack.

It is particularly important when buying a flat to ask whether there are any plans to collectively enfranchise. And if there is anything you don't understand or which is not clear – walk away, as flat ownership can be complicated. Not only is it MORE complicated when you are a BTL investor, it is even more vital to understand all the ramifications, as your bottom line is that you want your investment to be a financial asset.

Making the property lettable

How much would you have to spend on the place to get it into lettable condition? Although when letting privately you can rent it out in any condition at all, provided you can persuade somebody to pay rent for it, if you go through a letting agency, certain standards have to be maintained. There is also the consideration that the better the property, the better the tenant – as a general rule. Also, you are likely to get a higher rent when going through an agency, so it is probably worth refurbishing your property to current standards and regulations.

Reputable agencies will not accept any property where current regulations relating to fire, gas and furniture safety are not met. It is against the law, and no agency wants to be seen breaking the law. It is a risk they dare not take. Nor will agencies these days take on their books a property that does not have a telephone and television point and, if applicable, an entryphone system.

There must be a working shower and a usable kitchen. Agencies vastly prefer properties that have a washing machine and tumble dryer, fridge-freezer and microwave. Although not all of these amenities are essential, the more there are, the easier the property will be to let. All have to be bought, all have to be in good working order, and instructions and guarantees should be available with every appliance.

Your letting property does not have to be in good condition when you buy it, but it should look like a show home by the time it is ready to let. Clearly, then, you have to assess not just how much money you would need to spend on it to make it habitable and attractive, but how long this work will take.

One investment landlord makes a point of buying vacant properties in bad condition, and allowing one month between exchange of contracts and completion. During this month, the workforce move in, install a new kitchen and bathroom, paint and decorate throughout, and rewire and re-plumb as necessary. Once contracts have been exchanged, he alerts his local letting agency that a new property will soon be available. They advertise it and, assuming all goes according to plan, on the very day the workforce move out, the new tenant moves in.

This particular landlord reckons to spend between £15,000 and £20,000 on the refurbishment of each property. This sum does not include furniture, as all of his properties are let out unfurnished.

If you are considering buying a property in bad condition, it is worth asking local agents how much extra rent you may be able to achieve if the place is done up superbly, rather than if it is just adequate. In some areas, such as South Kensington in London, for example, there may be a striking difference. In other areas there is a definite rental ceiling, however wonderful the condition of the place, and this cannot be exceeded. In such cases, it may not be worth going for the most expensive kitchen, bathroom and so on.

In many areas, achievable rents will be closely linked to average wages and salaries.

On the other hand, it is rarely worth going for the cheapest you can get, as you only want to install a kitchen and bathroom once. Bearing in mind that a place that is tenanted gets quite a lot of wear and tear, spending more money upfront may save you repair and renovation costs later. Second-hand appliances, such as a cooker, fridge, washing machine and so on, may be a false economy.

If you already know an excellent and not too pricey team of local builders, then it may be worth your while buying somewhere in bad condition. My south coast studio flat was in truly terrible condition when I bought it in 1998. Indeed, it had not been inhabited since 1972 and needed total gutting. But I already knew a good local builder, and so had the confidence to go ahead and buy the place. Small as it was, the renovation cost over £3,000 and it took a year for this to be recouped in rent. Six years later, the flat collapsed when flooded from the one above, and this time renovation cost £12,000 – plus the property was untenanted for three months. It's the kind of thing that can happen all too often with property.

Although it is always tempting to buy a place cheaply and then do it up, as this represents a challenge to the property freak, it is not always a good idea. In some cases renovation can be so expensive that it takes years to recover the amount in rental income. If there is serious structural work to do, as may be the case with an older property, you may not be making a wise investment.

Once you have worked out the likely cost of refurbishment and any furnishings, plus theoretical length of time taken to complete everything (some sofas take three months to deliver), you must add it all to the cost of the property. One property I bought for £82,000 had cost me £85,000 in fees and costs by the time it was ready to let. Also, after completion, there was a month's gap before it was ready to let, meaning that I had a 'void' of one month to take into account.

Although you can claim repairs and refurbishment on tax once the property is let, you cannot do this while you are not receiving income, so you must add it to the capital cost of the investment. These costs can, however, be deducted from your capital gains tax liability when you sell.

Professional and legal costs

Solicitors' fees will be £900 at least; more if there are complications to work out on the lease. There may be other costs for local searches and surveys and you also have to remember to add on VAT for all prices quoted. The cost of searches and surveys are increasing all the time. In normal circumstances, you will not be able to recover the VAT, which, at 17.5 per cent at the time of writing, can add considerably to your purchase costs.

Since 1 December 2003, stamp duty land taxes on residential property, levied when you buy but not when you sell, have been as follows: properties selling for up to £125,000 attract no tax at all; properties going for between £125,000 and £250,000 attract stamp duty of 1 per cent; at over £250,000 and under £500,000 the duty is 3 per cent; and for properties over £500,000 the duty rises to 4 per cent.

So far as the Buy-to-Let investor – or indeed any property purchaser – is concerned, this is purely money down the drain. You get nothing whatever for it, but it has to be paid before the property can be yours. Many investors forget to add stamp duty (land tax, as it is now called) on to their set-up costs, but it must be done if you are to take a professional approach.

What about surveys, also very expensive items? I have a personal confession here, which is that I never, ever spend money on a survey when paying cash for a property. Surveyors may say this is foolish (well, they would) but it seems to me that you can tell by looking and smelling whether a place has subsidence, damp, a leaky roof or unsafe wiring. I once viewed a one-bedroom flat, in bad condition, as a prospective investment. The price of the property was £24,000 and the attic flat was characterful and charming. With a little work and expertise, it could have made a wonderful renter, except for one thing: the roof was extremely dodgy, and there was a huge damp patch in one corner. Because of this, I decided against it.

But I didn't need an expensive survey to tell me this. It was possible to assess the condition of the roof just by looking. When surveys cost upwards of £300, doing without one can represent a considerable saving. Over the years I have bought very many properties, both for myself and as rental invest-ments, and I have never once had a full structural survey, not even when buying a totally dilapidated Queen Anne property containing squatters. And I have never once regretted it.

Of course, when you buy an investment property on a mortgage, the mortgage lender will send a surveyor round to check that its money is safe. Although this is not a full structural survey, it is good enough, as the money will not be forthcoming if the property falls down on survey.

However, it must be stressed that if you do not have a proper survey you are taking a risk, especially with an old building. One property investor bought a Buy-to-Let flat in 2006 and did not have a full structural survey. Some months later, new regulations came in on asbestos removal and the upshot was that his half-renovated flat had to be quarantined until the asbestos work was carried out.

The investor lost a lot of money but it was a case of buyer beware – it was up to him to find out whether or not the property was contaminated by asbestos, or whether the asbestos would be disturbed by the renovations. If he had left the flat as it was there would have been no danger from the asbestos.

There are many instances of investors buying tired or old properties cheaply – and then discovering later that they have not got such a bargain after all. This is a particular trap for new and inexperienced investors.

In most cases, if you are buying to let on a mortgage, you would not need to go to the extra expense of a full structural survey.

Home Information Packs

Few housing decisions have caused as much controversy and comment than the Home Information Packs, which were not even a tiny gleam in the eye of government when the first edition of this book was published. Now they are a reality and have important consequences for BTL investors.

As a buyer you will now receive a HIP, usually from the estate agent, free of charge. This will contain a number of documents, some compulsory and some optional. The main compulsory item is the Energy Performance Certificate, which has to be commissioned from an accredited Energy Inspector, who visits the property and creates the certificate. This is based on the energy efficiency or otherwise of the heating, double glazing, insulation and any other energy-using elements in the property.

Very many older buildings are extremely energy-inefficient, and the good news for investors is that they may be eligible for a grant from the Energy Saving Trust to make the property more energy-efficient. Many of today's younger tenants and buyers are extremely concerned about energy issues and will choose an energy-efficient property over any other.

Most estate agents are now well geared up to produce HIPs, and of course you will have to provide one when you come to sell your property – unless of course, a different party comes to power and scraps them. But at the time of writing that has not happened and the present government is still committed to these packs.

Utilities and council tax

Suppose you have now bought your property. It has been refurbished, all the legal work has been done, and you are ready to let. There are still more costs to come. First of all, if the property contains a gas cooker or gas central heating, you must obtain a gas safety certificate from a fully qualified CORGI engineer, every year. There is a standard annual fee for this job, but it must be done. For this reason, many landlords renovating properties from scratch decide not to have gas. Instead, they go for electric cookers and storage heaters, thus avoiding the expense and organization of getting annual gas certificates. Small flats may not need central heating, and can be heated perfectly adequately with storage or Dimplex heaters.

Because of the need for a gas certificate, wherever I have a choice I won't buy a property with gas heating or gas cookers. Sometimes, though, the property is so perfect in other ways that I sigh and put up with the gas cooker and boiler, and the hassle and expense of obtaining the yearly gas certificate. It has to be said, though, that gas is by far the best fuel for heating, and properties without central heating may be difficult to resell.

Every year, it seems, more certificates and inspections are required for tenanted properties. The yearly gas certificate has been law since 1994, owing to the potentially lethal effects of carbon monoxide poisoning from unsafe gas appliances. Although instances of fatalities from carbon monoxide poisoning in rented flats are tiny almost to the point of non-existence, gas is – as everybody knows – a dangerous substance, so the annual certificate is a good precaution.

Electrical and energy certificates are more difficult to justify, but nevertheless they are creeping in. All new tenancies created from October 2008 will need a HIP-type energy certificate, and by the end of 2008 new tenancies will also need an NICEIC electricity certificate, to ensure the wiring and electrical connections are safe. Unlike the gas certificate, the electricity and energy certificates are one-offs and do not need to be renewed each year.

If you rent your property out through an ARLA (Association of Residential Letting Agents) agent they will have details of what you need to do to acquire the relevant certificates. Landlord associations such as the National Federation of Residential Landlords – which I can highly recommend as I have been a member myself for many years – will have up-to-date information on the latest safety and efficiency requirements for landlords.

Local councils may, though, legally order tenanted properties to be inspected from time to time for electrical safety. The ARLA leaflet, *Lets Make it Safe*, can be downloaded from their website www.arla.co.uk.

While your property is not let, you will be responsible for paying all utilities, including council tax. In 2004, the rules on council tax changed, so that now in most areas you have to pay 90 per cent of the full council tax for second homes, holiday homes or investment properties, instead of 50 per cent as before. If the property is tenanted on an Assured Shorthold Tenancy, then the tenant pays the council tax, at 75 per cent of the full rate for a single occupant, or 100 per cent for more than one occupant over the age of 18. Bona fide students are exempt from council tax, but every other adult has to pay it somehow.

Whenever the property is untenanted or there is a void period between tenancies, you as the landlord become liable for 90 per cent of the full whack. Council tax is also payable by you, the owner, on holiday lettings and short lets.

Properties that are unoccupied and uninhabitable – ie being renovated – can be exempt from council tax for up to a year. In this case, you have to contact HM Revenue & Customs, who will send somebody round to inspect your property and decide whether or not it can be deleted from council tax records for the time being. Then you have to inform them again when the place is ready for habitation, and they will decide on the council tax banding and whether you now have to pay the full whack.

Whenever a property is unlet, for any reason, council tax liability comes back to you, the owner. Never imagine, either, that the local council will ever forget about council tax. Although they may be remiss about collecting rubbish or other services, one thing they do do is issue council tax demands without delay.

Gas, electricity and water rates do not stop coming just because you do not have a tenant. And although you may not have to pay council tax while the place is empty, unfurnished and uninhabited, you do have to start paying as soon as it becomes lettable. In my experience, it is not worth trying to dodge these payments.

Finding a tenant

Whichever way you do it, it costs money to find a tenant. If you decide to go it alone rather than use a letting agency, you will have to factor in the cost of advertising in local or national newspapers, and time spent answering telephone calls and showing prospective tenants round. You will also have to obtain an Assured Shorthold Tenancy form from a stationer. These forms are perfectly legal, and absolutely essential to make the tenancy agreement viable.

Whether you let privately or through a lettings agency, it is essential to take up references. Usually, these come from the prospective tenant's bank, current employer and previous landlord. You also have to take one month's rent plus one month's deposit in advance. The deposit is returnable to the tenant at the end of the tenancy, in full – so long as you are satisfied that she has left the place in the condition she found it.

Using an agency

You may well decide that it is safer and better to go through a lettings agency than to risk renting out a property by yourself. Again, there are pluses and minuses. The minus is that you have to pay the agency at least 10 per cent of the rent plus VAT. The plus is that all the proper checks are made, tenants are properly vetted, and you may well get a higher rental than through private ads. You may also find that the cost of advertising the flat yourself comes to almost as much as six months' commission for the agency.

Although professional lettings agencies can reduce many potential risks of a non-paying or otherwise unsatisfactory tenant, they cannot cut them out altogether. When I first became a landlord, I let my flat through an ad in a local newspaper. This proved so successful that I used the same method for three successive tenants. I came unstuck, however, when I tried to find a fourth tenant. Although many people came to view the property, none took it. Seeing an endless aching void opening up in front of me, I contacted a lettings agency, which found me a tenant straight away.

They took up references, one month's rent and the deposit and the tenant moved in, professing herself 'delighted' with the clean white space of the flat. She proved to be my one and only tenant from hell. First she moved her boyfriend in. Then a little dog came. Then she refused to pay rent, complaining that the street outside the flat was 'noisy'. Finally she had to be evicted. She had, naturally, trashed the flat, and it took me two full weeks to get it back into lettable condition.

I chased her through the courts for unpaid rent but never got it, as she had been sent to prison for other offences. After her release, she left the country and I never saw or heard from her again. She left a trail of unpaid bills behind her – the telephone bill, water rates, electricity and council tax. All of which goes to show that, however careful you or the agency may be, it is impossible to be clever all the time.

A friend let a very nice flat, again through a long-established lettings agency, to a tenant who apparently had a millionaire brother. This tenant had recently got divorced, and his ex-wife had been awarded the marital home. He had a good steady job, though, and a reliable income. None of this prevented him from losing his job not long after moving in and absconding after two months, leaving unpaid rent and quite a lot of damage in the newly refurbished flat.

If using an agency, you should make sure you go to one that is a member of ARLA, the Association of Residential Letting Agents. ARLA was founded in 1981 as the professional and regulatory body for letting agents, and is regularly consulted on matters pertaining to the private rented sector by government, local authorities, housing interest groups and researchers.

In order to become a member of ARLA, an agency must have successfully run a lettings business for at least two years, hold and operate separate client accounts and carry professional indemnity insurance to a required standard. A copy of this insurance policy must be lodged with ARLA in order to comply with the requirements of the ARLA Fidelity Bond.

A firm that has been in business for less than two years may apply for intermediate membership until the Association is satisfied that all the criteria have been met. Letting agents who are members of ARLA usually display the logo prominently, and use it on all their advertising and company literature. There should also be a certificate of membership available for inspection in their offices.

This safeguard is designed to protect the landlord's rent. Mainly there have been all too many cases of rogue letting agents using clients' money to pay staff, rather than keeping it in a separate, untouchable client account.

There is much useful information for landlords and tenants on the ARLA website (www.arla.co.uk) but beware – it can sometimes be a little out of date. Dedicated browsers can also read through ARLA's Code of Practice for agencies, and this may help new landlords in particular understand just what a modern lettings agency does, and why it can be risky to go it alone when you may not be au fait with the ever-changing rules and regulations.

Agency fees and services

So, what about their fees? These may vary slightly from agency to agency, but in practice there seems little deviation. Most charge 10 per cent of the monthly rental, and this is payable upfront in its entirety for the length of the tenancy. So if your tenant signs on for a year, you will have to pay the agency a year's commission. Refunds are usually given when the tenancies end before this time, although not always.

Most agencies operate on a sliding scale, whereby the longer the same tenant is in place, the less commission you pay. An average commission would be 10 per cent for the first year, 7.5 per cent for the second year and 5 per cent for the third and successive years.

Landlords are often tempted to tell the agency that the tenant has now left, to avoid paying this commission. Some landlords feel that as the agency is now doing nothing to earn its commission, it should not be paid. But this is illegal. Should the agency discover that the same tenant is in place, they would be able to sue you for unpaid commission. And they usually win.

The lettings director of one large London agency let it slip that these repeat fees constitute a very large proportion of her company's income, as lettings agents charge both the landlord and the tenant to renew the tenancy agreement.

Is there any way round it? Some agencies offer what they call an 'introduction' service, whereby they charge a certain amount, usually the equivalent of three weeks' rent, to introduce you and the tenant. This service includes making all the reference checks, showing tenants round and drawing up the agreement. Then the agent withdraws and plays no further part in the transaction.

I usually go for this service, where it is on offer, but not all agents do it. After the initial six months, or year, the arrangement then goes into what is known as 'periodic tenancy' which proceeds on a month-by-month basis. Here, you as the landlord have to give the tenant two months' notice to quit, but the tenant has to give only one month's notice.

There has been a lot of talk in lettings circles recently about extending tenancies, now that renting is becoming more popular. But agents are resisting this, as it means they do not get their yearly, or six monthly, fee for renewals. They also argue that on renewal, the landlord is allowed to put the rent up by around 3 per cent – or the current rate of inflation – so every year the landlord gets more rent and the renewal fee is therefore justified.

Sounds good in theory, but in practice renegotiating the tenancy agreement often involves putting the rent DOWN. The tenant will only agree to stay on if the rent is renegotiated down instead of up. Where tenants have a lot of choice, they can drive hard bargains and the landlord, not wanting to risk a void, has little choice but to agree.

Real estate agents tend to be wily operators, which is probably why they entered the business in the first place.

Most letting agents have a complicated structure of fees charged, according to the service provided. There may, for instance, be a fixed sum, usually about three weeks' rent, charged for an 'introduction' to a suitable tenant. Once the tenant is in and the various checks completed, the agent withdraws and plays no more part in the transaction. This system works when you live nearby and can attend to your tenant's problems yourself.

Other services may include rent collection, responsibility for repairs and renovation, and attending to the tenant's problems. Every extra service comes at extra cost. Fees for short-term lets, where the tenant stays for a shorter time than the standard six months, may go up to 26 per cent, although as you almost always get a much higher rent for short-term lets, you may still be well in pocket.

The standard 10 per cent that most agents charge includes advertising for and finding a suitable tenant, showing prospective tenants round, checking references and bank statements, taking a holding deposit (usually £200 or so, to secure the property for the tenant) and, later, taking the full deposit and a minimum of one month's rent in advance.

Agents will also set up a standing order whereby the rent is paid monthly into your account. They will also draw up the tenancy agreement. Most agencies will also, at the same time, arrange for all utilities to be put in the tenant's name, telephone reconnection and council tax.

All this paperwork takes on average 10 working days. Agents will also introduce you to your tenant, but after the initial work has been completed, they do no more work apart from taking their commission when it becomes due. And don't think they will ever forget: letting agents have elephant-like memories when it comes to taking their commission.

For another 5 per cent, on average, you can have 'management'. This is a more comprehensive service and includes rent collection, holding the deposit, arranging repairs and calling out plumbers, for instance. If you go for 'management' this means, in theory at least, that all the cares of being a landlord will be taken off your shoulders. But, of course, for this luxury you pay an extra 5 per cent, plus, as ever, VAT.

Management is probably essential if you live abroad, or at a great distance, and simply cannot manage the place yourself. It can also be a good idea for new and inexperienced landlords. But if you live locally, I would say that management is a luxury that most landlords can do without. Management may make sense, though, if you have a very large or extremely valuable property to let.

Some agencies will also arrange to have your property furnished, and all the requisite appliances delivered and installed. Full management, which may include furnishing and kitting out a property, is probably only sensible with very expensive central London properties. It is a good idea in any case to go to several letting agencies and compare prices and services.

You can also have a professional inventory carried out. This will cost you another £100 or so, and only you can decide whether it is worth it or not. Again, if you are renting out an expensive property that contains valuable antiques and paintings, a professional inventory is a must. Letting agents can arrange these. Usually, inventory clerks do a very thorough job, but they are another luxury and another cost to be taken into account. If you have a very standard type of property, containing only the basics, you can perfectly well write out the inventory yourself. It's not a difficult job. An example of a typical inventory is given in the next chapter.

Guaranteed rental schemes

As well as developers offering guaranteed rental schemes as part of their inducement to Buy-to-Let investors, a growing number of letting agencies are also offering guaranteed rentals.

Here, a letting agent will guarantee the rent on a particular property for a landlord for a specified time, which is usually a year. This guaranteed rental operates whether the property is actually rented out or not, which means that the letting agency takes the risk. This scheme means that in effect you are letting your property to the agent, who then takes total responsibility for it.

Again, these schemes may not always be what they seem, as you will not be paid the full market rental for such a property. You could even be getting 30–40 per cent below the current market rate, although some agents operating such schemes maintain that the rental is only 5–7 per cent below the market rate. What you can be very sure of is that the rental will be below market rate – how much below may be difficult to ascertain.

Letting agent Robert Jordan, president of ARLA, is not in favour of these schemes as he believes letting should be hands-on. His view is that owners or investors who do not like handling their properties themselves and want to offload everything onto somebody else should probably not be in the lettings business in the first place.

I must say I tend to agree. There are of course the 'reluctant landlords' who are renting out properties they cannot sell or who for some other reason have not positively chosen to be landlords, but it is a fact that if you want to make money from your rental investment, you must do as much as you can yourself. The more you hand over to somebody else, the more control – and money – you will inevitably lose.

Also, in these days when very precise number-crunching is the only way to ensure success in this business, the more services you pay for, the more likely you are to end up out of pocket.

If a property won't rent out, your best bet is to sell it – and move on to another one which will attract paying tenants.

The Tenancy Deposit Protection Scheme

The Tenancy Deposit Protection Scheme, which has been gathering momentum for several years now, has finally become law.

This means that any landlord or letting agent who takes a deposit – usually of one month's or six weeks' rent – will have to 'protect' it by signing up to one of three government-backed and authorized schemes.

One scheme, free to use, is custodial and requires the deposit to be handed over. The other two schemes allow the landlord or agent to keep the deposit on payment of a fairly hefty premium.

Penalties for non-compliance are severe. Tenants can check to see whether their landlord has joined an approved scheme and if this has not happened within 14 days of creating a new tenancy, the landlord has to pay three times the deposit back to the tenant. In addition, any such landlord cannot evict a tenant, however bad, by the usual means of serving a Section 21 notice.

These penalties are designed to dragoon every landlord in the country – around 900,000 of them – to use one of the official schemes. The government is confident that these measures will prevent landlords from unfairly hanging on to deposits at the end of a tenancy. The scheme also provides a free and speedy dispute resolution service for both parties to use.

Landlords who do not take deposits do not have to sign up to a scheme.

The legislation is extremely fierce – but is it necessary?

Apparently so, says civil servant Phil Alker. Phil, head of the Government's Tenancy Deposit Protection team, says: 'There are 2.6 million private tenancies in existence, and 1.4 million new ones are created every year. The evidence from two recent Surveys of Housing shows that around one-fifth of tenants' deposits are never paid back. And as 85 per cent of all landlords take deposits, this means that 50,000 deposits are being withheld. Put another way, this also means that a total of £80 million is never paid back to the tenant.'

Around 17 per cent of landlords, added Alker, withhold at least part of the deposit.

'There had been a voluntary scheme in operation, but there was so little take-up the government felt that there had to be a hard-hitting, legislative solution for it to have any effect. The scheme has all-party support and is self-funding so will not require any government money.

'We acknowledge that deposit fraud is a minority problem, but no government can legislate selectively. So the majority of good landlords have to comply along with the minority of bad ones.'

The main attraction of the protection schemes, according to Alker, is in their swift and effective dispute resolution. 'If a landlord wants to withhold the entire deposit for a bad stain on the carpet, say, and the tenant argues the stain was there anyway, the Alternative Dispute Resolution service comes into play immediately. This is free to both parties and avoids the need to go to court.'

In fact, most disputes are resolved amicably, but where there is a severe sticking point the dispute resolution service comes into its own.

Letting agent David Salvi of Hurford Salvi Carr says 'We take the deposit from the tenant, put it into a dedicated account and return it at the end of the tenancy minus any agreed charges. Most agents work this way and have done for years.

'At our end of the market in Central London, disputes are extremely rare. We did not have a single one last year. But as agents we have the extra cost of joining the scheme.' This cost will, of course, be passed onto the landlord, not the tenant. 'The Government has been very concerned that the scheme should not involve the tenant in any extra expense', says Salvi.

'But apart from the expense, understanding and using the scheme is a lot for landlords to handle.'

Landlord Simon Cutting is so incensed with the scheme that he has set up Tenant Assure, a legal alternative which completely bypasses the need to take a deposit or sign up to a scheme. He says: 'To my mind the whole thing is ridiculous as it penalizes all landlords for the 17 per cent of bad ones.

'Most landlords have two or three properties, at most, and signing up to the schemes will involve them in a lot of extra work. If they choose an insurance-based scheme, this will also cost them around £30 per tenancy, plus a membership fee of £58, at a time when most landlords are not even taking enough from rents to cover their mortgage.'

But, says Simon, landlords do not have to take a deposit and this is where his scheme comes in. 'We are offering a tenant letting service whereby we vet all tenants and stand as guarantor. The whole thing can be set up online, and should the tenant default, we will pay the landlord two months' rent.

'Our charges, to both tenant and landlord, are in line with other agencies, but if we reject a tenant, we don't make charges.'

Other landlords say they will no longer take deposits, or will take two months' rent upfront, to avoid joining a Tenancy Deposit Protection Scheme.

But most, it is expected, will take a deposit as before, and comply with the legislation. In fact, figures from ARLA after the Scheme had been up and running for just four months, showed that over 225,000 deposits had been safeguarded by the scheme, and those combined deposits were worth a total of £150 million. Around 7,000 new tenancies were being registered every single day, the report continued.

After the four months, more than 125,000 landlords had signed up to the scheme, mostly through established letting agents.

All landlords or their agents must by law sign up to one of three schemes which were awarded contracts by the government on 22 November 2006.

The Deposit Protection Scheme (DPS) is a custodial scheme whereby landlords or agents must hand the deposit over in its entirety. The scheme, managed by Computershare Investor

Services Ltd, which set up a similar scheme in Australia, is free to use and will be entirely funded by the interest earned from deposits held. The deposits are held in a segregated client account and tenants will receive interest on their deposits. Assuming no dispute, the deposit, plus any interest accrued, will be paid back to the tenant within 10 days.

If there is a dispute, the Chartered Institute of Arbitrators will adjudicate. This is also free to both tenants and landlords. Landlords can sign up to the scheme via the internet or obtain paper forms. More information from www.depositprotection.com.

Tenancy Deposit Solutions Ltd (TDSL) is an insurance-based scheme whereby the landlord or agent holds onto the deposit but pays a one-off membership fee plus a premium for each new tenancy created. Fees are around £58 to join the scheme and £30 for each tenancy. Assuming no dispute, the landlord will hand the deposit back to the tenant on checkout. As with the custodial scheme, disputes will be handled by the Alternative Dispute Resolution (ADR). Should there be a dispute, the amount disputed must be handed over to the insurance company until it is settled. For more information, visit www.mydeposits.co.uk.

The third scheme, The Tenancy Deposit Scheme, also insurance-based, is aimed primarily at agents whose offices pay a yearly fee of between £521 and £1,609 per office to the insurance company handling the scheme. With this scheme, the deposit is held by the agent. Again, any dispute is handled by the ADR. For more information, visit www.tds.gb.com or call 0845 346 7837.

All Assured Shorthold Tenancies (ASTs) created after April 6 2007 will require protection if deposits are taken. Existing tenancies do not need to register, but every time a new tenancy is created with the same tenant, the deposit has to be re-protected. Other types of tenancy, such as Assured Tenancies and periodic tenancies, do not need to register. For more information visit: www.tenancydeposit.gov.uk.

Case studies

The following cases were adjudicated by the ADR when the Tenancy Deposit Scheme was still voluntary:

Case 1:
Deposit £2,910
Amount in dispute: £1,525
Awarded to landlord: £598.67
Awarded to tenant: £926.56

Here, the landlord was dissatisfied with the condition of the property on several counts, but the adjudicator ruled that the property's condition was not perfect at the start of the tenancy.

Case 2:
Deposit: £1,500
Amount in dispute: £759
Awarded to landlord: £1,500
Awarded to tenant: £0.

In this case, the neglectful behaviour of the tenant resulted in complete deposit loss. The tenant does not always win, by any means!

Now that the tenancy deposit schemes are up and running, it is even more important to take a careful inventory, as if you consider the property is not returned in good condition, you must be able to prove that it has deteriorated since that particular tenant moved in. It is a good idea to photograph the property beforehand and label and date the pictures.

The NFRL also recommend that you record the model and model number of any white goods, appliances or fittings, and also describe any furniture or paintings very carefully – if, that is, you are concerned about the items. Personally, unless the items and of some value, I don't record the actual details. I don't really care all that much if a cheap mug from Woolworth's is broken, or if a picture I have just put up as décor is taken.

Sometimes ironing boards and waste bins are taken when the tenant moves out; usually because they are not recorded on the inventory and nobody can remember whether they were there or not. In any case, I only ever put very cheap items such as these in rented properties, so that replacements cost hardly anything.

Shower curtains, for instance, almost always have to be replaced after a tenancy, but as you can get perfectly good ones for £5 or so, I don't bother to put them on the inventory. You can be too anal about these things.

Of far greater concern is the fabric of the property, as this can be expensive to repair. So it is vital to write down very carefully the condition of the walls, carpet, ceiling, windows and so on, and then make sure both you and your tenant sign the inventory and agree to the condition of the place.

One piece of advice is never to leave the inventory with the tenant for them to complete at their leisure, as mostly they never do, and never return it. It is so often one piece of paperwork too many at the beginning of the tenancy.

Landlord's contents cover

Landlords who rent out furnished properties, or who have expensive carpets and curtains, can take out contents cover, which protects items in the event of their being ruined by the tenant, or by accidental damage such as flooding from above, fire or a break-in.

In order to be eligible for this type of cover, you will have to fit compliant window and door locks. Again, as with any insurance, only you can decide on the risk–benefit ratio.

Energy efficiency

Very many rented properties are old and as such, difficult to make energy efficient for today's standards. But the government-funded Energy Saving Trust is now targeting landlords with various schemes and incentives to ensure that rented properties meet at least minimum standards for energy efficiency.

Some of the provisions of the Housing Act sound like a good idea until the reality of implementing them impinges.

At present, there is a 10 per cent wear and tear allowance for furnished properties, although unfurnished properties do not attract this allowance. Once the energy efficiency ratings bite, this allowance is going to be conditional on properties meeting a certain level of energy efficiency. Local authorities will set minimum standards and these, of course, could change dramatically from one authority to the other.

Some energy experts believe that the private rented sector contains the most energy-inefficient properties in existence. Energy-efficient measures include: gas central heating instead of electric; double-glazing the windows; replacing old boilers; lagging the roof and putting in cavity wall insulation.

One tenant who welcomes the proposals is investment analyst Laura Bennett, who has lived in a variety of cold, draughty, difficult to heat rented homes in London. She says: 'Mostly, the windows have not been double-glazed, wind whistles down the fireplaces and there are draughts every-where, and as a result our heating bills are astronomical, through no fault of our own.

'However energy-efficient you as a tenant want to be, the landlord has control. In any case, you are not usually in the same rented property for long enough to make it worth carrying out energy-saving procedures yourself, as a tenant. You just have to put up with it, so I am in favour of any measures which force landlords into energy efficiency.'

The Housing Health and Safety Rating System (HHSRS) is a new way of assessing the fitness of a particular property, including rented property. The aim here is to provide a system rather than a standard, but if your property is licensable under the new HMO rules (see below), there is a legal obligation on the local authority to carry out an inspection. Otherwise prop-erties are unlikely to be inspected.

Potential hazards include:

- asbestos;
- carbon monoxide;
- overcrowding;

- noise;
- hygiene;
- fire safety;
- structural problems;
- damp and mould.

Obviously it is not possible to remove every hazard from every building, but the aim is gradually to improve the quality of housing stock.

Landlord Action

An alternative to legal expenses insurance is Landlord Action, founded by landlord Jonathan Chippeck after he became traumatized by the vast amount of money he lost on account of a bad tenant. This three-step scheme allows landlords to get ghastly tenants evicted cleanly and speedily for a fixed sum.

Step One costs £115 incl. VAT and involves a member of the team visiting the tenant and serving an eviction notice. Step Two, enacted after 14 days if the first step fails, involves a solicitor issuing proceedings, setting a court date and instructing a barrister. This costs £565 incl. VAT. If that doesn't work, Step Three means the court bailiffs are sent in to ensure the return of the property. Debt collection can also be arranged.

Jonathan Chippeck believes that landlords are often their own worst enemies when it comes to unpaid rent. 'Most are small-time amateurs who don't like bothering tenants for rent', he says. 'They keep hoping it will be paid next month. But I've learnt that tenants who miss one month will usually never pay again. They have to be chased up within a week, at most.

'Unlike insurance, where you pay for cover whether needed or not, Landlord Action only comes into force when there is a problem.' Landlord Action can be contacted on 0870 765 2005.

Otherwise, legal expenses insurance costs around £50 a year, and rent guarantee insurance another £50 a year, at least. Most policies cover up to £50,000 of legal expenses, so long as an

Assured Shorthold Tenancy is in place. As with all insurance, it's vital to read the small print (which, to my mind, should be extremely large print instead).

It is also possible to get contents insurance if you are letting out a furnished property. Again, this is probably only sensible if your property contains extremely valuable and not easily replaced items.

Here is a rundown of costs and revenue on a typical Buy-to-Let flat costing £200,000:

Purchase of property	£200,000
Stamp duty land tax	£2,000
Legal, survey, set-up costs	£7,000
Renovation	£15,000
Redecorating	£2,000
Total acquisition costs:	£24,000
Total price of purchase	**£224,000**
Rent @ £1,000 pcm	£12,000
Letting fees @ 10 per cent + VAT	£1,410
Tenancy agreement fee	£146.87
Service charge on property	£700
Gas certificate	£70
Deposit protection	£83
Contents insurance	£200
Annual cost of letting	£2,509.87
Net rental yield before tax:	£9,567

Gross rental yield: 6 per cent – about the best that can be hoped for at the time of writing.

In general terms, acquisition and capital costs are not tax-deductible until you come to sell, but ongoing costs such as the service charge, letting fee, deposit protection and gas certificate, plus minor repairs while the property is let, are tax-deductible.

Note that this rundown of costs does not take a mortgage into account, but if you have a mortgage, the interest is tax-deductible on a BTL property. This is a controversial allowance

in some quarters as some commentators believe it gives landlords an unfair tax advantage. So – it may change if the
agitators win out.

If you have a mortgage, you will typically be borrowing 75
per cent of the purchase cost of the property. On a standard
Buy-to-Let mortgage at, say, 6 per cent, your mortgage
repayment costs will be £9,000 pa, leaving you just a few
hundred pounds over. There are also likely to be mortgage
arrangement fees.

These figures are for guidance only, and exclude any void
periods. But it is important to bear in mind that the value of
any investment, including property, may go down as well as
up.

E-letting

The idea of e-letting, where landlords and tenants can do the
whole thing online, thus completely bypassing the high street
agent, has not proved particularly popular with either tenants
or landlords. It seems that, with letting property, nothing beats
the personal touch!

There are a number of dedicated sites where you can post
your property, and the vast majority of letting agents now
have websites where properties can be posted and viewed.
But nobody is any longer offering a full e-letting service, and
the last e-letting site closed for business in March 2004. Jason
Cliffe, co-founder of Froglet, one of the original full-service
sites, said: 'People were enthusiastic initially, but it didn't
seem to work and I am back to doing business in the high
street.' Jason's new company, Johnson Wood, has no plans to
return to e-letting.

The nearest approach to e-letting is lettingzone, founded by
private landlord Mark Garner in 2000. This site, now the
largest in the United Kingdom, has a facility whereby your
property appears on 23 other websites. Mark says: 'We are now
the number one uploader, and the leading advertising service
for landlords and agents in the UK.' Lettingzone works closely
with the National Federation of Residential Landlords, and
enables new members to join the Federation by logging on to
the website.

So although e-letting as such appears to have died the death, the concept of advertising properties to let on the internet has proved highly popular, and indeed around 70 per cent of tenants now make the web their first port of call.

What has happened is that different components of the industry, once extremely scattered and fragmented, are now working together to improve and modernize the service for all concerned. Lettingzone, for instance, is visited by over 400,000 landlords, letting agents and property professionals every month, and new services are always being added to the site.

Buying at auction

Very many investment properties are bought at auction. In fact, it is a fair bet that the majority of people at house auction sales will be there with a view to buying an investment property, either to rent, or to do up and sell on. Usually, estate agents arrange block viewings when properties are to be sold at auction, so at least you will get a preview of your fellow bidders.

You can now get whole books and reams of advice on buying at auction. As with any other form of purchase, there are pros and cons.

Prices at auction sales often seem to be very low, but properties are usually sold at auction for a very good reason – they are unsaleable by other means. They may be in terrible condition, there may be outstanding service or other charges on them, they may have had squatters in for many years. There may be legal problems, there may be serious subsidence, or a major road may be planned to run right past the property.

Auctioneers and estate agents have a duty to point out the defects of each property coming up at auction, but otherwise it is a case of *caveat emptor* – let the buyer beware. At auction sales, you will be up against hard-nosed experienced property developers and investors. However, you can certainly pick up a bargain, or what seems like a bargain.

One property developer bought a totally dilapidated London house for £230,000 at auction. At the time, similar houses in the street were going for around £500,000, if in impeccable condition. His house took over a year and cost £150,000 to renovate. It looked good when finished, and went on the market for £600,000. But – it didn't sell, and in the end the buyer was forced to rent it out for £800 a week. This represented an extremely slow way of getting his money back. The problem was that houses in that particular street simply would not sell for the high price this buyer needed, because they did not have gardens. Nor could he get more than £800 a week in rent, in that particular area. So in the end, that house was hardly the bargain it first seemed.

In another case, an investor bought an unmodernized studio flat at auction for £46,000 cash. This seemed a terrific bargain – until he came to renovate it. The property was Grade II listed, which meant he had to get Listed Building consent in addition to all the other planning permissions. In the event, he was prevented from carrying out the renovation for three months while the relevant consents were considered.

It was by no means a foregone conclusion that permission would be granted, and in any case he had to wait while the applications were posted through residents' letter boxes and put on lamp posts, and for the consultation period.

In the end, the renovation took him over a year and cost £25,000, during which time he also had to pay service and maintenance charges on the property. He put it on the market but could not sell it and again, decided to rent it for a year, after which he managed to sell it for £69,000 – meaning that from a financial point of view the whole exercise was a complete waste of time.

It is very common for Buy-to-Let properties which won't seem to rent out to be sold at auction, and hopeful but naïve investors often find they end up losing a lot of money.

Buying at auction assumes all the preliminaries have been made, because when the hammer comes down, the property becomes yours. The knock of the hammer signals that contracts have been exchanged. Therefore, solicitors must have been instructed, mortgage valuations made (if appropriate) and surveys and searches undertaken well in advance of the auction date. You must be financially ready to take possession of the property on the very day of the sale.

If you do not manage to secure the property at auction, you will lose all the money incurred in instructing solicitors, carrying out local searches and so on. You will have to put it down to experience, as there will be no way of recovering your money. So far I have never dared to buy a property at auction, although as I get bolder, that day may come. Many investment landlords I know have done extremely well with auctioned properties, although most, it must be said, are able to call on a reliable team of builders to renovate the property.

Although buying at auction is becoming ever more popular with property investors, it is essential to know what you are doing. A regular newsletter, *Property Auction News*, gives details of all the main property auctioneers nationwide. It is worth getting the catalogues and going along to some auctions to get a feel for them before deciding whether this method of buying is for you.

Here are two opposing views of buying investment property at auction. Property developer Mark Nathwani, who rents out more than 50 apartments, believes the days when you could get bargains at auction are over. 'My view is that you now pay more at auction than through estate agents', he says.

However, Peter Parfait, a dedicated buyer at auction, insists: 'Almost everything I possess has passed under the auctioneer's gavel. My first property was bought from auction, as was the house I live in and my investment portfolio. The vehicle I drive came via a car auction, as did the previous one, and my mother-in-law's car. The furniture in my house and in my office almost exclusively came from antique and fine art auctions, and I furnish my rental properties from chattel sales.'

He adds that he does it because it makes financial sense. 'Why pay £X plus the vendor's mark-up for an item when you can so easily bypass the middlemen and purchase from the source?'

As with everything else, whether you like the idea of buying at auction comes down to personality. Some people enjoy bidding, while others are frightened and intimidated by it.

Buy-to-Let

So far, all figures have been worked out on the assumption that you are a cash buyer who does not need to borrow money to buy your investment property. Until 1996, the great majority of private landlords were people who had paid cash for their letting properties, simply because it was extremely difficult to rent out any other type of property. As a rule, you were not allowed to rent out a property on which you had an outstanding mortgage, although some mortgage lenders gave permission for this if certain conditions were satisfied. However, the now famous Buy-to-Let scheme then came in, and has proved extremely successful. This was an ARLA initiative, and has completely transformed the private rented sector.

Previously, those who wished to buy investment properties were either surcharged or forced to borrow at commercial bank rates. In these cases, potential rental income was not taken into account for servicing the loans. From 1996, however, a number of mortgage lenders have brought their interest rates in line with rates for owner-occupied properties, and also take rental income into account. These changes came about, says ARLA, because of the new confidence with which mortgage providers regarded ARLA members. If professional letting and property management agents were involved, then, the thinking went, the risk to lenders would be very slight indeed.

Here is a typical Buy-to-Let scheme, as offered by Mortgage Express. Note: other lenders' figures and conditions may vary slightly, but are unlikely to differ dramatically from the information given.

You can buy an unlimited number of properties, either privately via an estate agent or at auction, up to a maximum value of £5 million. It used to be the case that most lenders required proof of minimum income. Mortgage Express at least has now scrapped this requirement, although they will still need to see at least three years' audited accounts for self-employed people.

The ability to repay the mortgage is not based, however, on your income, but on the rent received from the property or properties. This must usually be between 130 and 150 per cent of the monthly mortgage payment. For instance, if your mortgage repayment works out at £100 a week, your income from rent must be at least £130 a week. The minimum age for eligibility for an investment mortgage is 25, and the maximum age 75. The minimum term for borrowing is five years and the maximum term is 25 years' repayment.

Once you have bought your property with an investment mortgage, you must let it out on an Assured Shorthold Tenancy agreement (known as 'Short Assured' in Scotland) within three months of purchase. It must be let, or be available to let, for the whole duration of the mortgage. You cannot live in it yourself.

Multiple tenancies and social or diplomatic immunity lets are not usually allowed, and properties must have one kitchen and not more than five bedrooms. Rooming houses, or houses where facilities such as kitchen and bathrooms are shared, are not suitable for Buy-to-Let schemes. Under certain circumstances, though, it may be allowable to let to local authorities.

The rate of interest payable is linked to the Bank of England base rate, so is liable to change as interest rates fluctuate. You can borrow up to 75 per cent of the purchase price of the property, provided always that the rental is at least 130 per cent of the mortgage repayments. In recent years, some lenders have been offering rent-to-mortgage deals of 100 per cent, but this gives no margin for error whatever and is emphatically not recommended.

Some part of the loan may be available for repairs and renovation, or as a deposit for a new investment property. Usually, you will not be required to purchase insurance cover, and the standard mortgage arrangement will be straight repayment or interest-only repayment. Most Buy-to-Let mortgages are quite flexible, and it is advisable to discuss the possibility very thoroughly with a mortgage provider so that you are aware of all the pros and cons before taking the plunge.

In fact, it is quite difficult to buy a pig in a poke on a Buy-to-Let scheme, as you are required to have an inspection and valuation of the property you are interested in buying. The valuer will also advise you on the suitability of the particular property for rental purposes. The valuation fee is based on the value of the property and can vary (at the time of writing) between £117 and £205, or thereabouts. There is also a fee of around £250 for setting up the mortgage and this will be added to your loan on completion of the deal.

You can make capital repayments to reduce your loan at any time, but if the mortgage is redeemed within three years, a redemption fee of three months' interest will be payable.

Here are some typical figures: if you borrow £30,000 to buy a property valued at £50,000, repayable monthly over 25 years on a repayment basis, the total amount payable will come to just over £73,000. With any luck your investment property will be worth at least that after 25 years. If you are paying back £100 a week on your investment property and you achieve £130 a week in rent, that leaves you with just £30 a week pocket money – hardly a billionaire's income. 'It provides a holiday for you,' said one mortgage company, 'but that's about all.'

Investment mortgages are aimed at the small-time landlord, for those who have savings on deposit they are looking to increase. Investment properties, provided the right checks are carried out, are relatively safe, and Buy-to-Let schemes are not for what one agent termed the 'pork belly speculator' interested in high risk and high returns. They are not aimed at people with a gambling mentality, but rather, the more timid type of investor.

Feedback from those who have taken advantage of Buy-to-Let schemes shows that they tend to be cautious people who are attracted by the idea of something tangible as an investment, 'something you can walk past', rather than an abstract share portfolio.

ARLA gives some useful tips for Buy-to-Letters:

- *Do* think of it as a medium- to long-term investment.

- *Do* make sure the rent covers borrowings and costs, after allowing for void periods of between one and two months a year.

- *Don't* purchase anything with serious maintenance problems, such as a thatched roof or a very large garden. These add nothing to the rental value and cost a lot in upkeep.

- *Don't* imagine that investment properties can be left to friends or relatives to look after. Professional services are essential.

Since it was first instigated, the Buy-to-Let lending industry has become extremely complex and sophisticated. There are currently many lenders offering Buy-to-Let mortgages, and lenders now offer the full range of mortgage options: fixed, capped, repayment and so on. As this market is highly competitive, it is worth shopping around for the best mortgage you can get – not necessarily the cheapest.

Arrangement and exit fees

In response to repeated campaigns, many lenders have now scrapped their exit fees. But in order to make up for this loss of easy revenue, many have greatly increased their mortgage arrangement fees. So whenever arranging a Buy-to-Let mortgage, ask about any extra fees for 'arranging' this mortgage.

It is impossible to give specific advice on Buy-to-Let mortgages, as changes can occur almost hourly, especially as interest rates are liable to frequent fluctuations. Investors should talk to a mortgage broker and think long and hard about the long-term consequences of each type of loan. Don't forget that mortgage lenders show no mercy to Buy-to-Let investors who default on their repayments. There is not the same leeway or leniency as when lending on your own home, and mortgage lenders, like you, are in it for the money. However sweet and seductive their words, they are not charities, or 'out to help you'; they exist to take your money off you.

Most Buy-to-Let investors nowadays will go for an interest-only, fixed-rate mortgage, as this makes investment property easier to keep a financial eye on than with a mortgage that keeps fluctuating. Matthew Grayson from Birmingham Midshires, one of the biggest lenders in this market, says: 'It is easier for investors to budget with a fixed rate, as this means your payments don't change when the base interest changes. A Buy-to-Let mortgage is not necessarily set at a higher rate than your own mortgage, as we take into account expected rental.

'If somebody comes to us wanting a Buy-to-Let mortgage, we will send out a valuer to that property. On one property we viewed, the next-door house had all its windows boarded up; as a result, we decided not to lend on that property.'

But beware! When buying property as an investment, expect far more red tape than when you are an owner-occupier. PR executive Anne Diamond could not believe the detail her mortgage lenders required when she wanted to invest in property. She says: 'First of all they wanted three years' accounts. Then they pored over bank statements, loan state-ments, credit card statements, business bank statements. They even wanted my passport. The amount of paperwork I had to supply was unbelievable. The chap at the mortgage shop told me Buy-to-Let loans were more difficult because the property would not be your place of residence.' Anne's mortgage took three months to sort out, but she does feel that eventually she got a good deal. 'I now have to stick with this lender for five years and can't change. Nor am I allowed to pay the mortgage off fast. It has to be over 25 years and I can't renege on the arrangement.'

Greg Shackleton, however, believes that Buy-to-Let borrowing has now become professional, which it was not when he began in 1994: 'When I first started, you had to get bank loans from people who hadn't got a clue. They asked silly questions and you had to borrow at a punitive rate. But nowadays there are experts in the business. You can get specialized Buy-to-Let mortgages at competitive rates.'

However, Greg has this to say about borrowing: 'You have to regard the purchase price as a cash deal, even when you have a mortgage on it. Think of it as your own money you are spending, not the bank or building society's.' In common with other sensible property investors, Greg advises going for yield over capital increase, every time. 'If we went into negative inflation, which could happen, your properties would lose value. But if you go for yield, you will always be getting rent.'

Buy-to-Let lenders will also advise on how to deal with possible rental voids, coping with capital gains tax and repairs, and all the other costs which so relentlessly stack up when investing in something as big and complicated as bricks and mortar. Anne Diamond says: 'I imagined in my naivety that I would make an instant profit. But by the time I had paid all the fees and costs, I only just about broke even for the first year on a rent of £450 a month.' After that first year, though, Anne did come into profit, and feels that, now the horrors have receded, it was definitely worth it.

Here is a typical run-down of how it all works out, according to the Clydesdale Bank. First of all, the bank takes into account the expected rental income, and will lend on 10 times the annual rent. So if you expect to receive £750 a month in rent, or £9,000 a year, the maximum loan on that property would be £90,000.

The most popular Buy-to-Let option is interest only, usually granted for five years, when the mortgage will revert to a capital and interest, endowment or pension plan basis for the rest of the loan term.

Good news from the Council of Mortgage Lenders is that very few, if any, Buy-to-Let mortgages fall into serious arrears. So, it seems that it does all work out, so long as careful research is carried out beforehand. For more information, contact the Council of Mortgage Lenders on 020 7440 2255, or the ARLA website at: www.arla.com.

Sell the 'dogs'

Most Buy-to-Let investors believe that, however clever you are, not all properties perform. Or, some may perform for a time and then fail to let; others may never perform properly at all.

Property investor Lesley Cooper believes that you should always be prepared to sell a property that has not proved to be such a good buy as you thought. Cut your losses and move on.

She says: 'Always be prepared to sell the dogs, rather than throw good money after bad.'

Gearing up

Gearing up means gradually increasing your property portfolio by borrowing further amounts secured on the first property you buy. Most serious investment landlords, such as Greg Shackleton and Mark Nathwani, have built up their property empires through a process of gearing up with successive loans. In fact, they could not have done it otherwise. Greg Shackleton acquired a rundown property by accident in lieu of a fee, and used this to 'gear up' for future purchases.

Mark Nathwani, who started buying properties at 19 and was able to borrow £12,000, advises: 'You should take advantage of low interest rates and let your property empire grow. The answer to doing it properly is, research, research, research.' Mark adds that in order to make it all work, you must have an instinct, an inbuilt feeling, as it were, for property. 'I was about to go to university, but in the end I couldn't be bothered to take yet more exams and started investing in property instead.' Twenty years later, Mark has no regrets about elbowing university to climb up the property ladder instead.

Here is an example of how gearing up works. Your first property is a cash purchase of, say, £25,000. If you buy it in a rundown condition, you obtain an independent valuation once it is renovated. This property attracts a rental yield of 15 per cent, or £3,750 a year (£72 a week). You then arrange a Buy-to-Let mortgage on a subsequent property, releasing cash invested in the first property. This cash is then used to purchase another property, and the process can be repeated until your portfolio is considered to be complete.

The 'gearing up' process is relative to the number of properties bought in the first stage. If you start with one property, you can only gear up one at a time. If you start with five properties, you can gear up five at a time, assuming the properties are of roughly equal value.

This means that a 10-property portfolio could provide an annual rental return of £37,500 for an initial investment of £25,000.

These figures work on the assumption that all 10 properties are fully let at all times – and nobody can guarantee this, of course. You also have to bear in mind that much of the nearly £38,000 you receive annually in rent will be going straight to the mortgage people. However, it is the case that the more properties you own, the more useful the rental income becomes.

Property seminars

As Buy-to-Let becomes ever more popular, very expensive weekend seminars are being offered which purport to impart all the secrets of property investment. These seminars can cost up to £7,000: are they worth it?

Mark Nathwani, who has attended many such seminars over the years, believes that some constitute money well spent, whereas others are a definite rip-off. 'I've been on most of these expensive courses,' he says, 'and they make it sound very easy indeed. But that's like saying it's easy to fly to the moon. I went on a Tony Robbins wealth mastery weekend which cost £700, and that was definitely money well spent. On the other hand, I booked up a £4,000 course in Switzerland which cost me £7,500 by the time I'd paid for flights and hotels, and it wasn't worth 20p.'

Before becoming a property investor, Margaret Sceats attended a £3,000 weekend seminar arranged by Russ Whitney, an American company. Her view was that attendance at the course gave her the confidence to start buying, which she would not have had otherwise. Margaret was able to take a friend on the course, so it cost them £1,500 each, and there was useful support and networking afterwards.

As a direct result of attending the seminar, Margaret bought two properties in the North-East, and tenants were obtained right away. She used some of the equity in her home to finance the purchases, and believes it has worked out well.

'I thought the course was brilliant, as it went into every last detail about Buy-to-Let. Although I live in London, I soon realized London would be too expensive for me, but the course identified several property hotspots, of which the North-East of England was one. I went to view some northern properties with other people from the course, and took the plunge.'

Property investment seminars and workshops are a quickly growing industry, with more seminars and conferences seemingly held every week. All the main landlord organizations offer masterclasses in Buy-to-Let, often at much cheaper prices than the commercial organizations. Expect to pay in the region of £300–£400 for seminars organized by non-profit landlord associations. You do, though, have to be a member of the relevant landlord organization to attend these events.

Some lettings agents are now also holding seminars and conferences about Buy-to-Let. These are usually free, but sponsored by banks, accountancy firms or other financial institutions, which naturally hope to gain business from the occasion. Again, they are only available to clients of the lettings agency, not to the general public. They are, though, highly informative, with expert speakers, and are worth attending to update yourself about changes in the law, which are happening all the time and about which understandable information is not always easy to access.

There are also ever more property investment shows held around the country at several venues. These too offer a huge range of workshops and speakers, again at varying prices.

But there are signs that the popularity of expensive property seminars, as opposed to the low-cost or free ones, may be coming to an end. In March 2008 Inside Track, one of the biggest such companies, announced that it was suspending its seminars and at the same time cutting 40 jobs at its Kingston, Surrey, headquarters.

The reason? Managing director Tony McKay stated that the current market conditions in the UK were too difficult to attract new investors. In fact, the number of attendees at its £2,500 two-day, non-residential seminars had been steadily falling for the past year. At the seminars Inside Track also asked attendees to fork out another £5,000 or so to obtain membership of its investor club, so as to secure discounts on offplan properties. Yet throughout 2007 and 2008 there had been steady warnings that buying offplan could be a high-risk strategy for existing or potential Buy-to-Let investors. Also, many newspaper articles questioned the value of these pricey seminars, when you can buy a perfectly good book on letting for under £12!

Some property seminars, such as those run by landlord organizations, are purely educational, but a number of companies are starting up, warns ARLA, that are side-tracking the unwary or naïve potential investor into buying properties that purport to be Buy-to-Let, as this is the buzzword of the moment, but which are not true Buy-to-Let opportunities. ARLA's president Robert Jordan says: 'True Buy-to-Let is an example of private enterprise fulfilling a social need for choice in housing. It is about fair returns and quality accommodation, not get-rich-quick schemes.'

Examples of property dealing that might be improperly linked to Buy-to-Let, according to ARLA, include speculative buying offplan, buying in foreign markets and buying holiday homes in the United Kingdom and abroad. With offplan buying, you are speculating on the increase in house prices. The 'guaranteed rent' mentioned earlier is, says ARLA, in effect no more than a delayed discount and no real guarantee of the rent that can be achieved, or even of whether the property can be let at all. Robert Jordan also warns that the competition is fierce in these new areas, and some property seminars may be disguised attempts to get attendees to buy there and then, particularly in the foreign market.

Dominic Farrell, a former Army major, has made a great success of his 'Jet-to-Let' seminars which cost a few hundred pounds each, in contrast to the five-figure seminars held by some other similar companies. These seminars concentrate exclusively on buying offplan apartments in selected countries.

Note: in the main, these investment seminars are aimed at selling offplan or newbuild apartments rather than existing or resale properties. As we have said before, the overriding problem with buying offplan is that as these properties have not been tried and tested on the open market, nobody knows for sure whether their value will rise or fall.

As with buying new cars, there is very often a premium on newbuild properties, so you could easily find yourself paying over the odds. Also, there is very often a chain of operators and middlemen at work, whereby the developer sells to a middleman, that company sells a block of apartments to a company specializing in selling offplan investments, and so on. These chains are often very delicate and in the same way as with ordinary housing chains, any link can easily break.

Bankruptcies and takeovers are not uncommon in this business either, so be very careful indeed. The other aspect to bear in mind is that each company and operator will want to take a cut – they are all in it for money, after all. This means that the person at the very end of this complicated chain – you – could find yourself bearing the brunt of all these costs, commissions and cuts.

Before buying anything offplan, either in the United Kingdom or abroad, you need to know how many companies are involved in the chain, and exactly what their role is.

The couldn't-care-less landlord

The rise of the speculative investor has given rise to a new and disturbing phenomenon: the landlord who couldn't care less. Such landlords don't care about tenants or the condition of the property, but are interested only in making a quick profit. In this, they hark back to the bad old days of Rachman and van Hoogstraten, who were also property speculators rather than genuine landlords.

All lettings agents have become aware of the couldn't-care-less landlord in recent years, and when agents get to know about them such people go onto an immediate blacklist. ARLA believes such people should not be given access to Buy-to-Let mortgages, but how do you tell the difference between a caring and a careless landlord – except as time goes on?

The right attitude for a landlord to have, says ARLA, is to want to give a good service for a fair return and to be interested in the long term, rather than gambling on a quick profit. The main difference between property letting and other types of investment is that tenants are people, and landlords are providing a basic need, not a luxury service. This, coupled with the centuries-old laws of tenure, means that uncaring landlords could be giving the new and so far very successful Buy-to-Let industry a bad name, as in the past.

If you do not really want to be bothered with tenants and are only looking at the profit and loss account, Buy-to-Let is not for you. I have always said this and now ARLA is endorsing it.

Join a landlord association!

There are a number of associations for private landlords and those who want to make the most of their investment should consider joining one. For instance, I am a member of the National Federation of Residential Landlords (NFRL), which is a nationwide non-profit organization. It holds free seminars in many parts of the country, training days and also runs a helpline.

These associations are non profit-making and you join by paying a yearly membership fee, typically around £75. This is tax-deductible, an allowable expense. In return you will receive a regular newsletter or magazine giving all the latest information, regulation and comment on the private rented sector, and also be invited to attend, free of extra charge, a number of seminars, social evenings and talks.

The NFRL, for example, holds regular landlords' social evenings, where members can pool ideas and discuss strategy, and also seminars and talks where experts will be on hand to discuss matters of import and interest to landlords, such as tax matters, inventories and Tenancy Deposit Schemes, building up a portfolio, getting the best type of mortgage, décor and renovation, and where to find the hotspots. There are invaluable opportunities for networking, sharing experiences and making friends. There will also be meetings to discuss implications of new legislation, such as Home Information Packs, licenses for HMOs and energy efficiency measures. As ever more legislation and control comes in, landlord associations will become increasingly essential, as it is not always easy for laypeople to get their heads round the labyrinthine implications of new bills, acts and directives.

The NFRL also runs a free helpline whereby members can get advice on evicting troublesome tenants, collecting unpaid rent, the merits or otherwise of going to court, and securing the best type of mortgage.

Being a landlord can be lonely and bleak, especially when things go wrong, and local landlord associations provide help and support as well as expert advice. Senior members of landlord associations also frequently sit on government committees and advise the government on strategies and ways forward in this sector. Whether the government takes any notice is another matter!

You can also learn through membership of such an association which are the good letting agents, and which are the ones to avoid. Members can also often secure useful discounts on insurance, furniture packages and kitchens and bathrooms, through their membership.

In my view, membership cannot be too highly recommended! Landlord associations are particularly useful for new landlords, as they frequently hold meetings where all rules, regulations and obligations are explained. Most associations hold Development Days, aimed especially at the rookie landlord. The associations can also give details of Landlord Accreditation Schemes, as, if you want to be super-professional, you can now obtain an accreditation certificate to show you are highly competent in the ever more complex business of renting out property to others.

Many local authorities now run Landlord Accreditation Schemes. In order to become an Accredited Landlord you have to attend a one-day development course which will bring you up to date with all current legislation and requirements. You will agree to follow a Code of Conduct and you have to be a 'fit and proper person' to run a lettings business. This means you have not been in prison or convicted of any major offence.

The one-day course costs around £80 (in 2007) and accreditation lasts five years. The scheme is open to private landlords, agents and big investors who want to make a success of their lettings business. Local authorities will have details of such courses.

Tax

Now we come to the thorny but unavoidable subject of tax. Net rental income is subject to income tax at the marginal rate (10 per cent, 20 per cent or 40 per cent in 2008, whichever is applicable). 'Net' income means that amount of income left over when all expenses incurred in letting, including loan interest payments, are taken into account. Insurance cover and any VAT incurred are also allowable. A wear and tear allowance of 10 per cent of the rent is available where properties are furnished. All income from letting is subject to tax, and this applies whether you are letting rooms in your home, you are an investment landlord, or you are letting your home while you are abroad. UK landlords living abroad are subject to UK tax on their rented properties.

If you carry out any refurbishment while the place is let, you can claim this. But in order to set costs against income tax you must be receiving income, however small. One friend got round the refurbishment problem by allowing a relative to live in her flat at a peppercorn rent, while she refurbished it with a view to letting it.

Your accountant, if you have one, will work out the figures for you. Some of the larger letting agencies can also give information on your tax situation. Although novice landlords are understandably frightened of having to pay huge taxes on investment properties, especially when there are so many other costs to consider, in fact there are very many items you can set against tax.

When you come to sell your investment property you will most probably incur Capital Gains Tax.

If you have been renting out rooms in your own home, the situation gets even more complicated. If you have a lodger with her own bedroom, you are not liable for Capital Gains Tax when you sell. But if you have been letting, say, a self-contained basement flat you could be liable for a proportion of the gain on your home. This proportion will depend on how much of your home you have let out, and the length of time for which it has been let.

As Capital Gains Tax is not straightforward, you should talk to your accountant or tax adviser before selling any investment property, as you may gain or lose according to when the tax year falls. To take a personal example, in one single tax year I sold two investment properties, and so had to pay Capital Gains Tax on both. But if I'd waited just three days to complete on the second property, I would have been liable to pay for this in the following tax year. I shan't make such a mistake again. A useful leaflet, CGT1, is available from your local tax office.

A very useful and comprehensive CD, Buy-to-Let Tax explained, takes you through all the many ramifications of the tax implications when you are letting property. It is compiled by tax experts, is very easy to follow, and is available from Dolomite Publishing, 107 Kings Road, Godalming, Surrey GU7 3 EU, e-mail: bruno@dolomite.co.uk.

Capital Gains Tax used to be extremely complicated, with business asset taper relief, indexation, your own personal liability and the length of time you had owned the asset all affecting the eventual tax payable. Although this made a lot of lovely extra lucrative work for accountants, since April 6 2008 CGT has been vastly simplified and now comes in at a flat 18 per cent of the profit made on the asset, however long you have had it and whatever your personal tax band.

You may still need expert advice, however, to help you work out exactly what you can set against this tax, as it is payable only on the actual profit and not on the price the asset eventually fetched.

Choosing an accountant

As Buy-to-Let can be complex, it is recommended that you choose an accountant who is also a landlord. Working out the numbers can be difficult as you are dealing with many imponderables; also, tax laws are always liable to change. Accountants who are themselves landlords tend to have more understanding of the market and what is involved than others.

Capital Gains Tax

Capital Gains Tax can still be complicated, but as a general rule you will have to pay CGT on any asset considered to be a capital sum that does not form part of your income, ie your own home, or 'principal private residence'.

Just to make matters even more difficult, properties rented out as holiday lettings are counted as a business asset, while other types of residential property you may let out are regarded as non-business assets. That means a holiday lettings business is counted as earned income, while letting on an Assured Shorthold Tenancy is regarded as unearned income. (There's absolutely no work or effort involved, you see, at least according to HM Revenue & Customs.) However, it's still counted as an asset so you still have to pay CGT if and when you sell the property. If, however, you sell or give this asset to your spouse or civil partner, you will be exempt from the tax.

The rate you have to pay on disposal of your asset, which could be property, stocks and shares, land and buildings, or machinery, used to depend on many variables such as income and length of time the asset was held. It is now a flat rate of 18 per cent of the gain.

A chargeable gain is defined as an asset that is worth more when you dispose of it than it was when you acquired it. You can set against this gain certain allowable costs. For a property these could include costs of acquisition; incidental costs of acquisition (legal fees, survey fees, for instance); enhancement costs, such as putting in a new bathroom and kitchen or a new roof; costs of establishing or defending the title, and incidental disposal costs – again, such as legal fees.

Any VAT paid as part of acquisition or disposal costs is treated as allowable. Indexation – an allowance that reduces gains for the effects of inflation – no longer applies. If the property has created an overall loss for you, the rate is capped at zero.

All very involved, but the bottom line is that you will almost certainly have to pay *something* to the tax office when you sell your rental property. In the meantime, while you own the property make sure you keep all bills related to improving the asset, such as those from plumbers, painters and decorators, builders, electricians and so on.

Costs such as utility bills, service and maintenance charges will not normally be allowable on rental properties as you can claim tax relief on these out of the income gained from renting.

By now, most tax loopholes regarding Capital Gains Tax have been severely plugged, and there is no real way of avoiding payment – unless you are determinedly dishonest.

HM Revenue & Customs staff these days are extremely helpful, and can give you chapter and verse on Capital Gains and other tax liabilities relating to furnished and unfurnished lettings. As the tax position can be complicated, and vary according to other circumstances in your life, each case has to be assessed individually. What we can say is that income derived from lettings is subject to tax: nothing is more certain than that.

There is one notable exception, however. Under the government's Rent-a-Room scheme, you do not have to pay tax on rent from a lodger in your home if the gross annual amount of rent is less than a specified amount. Obviously this is liable to constant change, but in 2006, the first £4,250 could be tax free. To find out more, you can obtain the HM Revenue & Customs leaflet *Letting and Your Home* (IR87) from any tax office. The Rent-a-Room scheme was designed to encourage more people to provide accommodation by letting spare rooms in their home. Previously, fear of tax liability put people off doing this.

Generally speaking, expenses that are 'wholly and necessarily' incurred in letting out property can be set against tax. Food, if provided (as with a lodger or B&B guests), is an allowable expense.

SIPPS

In December 2005, the government suddenly backtracked on its intention to allow residential property investments to be put into a tax-efficient Self-Invested Private Pension (SIPP). Many new flats in major cities had been built, or were being built, in anticipation of this tax break, but the whole thing has fallen flat on its face, especially as increasingly, mortgage lenders are tightening their lending criteria on new flats. With some lenders, the minimum deposit on new flats has increased from 15 per cent to 25 per cent.

Although residential property, in most cases, cannot now be put into a SIPP, halls of residence are still allowed. Children's homes and prisons are other residential categories which are still allowed within a SIPP.

But for property investors, student accommodation is likely to be the best bet. With student numbers set to increase every year from their 2006 level of two million (in England and Wales), there is a strong market for student accommodation, and an opportunity to invest in this sector while satisfying the altered SIPPs requirements.

Obviously this is a complex matter, as it is not a direct investment, so advice has to be taken from somebody who knows what he or she is talking about. A good start, if you are interested in investing in student halls of residence, is to talk to the accommodation department of your local university, which can give general advice; then you would have to hammer it out with a tax advisor, before making any such investment.

REITS

The REIT – Real Estate Investment Trust – is an idea the government have pinched from Australia and the United States. Again, it is a scheme whereby your property portfolio can be put into a tax-transparent vehicle that avoids Capital Gains Tax.

At the time of writing, it is not yet known how these new government plans might benefit the small investor, as they are mainly aimed at the big investor, with the intention of enabling the private rented sector to grow.

These will, though, affect the small investor in time and some funds have already been established whereby people can invest in properties in much the same way as they might invest in stocks and shares. The investment is indirect, rather than direct, in that you will not be buying a property as such, but instead putting money into a fund which buys properties for Buy-to-Let purposes.

Some financial experts believe that investing in a REIT may be safer than buying property direct, as many checks are carried out before the investment takes place. Well, that remains to be seen, but the performance of many big and high-profile financial companies in recent years has not been all fabulous, to say the least.

REITS will be allowed in a SIPP, so by investing indirectly in residential property through a trust, you can still gain the tax advantages cruelly wiped out – as some see it – by the Chancellor at the end of 2005.

Again, expert advice must be taken from a reputable tax planning company, as these investments are not always easy to understand. As always, the overriding advice is: never invest in anything you do not fully understand, especially where large sums of money are involved.

So far as Capital Gains Tax goes, it is possible to reduce the amount payable, if you live in your Buy-to-Let property yourself for long enough for it to count as your main personal private residence. Even if you have only lived in the property for a very brief time, there will be an element of exempt gain when you come to sell. But be very careful if you have a Buy-to-Let mortgage, as strictly speaking, these are not intended for your own home or main residence.

Income tax is payable on all Buy-to-Let properties when rented. Very many investors in this sector buy properties in bad condition, and then renovate them to make them lettable. This puts the investor in a difficult tax situation, as tax relief cannot be obtained on a property before it is let. If, however, you can persuade the tax inspector that it was lettable in its original condition, tax relief applies.

Confused? This example should make it all clear: a friend inherited a two-bed flat when her parents died. She intended to do it up as a Buy-to-Let, but at the time she inherited it the flat was extremely dilapidated and needed total renovation. It was, however, just habitable. At the same time, my friend's ex-husband was between homes. He had sold his house but had not yet found somewhere suitable to live. The arrangement was that the ex would live in the dilapidated flat, paying a peppercorn rent, until he found his new home. As it turned out, the ex lived there for nearly a year. As soon as he moved out, my friend had the place completely renovated – and gained tax relief on repairs and renovation, simply because she was receiving income from the place in its original state.

Hidden costs

Don't forget, when working out the numbers, that there will always be hidden and unexpected costs. These can include levies for renovation and repair; installing a new kitchen or bathroom; legal costs if trying to evict an unsatisfactory tenant; service charges being increased; paying for your share of buying the freehold; and stumping up for redecorating the common parts, or for new lifts.

The common parts in one of my properties suddenly developed dry rot, or at least, dry rot became apparent. This was not included in the insurance, and cost all the owners several thousand pounds to put right. With another property, the freeholders decided to install new windows throughout the block, at a cost of £2,000 plus to all the residents. Any ill that bricks and mortar is heir to can crop up in an investment property, so be prepared.

Not every cost can be calculated in advance, so it is very wise to have a contingency sum in the bank for these eventualities.

It's worth it!

Although initially the figures on the debit side may look daunting, as there seem to be so very many costs to set against gross rental income, the fact is that most people who let properties find they do very nicely, and the extra dollop of income received every month from rent is very welcome indeed.

When I have gone through lean times in my 'day job', that guaranteed income, provided the tenant pays up, of course (and the vast majority do, I'm glad to say), has helped through many a crisis. In fact, if you have some savings, an inheritance or redundancy money, it's hard to think of any better way to use it.

The late newspaper columnist Auberon Waugh once wrote an article asking whatever do you do with a sum such as £90,000 – an amount he had received from selling an antique at auction. He complained that it was an awkward amount of money, too much just to spend and not enough to invest with any reasonable return. But clearly, the best thing to do would have been to buy an investment property and let it out to somebody who would be grateful for a decent roof over their head.

In fact, it's hard to imagine a better way of using spare cash than to provide somebody with a desirable home in return for rent. You gain, and somebody else gains. If it all works out well, it's a win–win situation.

Hodgkinson's Law of Landlord and Tenant

A sum of money that seems large for the tenant to pay is not much for the landlord to receive.

4 Décor and renovation

How 'desirable' does the property have to be to attract good tenants? And what constitutes a desirable property in today's terms? There is little doubt that standards of rental flats are getting higher all the time, and that clean, smart flats and houses are fast becoming the norm rather than the exception.

It must be said that the success of the Buy-to-Let scheme and the increased professionalism of letting agencies since the formation of ARLA have pushed up the standard of much rented accommodation, including even student accommodation.

Furniture stores selling mainly to landlords report that since letting became a middle-class, professional activity, there has been a new insistence on chic, matching furniture, plain carpets and neutral-coloured walls. The days of swirly carpets fighting with mildewed, faded-rose-patterned wallpaper and grim, brown, uncut moquette three-piece suites are, if not over, rapidly passing, thank goodness.

Hamptons International, which has produced a *Lettings Handbook,* makes the following recommendations for investment property:

- Carpets and walls should be in a neutral colour. Whites and pale creams make the freshest, cleanest impression.

- Paint finishes are easier than wallpaper to maintain, although wallpaper may be expected in very high-value properties.

- Good-quality curtains and carpets are essential. They are particularly important in unfurnished property, where they are highly visible.

- Kitchens should be well equipped, and this ideally means a dishwasher, large fridge-freezer, washing-machine, separate tumble-dryer and microwave.

- Bathrooms should have high-quality fittings and be well lit. Power showers and fully tiled floors and walls are expected by corporate clients.

- Bedrooms should have ample wardrobe space.

- If you are letting to corporate clients, high standards are expected. Woodstrip floors, low-voltage lighting and granite work surfaces will all impress premium clients.

- Laminate floors cheapen a property. Go for real wood or carpet.

To furnish or not?

If you have recently bought, or are considering buying, an investment property, you will at some stage have to make a decision as to whether or not to furnish it. There is little, nowadays, to choose in rent, and the days when unfurnished lettings gave tenants more security of tenure are over. At one time, unfurnished premises were considered more 'permanent' than furnished, as tenants could not be so easily evicted. For this reason, most landlords preferred to 'furnish' their property, even if the furniture consisted of broken chairs and collapsed beds. These days, both furnished and unfurnished lettings are governed by the same laws and tenancy agreements, so there is little advantage either financially or in terms of security of tenure either way. The only difference is that the annual 10 per cent 'wear and tear' allowance is limited to furnished properties. Tenants in unfurnished accommodation can be evicted as swiftly as those in furnished lettings. A landlord enjoys the same legal protection whether the property is furnished or unfurnished.

Generally speaking, the majority of properties in central London are let furnished, whereas country properties are more likely to be let unfurnished. Greg Shackleton, our super-landlord, always lets his properties unfurnished as, on the scale at which he operates, it is simply not practical to keep buying sofas and washing machines. By contrast, the former actress Fiona Fullerton, now a property magnate, says that she always lets her properties furnished, wherever they are, simply because they look so much nicer that way. It is certainly true that unfurnished flats can look bleak, bare and uninviting. They may not 'show' as well as furnished properties.

This is something all landlords must take into account: first impressions. It is not a scientifically proven observation that I am about to make, but it seems to me that women prefer to let places furnished, whereas men tend to let them unfurnished. This may be because female property investors can't bear to leave a place unfinished, and just love putting in little touches. I always put a vase of flowers, a plant or some ornaments in my flats, simply because I prefer them that way when showing tenants round. At the risk of seeming sexist, it also seems to me that women naturally tend to make a home of an investment property, whereas men, with a beady eye on maximizing profit, will be content to leave it as bleak and unhomely-looking as possible.

So in a sense, the decision to furnish or not depends on your temperament, as there is little to choose either in legal protection or in achievable rent. Agents do point out, though, that unfurnished properties may take longer to let, so there is an increased risk of void periods. Against this, it has to be remembered that furnishing a place will cost something, so it may be a matter of balancing possible void periods against the expense of furnishing a property.

Many agents report that unfurnished properties take longer to let than furnished ones, because they tend to look bleak without furniture. In fact, one agent said: 'If you want to let a flat unfurnished – furnish it first, even if you take the furniture out before the tenant moves in.'

Two friends of mine bought dingy, dated flats, renovated them to a high standard, then waited – and waited – for a suitable tenant to move in. One waited nine months, the other waited five months, before the flats were let. The reason? They were completely unfurnished and so had little 'eye appeal', even though they were clean, smart and modern.

In fact, when one of the owners put in a bed, table, sofa and chairs, his flat was let instantly. When considering whether or not to furnish, one has to ask oneself: why do property developers always have show homes? Simply so that prospective buyers can see for themselves how wonderful the place could look. The idea of 'staging' a property has now embedded itself into people's consciousness, thanks to very many makeover programmes on television, so that viewers now expect it.

Most tenants, it has to be said, have decidedly undeveloped powers of visualization when they are shown an unfurnished flat. They can't imagine how it could look. Another important factor is that rooms look far larger and more impressive when furnished than when empty. An empty room is just uninviting. Also, it may be difficult for potential tenants, giving the place a cursory glance, to see how a double bed, sofa, wardrobe, computer desk and so on could fit into the space available.

Many properties that are let unfurnished do have furniture in them, of course, which belongs to the outgoing tenant. It's the completely bare flat or house that can be hard to let, even to those who are actually looking for an unfurnished property.

Another option for those who do not want to be landed with dozens of tables, chairs and beds is to hire all furniture. This is a solution adopted by property developer David Humphreys, who buys properties to let both for himself and on behalf of clients.

He says: 'If you hire furniture, you can replace anything which is broken or past its best with a matching item. This may not be possible if you buy at sales or at places like Ikea or Habitat, which have a fast, unrepeatable turnover of styles.

'There is also the advantage that furniture on hire is tax-deductible, which is not the case when you furnish before letting.' An average price for hiring a whole flat full of furniture is around £175 per month.

The essentials

Whether a property is let furnished or unfurnished, it should *always* have a fully fitted kitchen that contains a cooker, washing-machine and dryer, fridge-freezer, and if the property is a three-bedroom house or flat, a dishwasher is recommended as well. There is no need to put a dishwasher into a studio or one-bedroom flat; indeed, it is most probably a waste of money, as tenants usually consider them too much of a hassle to use. Also, it's yet another possible thing to go wrong.

If putting in a new kitchen, I would always go for white units in tenanted properties. As kitchen units are basically all much the same, and it's only the doors that add the style or otherwise, there's nothing wrong with going for the cheapest units available. I have found that Wickes kitchen units work perfectly well. Tenants can add their own touches of colour. Also make sure all 'white goods' are white. Colours date a place.

A word of warning: if installing a new kitchen, do not on any account go for integrated units, whatever your level of refurbishment. The reason is that they have to fit exactly and may be difficult, if not impossible, to replace after a few years. Landlords Marion Mathews and Renske Mann bought an upmarket London property to let out, which already had a beautiful expensive kitchen with all integrated units. However, after a time every single unit broke down and had to be replaced. Renske spent days, weeks, on the Internet trying to find replacements for the units. Then the next job was to find somebody to install them. The whole process took over a month, during which time their long-suffering tenants had to manage without appliances. Yet if the kitchen had been fitted with ordinary pull-out units, the replacements could have been installed in less than a week. Also, integrated units cost more than twice as much as others, yet they are just as liable to break down or go wrong.

In fact, there is a lot to be said for appliances that can simply be chucked out when they go wrong. The age of the throwaway appliance is fast approaching, if it has not already arrived. A perfectly good washing-machine can be bought for

£200, yet engineers charge £60 or more just as a call-out fee. All white goods are rapidly coming down in price, and these days the expensive ones are rarely worth the extra cost. And don't forget that any replacement item is fully tax-deductible.

There should also be in all rental properties a good working heating system, a power shower, curtains and carpets. Also, service contracts, guarantees and useful phone numbers should be provided and left in the tenant's file.

Many landlords do not pay enough attention to the important matter of the tenant's file. From experience, I have learnt that it is essential to have important information in a readily accessible, durable file that remains in the property.

All guarantees and instructions that are likely to get wet, such as those for the shower and washing-machine, should be laminated. Also, take a photocopy for yourself, as it can be difficult to replace instructions once lost.

You should also give your tenant details of any peculiarities pertaining to the lease or the building, such as whether washing can be hung on the balcony, or relating to noise or pets. Some managing agents now prepare cut-down versions of leases especially for landlords to give their tenants. Ask your managing agents whether they do this.

Tenants often complain that landlords never leave sets of instructions or, if they do, they are in a tatty, unreadable pile hidden away in a cupboard. Leaving a smart file shows that you care – and this encourages the tenant to care as well.

All letting agencies say that properties should be 'in good decorative order' – but what exactly does that mean? There are certain golden rules that must be obeyed, the first of which is not to decorate in your own personal taste, if this is in any way eccentric or idiosyncratic, as the more individual the property, the fewer tenants it is likely to attract. The safest option is to go for white or, preferably, very pale cream, ivory or buttermilk. Magnolia now looks rather dated, and in any case has a rather nasty pink tinge. Paint all doors and woodwork in eggshell gloss. Use good-quality paint and, if you can bear it, put on three coats. Then the property won't have to be repainted for several years. In flats without picture rails or coving, I always paint the ceiling the same colour as the walls, thus avoiding the inevitably wobbly demarcation line and the expense of having coving professionally installed. You could alternatively put up a wallpaper border or polystyrene coving, but both require quite a lot of expertise and are expensive in labour.

Wooden floors are extremely popular with tenants, and some tenants even request them when going to letting agencies. Before going to the expense of laying a wooden floor, however, check that it is allowed if the property is leasehold. Some leases stipulate that floors must be covered in fitted carpet, for the sake of the residents below. Wooden floors tend to be noisy.

Letting agent Mary Hennigan-Lawson of Cluttons says that virtually every prospective tenant she gets in her office asks for wooden floors, preferably throughout the flat, including the bedroom. It seems, she adds, that everybody these days has a dust allergy and wooden floors are considered to be cleaner and more modern than carpets.

Properties with wooden floors tend to attract a premium over a carpeted property, and some leases may allow wooden floors if stringent soundproofing requirements are met. It is now possible to soundproof wooden floors, but this is very expensive indeed, and in period flats, it may not be possible to soundproof adequately, whatever the cost.

Even basement and ground floor flats with wooden floors must be soundproofed, as there are instances on record of noise rising up from people walking on wooden floors in the basement.

In one case, a landlord installed wonderful wooden flooring when he refurbished, but unfortunately did not pay enough attention to soundproofing. The resulting noise from occupants walking on the floors led to numerous complaints from other residents which eventually came to the attention of the Royal Borough of Kensington and Chelsea, which ordered soundproofing measures to be installed at once. The landlord put down thick expensive rugs and the tenants were ordered to walk around in slippers, although when those tenants moved out, the landlord had to carpet the entire flat at a cost of £3,000 before it could be re-let.

Wooden floors are expensive, carpets are expensive – so before fitting either, make sure you are effectively muffling the sound from occupants walking across the floor.

Whatever soundproofing requirements are in place, never put carpet in a bathroom. Vinyl is almost as soundproof as carpet and works well enough in most ordinary flats, although very high-end properties may require ceramic, limestone or other expensive tiling, which can again be noisy. A thick bathroom mat should solve this problem though.

Yes, I know I said earlier that I put carpet in one of my bathrooms, but that was a temporary measure until the bathroom could be renovated. That bathroom now has vinyl, and another rental flat is tiled. Sometimes the condition or type of floor means you cannot have an absolute choice with flooring, although the importance of the right flooring, both for appearance and noise reduction, cannot be overestimated.

I would say there are more problems over flooring in rental flats than any other aspect of the décor. But whatever you do, don't be tempted to put down 'landlord's laminate' as this has become a turn-off in all but the very cheapest and nastiest flats.

If putting down a wooden floor, make sure it is real wood and well fitted. In fact, expert fitting is essential in all rental flats, as tenants give the place very hard wear and badly fitted carpets and vinyl soon start curling up at the edges, or may 'ruck up' if not laid properly.

Carpets are more hard-wearing than wooden floors, and don't show up stilettos or scuff marks so much. Also, wooden floors ideally need sanding every two to three years – another expense. Ikea-type simulated wooden floors are not particularly hard-wearing and probably not ideal for tenanted properties. Carpets should be the same throughout the property, as this makes the flat look more spacious and streamlined. Don't use cheap off-cuts and bits of carpet; do it properly. The best colour is beige, not too light and not too dark. Light carpet shows the dirt, and dark carpet shows up all the bits. A beige carpet with a darker fleck in it is probably the most practical of all.

Some landlords maintain that it's essential to put down good-quality carpet. I'm not so sure. I have found, over the years, that cheap cord carpet works perfectly well for rented flats.

Curtains are a potential problem. Professional inventory clerk Jennifer Reigate, who visits several properties a week to check inventories, said: 'Even these days, I rarely see nice curtains, yet these, more than anything else, absolutely make a property.' My number one rule is: if you can't afford, or don't feel inclined to buy, expensive furniture, don't economize on curtains. This doesn't mean you have to go for the most expensive curtains you can find, but it is a good idea to have them specially made, in fabric thick enough to hang well, floor-length, with rope tiebacks, lined and interlined. You only have to curtain a place once, as curtains get very little wear at all, and can look as good as new many years later.

A number of my flats have been enthusiastically snapped up purely because of the luxurious-looking curtains. They can be in cream or off-white thick cotton, and they add a definite touch of luxury to even the simplest flat. Second-hand designer curtain shops are good places to look if the prospect of paying for specially commissioned curtains makes your eyes water.

Many younger tenants like wooden and Venetian blinds, and these may be a good idea where floor-length curtains might cut out too much light, or look too 'staid' for younger tenants. These blinds look trendy and are extremely versatile as regards the amount of light they let in, but they can get sticky and dusty and be difficult to clean. Also, they can get stuck or become difficult to operate in time. There is virtually nothing to go wrong with curtains once they are up, which is another major factor in their favour.

Bathrooms and kitchens should have roller blinds rather than curtains, which can get in the way of sinks and washing up, for instance. Slatted blinds in kitchens, whether of metal or wood, can get very greasy and in any case are difficult to clean.

If you're putting in a new bathroom, this should be white. As with kitchens, tenants can add their own touches of colour with towels, soap and toiletries.

If you have decided to let your investment property unfurnished, then that's about all you have to do.

Furnishings

If you are furnishing your property, then more decisions have to be made. I personally always furnish my flats, providing at least the basics. Apart from the fact that furniture makes a place look immediately like a home rather than a daunting white space, it also means that people are not humping double beds, huge sofas, sideboards and dining tables in and out every six months, thus risking damage to carpets and walls, and increasing wear and tear on the fabric.

To be adequately furnished, a flat or house must have:

- a sofa;
- at least one easy chair;
- a coffee table;
- standard and table lamps;
- bedside lamps;
- a double bed;
- a chest of drawers;
- a wardrobe;
- a bedside cabinet or table;
- coat hangers;
- a dining or kitchen table; and
- kitchen chairs.

This is the minimum. It should be smart and, if not new, at least looking like new when you first furnish the place.

In the kitchen, you should provide cutlery and crockery, glasses, saucepans, kettle, toaster, iron and ironing board, cleaning materials, buckets, mops and tea towels. In fact, the kitchen should have everything needed to cook, eat and clean. Ever more landlords are providing microwaves, as so many tenants these days want to just pick up their microwave meal on the way home, then heat and eat. But a microwave is not absolutely essential. After all, tenants can provide their own if they are that keen.

Although the traditional advice given above still holds good, I am hearing more and more from letting agents that there is a trend now for tenants to provide their own crockery, cutlery, glass and china. This avoids worrying about silly little items on the inventory, of which more later, and also means the tenants can have fun choosing their own bits and pieces.

Martin Bikhit, of the London agents Kay and Co, believes that providing kitchen equipment is getting old-fashioned, as Ikea, Cargo, Woolworths and similar stores now sell trendy kitchenware at extremely cheap prices. Woolworths have white mugs at 28p each and plates for 50p.

In fact, the trend is ever more towards the throwaway – throwaway ovens, fridges, cutlery, crockery. The days when you bought kitchen items to last for ever are over, it seems. Also, fashions in homewares now change extremely quickly, and a five-year-old set of kitchen items can look extremely dated. Ikea, for instance, have trendy wine glasses for £1 each. Who worries about whether items so cheap get lost or broken?

Some agents maintain that, in order for a property to be presented fully furnished, it must contain bed linen and two spare sets for each bed. This is certainly the case when letting to short-term or corporate clients, but in my experience, most ordinary tenants prefer to bring their own bedding, including pillowcases and duvets. I always provide just one set of bed linen, a duvet and pillows, in case of emergency, but not a spare set. If tenants staying for a year do not have their own bed linen when they arrive, my feeling is that they can go out and buy it. After all, you can get new linen extremely cheaply from seconds shops and sales these days.

I have cheap white or off-white Indian cotton throwovers on the beds, as they make the beds look neater and more welcoming, and they are easily washable. I can't resist the temptation to scatter matching and coordinating cushions around, and often have a few made up in the curtain fabric, while I'm at it. But that's a personal quirk, not an essential. As a landlord, I feel I am somewhere between a cynical investor and a compulsive homemaker. Although a matching, specially made cushion may not be a very clever idea from an income-producing point of view, I have to have one if it absolutely makes the place.

A word on sofas and upholstered chairs: these must conform to the 1988 safety regulations. Sofas manufactured before this date are considered a fire hazard, and must not be used in furnished accommodation. Letting agencies, which have to abide by the law, won't allow these sofas. But sofas and couches manufactured before 1950 are safe, as these are upholstered in horsehair rather than foam.

Sofas should either have loose, washable covers, or be in materials and designs that do not show the dirt. A white sofa in a tenanted flat is asking for trouble: what if they spill red wine or Ribena on it? I once saw a lovely white sofa in a junk shop at an amazing price, £90. The only thing was, it was rather dirty. By some weird chance, a couple of friends of mine who run a carpet-cleaning business happened to be passing by as I was looking at the sofa. They inspected it and advised me not to buy, even though it seemed such a bargain, because it was not possible to clean the type of fabric that covered the item. Therefore, it would have been the opposite of a bargain and, thanks to their miraculous intervention, I avoided a nasty mistake. Loose covers on sofas, if you have to buy them, can cost as much as buying a new piece of furniture, so the best advice is not to buy any furniture for your investment properties that is not absolutely perfect at the moment of purchase. It is simply not worth it.

There are so many furniture bargains and sales around that you would do far better to shop at places like The Pier, Carpenter's, John Lewis First Furniture and Habitat than go to junk shops or auctions. Also, I've discovered that auction and junk-shop furniture is _just as expensive_ as buying new sofas in sales and on special offers.

For small rooms, wicker furniture can look smart, informal and welcoming, although it is not always particularly hard-wearing. A few stackable chairs are a good idea as they enable your tenants to have the facility to entertain guests without the rooms being totally bunged up with furniture all the time.

Flatpack furniture is fine for rental accommodation, and present-day designs are sleek, streamlined and functional. Do not ever be tempted to put your old cast-offs into an investment flat. It should look, if anything, even smarter than your own home.

If you have inherited a property that you are interested in letting out, it's a good idea to ask a letting agent to come round and inspect it, then advise on what renovation or refurnishing needs to be done to bring it up to present-day letting standards. Properties that have been lived in by very old people are unlikely to be considered safe or desirable by present-day standards, even though the old people concerned probably lived in them extremely safely for decades. But we are living in a nannying age, and rules and regulations are likely to increase, rather than decrease, in future.

Hamptons says that you should expect to spend around 5 to 6 per cent of the purchase price of the property on furnishings. On a £60,000 property, that would come to around £3,000. I've found that it's hard to spend less than this, at least if you want to take a pride in the place. It's amazing how a trip to Ikea adds up.

To sum up, whether you are letting furnished, unfurnished or 'part furnished', to use a new phrase now creeping into agents' jargon, your rental property should be decorated in neutral colours, have a clean, crisp overall look, and be professionally cleaned and well aired. Hamptons recommend using glass table tops rather than wood as this reduces staining and scuffing. Glass table tops are not recommended in Feng Shui, as wood is supposed to create better vibes in the place, but with rental investments you have to be practical.

How often should you redecorate/renovate?

These days, fashions in interiors change almost as quickly as fashions in clothes and, while you cannot expect always to

be up to the minute in every detail with investment properties, care should be taken that they don't start to look tired
or old-fashioned.

So, every few years, pretend to be a tenant and take a look at
the other properties on offer, to see whether you are getting
out of date. A dated rental property can be as off-putting as one
in bad condition. Also, as it gets more tired-looking, rental
yields tend to go down.

The thing is, again, to work out the figures, and discover how
much you could command in increased rent if you cheered up
the place. One landlord in Canary Wharf, East London, where
there are very many rental properties to choose from, was
getting £250 a week in rent, and there were also many voids. His
agent advised him to renovate the place using an interior
designer. He did so, at a cost of £20,000. But the minute the
makeover was complete, that same flat rented out at £320 a week.

Pierre Brahm, whose family owns many rental flats in
Cadogan Square, one of the most expensive areas in London,
decided that his properties, with their swags and heavy
curtains and patterned carpets, were looking decidedly old-
fashioned. He employed top designers to redesign the properties, which were immediately let out at double the previous
rent. He said: 'After a time, if you don't renovate, the rental
yield will start to go down, and the property will take much
longer to let. You should always make sure your investment
property has – and keeps – its wow factor.'

I know from experience how difficult it is to reach the
decision to redecorate. I always think: maybe it will do just one
more tenancy. But the difference in rent can be dramatic if the
place is really smart.

Renovating vs selling up

However smart and trendy a property is when initially let,
inevitably over the years it will become tired and dated, almost
imperceptibly at first, and eventually, you will be so ashamed
of it you won't want to show anybody round.

How long does a property take to reach a stage where it can no longer be let – and how do you decide whether to bite the bullet and give it a total makeover, or sell it, either as it is or when renovated?

From experience, I would say that 8 to 10 years is the maximum time a property can go before it needs a new kitchen, new bathroom, new carpets and curtains, new tiles and new flooring. In between these times, it will certainly need some cosmetic enhancement, such as redecorating, and possibly replacement of some appliances and furniture, if being let furnished.

But after a decade of tenant occupation, it will certainly need the full works. Even if it is not in bad condition, it will be in the style of a decade ago – and never forget that there is a lot of competition these days, and only the smartest, most up to date properties let out quickly. Of course, you can always get somebody to take it, in any condition, but they are not going to be the best tenants.

Another way of looking at it, especially with the Tenancy Deposit Protection Scheme now up and running, is that it is difficult, if not impossible, to compile a useful inventory if the property is not in immaculate condition. And now that deposits are held in government-backed schemes, deciding whether the property is significantly more dilapidated at the end of the tenancy than the beginning could be problematic if the place was tatty to begin with.

But, as always with investments, you are playing a numbers game, and the only way you can tell whether to renovate and re-let, or to sell is to work out the figures very carefully, bearing in mind mortgage repayments, possible void periods, cost of works and cost of selling or re-letting, including paying capital gains tax if you decide to sell.

Liam Bailey, Head of Residential Research for Knight Frank, believes the best way to work out the figures is to discover whether you can get a significantly higher rent for the property when refurbished. Supposing you were getting 5 per cent yield – about average these days – and the renovation is going to cost you £15,000. The increased rent must now give you a yield at least slightly higher than 5 per cent. Otherwise, you are probably better off selling.

A lower yield than before, after adding on the cost of renovation, is your indication that this may be the right time to sell. Liam Bailey adds: 'If you decide that residential property is going to remain in your portfolio you have to look at the impact of the investment on property improvement in terms of rental growth and rental return.

'If you are not seeing your gross yield declining after the improvement then you should probably go for it, bearing in mind that gross yields have reduced greatly in recent years anyway.'

Whether you renovate before you sell, if you decide on this option, depends on the type of property and the market; some properties do not fetch significantly more money after renovation. Again, take advice from a number of agents, or key into the PropertyPriceAdvice website for an impartial assessment.

Another way to look at it is to work out what return you are getting on your cash investment after the refurb. For example, if you were getting £250 a week in rent for a property before refurb, and £330 a week after spending £20,000 on renovation, that extra £80 a week represents a 20 per cent return on the renovation cost – better than you could get at the bank.

Here is a personal example: in 1999, I bought a large studio flat in Worthing for £33,000. Sounds cheap, but that was the going rate then. It needed redecorating, a new carpet and new flooring in the kitchen and bathroom, after which it was let for £380 a month, making a gross return of just over 13 per cent. Over the years I had to put in a new washing machine, new cooker and do some redecorating, none of which cost much.

The flat was let very successfully for seven years, during which time the rent went up very slightly to £400 a month. By now, though, it was in dreadful condition and needed a complete refit. It could no longer be toshed up and was no longer 'lettable' in its present condition. A complete refit was going to cost £9,500, after which I would be able to get maybe £450 a month in rent. The work was going to take a month, during which time I would be getting no rent at all but would start to incur utility bills.

But also during this time, the property value had increased significantly, and the place was now worth around £115,000. This meant I was getting, in effect, a gross yield of only 4.2 per cent. After renovation – assuming I could get the expected extra rent – this yield would go up to 4.7 per cent, but I would be £9,300 poorer. It would also take about 10 to 15 years to recoup the cost of this investment in increased rent.

What to do? Selling agents advised me to sell it in its present condition rather than do it up, on the grounds that new owners would want to put in their own kitchen and bathroom. My own feeling on this was that any buyer for a property at this price would be a first time buyer, probably struggling to raise the deposit and pay the mortgage, and would not be able to afford another £10,000 on immediate refurbishments.

Any mortgage company would most probably insist on a new kitchen and bathroom as a condition of the mortgage, and this could make selling and negotiating very protracted indeed – all the while the property would be costing me in council tax and utility bills.

As I felt it would be vastly easier to sell, if I chose that option, in perfect condition, I went ahead with the refurb and asked selling and letting agents to come round when it was finished, and value it for both sales and letting.

Most letting agents reckoned on another £50 a month rent, but the sales agents did not value the place significantly higher after refurb. I could get maybe another £5,000 – less than the cost of the refit. Yet I would have struggled to sell it at all without renovation. The bathroom was previously done in the 1970s but could go no longer.

In the end, I decided to rent it out again, especially as it rented out very easily in its renovated state. There is a school of thought which says Buy-to-Let investors should never sell – unless they have unwittingly bought a real dog – as property prices keep on rising and eventually, capital gains tax comes down to nothing, or very little.

It is never an easy equation, and when expensive refurbishment can no longer be avoided, probably the best question to ask yourself is: what do I want to do now – and what are my long-term goals?

Everybody's goals, aims and ambitions are different, but important questions always have to be asked whenever major renovations are in the offing. You can always sell it for something – there are companies such as AquickSale which will buy off you for BMV (below market value) and sometimes this can be a sensible option.

The most significant question to ask yourself, always, is whether you want to remain a landlord.

The thing is, tenants as well as owners have well and truly got their eye in from watching so many makeover programmes on television, and they now expect a place to be smart, with strategically placed candles, cushions and upmarket magazines.

The question as to how often a place needs redecorating is difficult to answer. I would say *at least* repaint professionally and thoroughly every five years, with kitchens and bathrooms needing to be replaced every 10 years. The only problem is that, when you have got a place absolutely sparkling again, you may not want a tenant to come in and mess it up!

The thing is, you as the owner may not notice how tired the place is getting, and very often agents never say a word. When I had an extension built on to my home, the builder remarked that the house could not have been touched for 10 years, as everything was in the style of a decade ago. He was right, but until he drew attention to it I had never noticed. The same goes for investment properties, especially as tenants may be viewing as many as 20 or 30 before making a decision.

You also need to keep a beady eye on how well the shower is operating, whether the oven is holding up, whether the central heating is working properly, and so on.

Letting out your own home

There may be a number of reasons why you want to let out your own home. It may be that you or your family are relocating to another country for a year or two, and want to return to your home at some future date. It may be that you are in negative equity, and can get more money from letting out your home to tenants and renting a cheaper place yourself. In this case, the mortgage provider's permission will have to be sought, and the lender may well want to see any tenancy agreement.

It may be that you are temporarily relocated to another part of the country, have accepted a contract for a few months which takes you away from home, or work part of the year in another country anyway. During this time, you do not want your home to be empty and a temptation to squatters and burglars. It may be that you are in a new relationship and living with a partner, but do not at this stage want to give up your own home.

Whatever the reason, it is unlikely that your own home will meet, in every aspect, the current demands of letting agents. You may have pre-1988 sofas, for example. As with an inherited property, the best thing here is to ask an agent round to inspect the place and give advice. If you are locating abroad for a year or more, you should have your property professionally managed.

ARLA's advice here is never to leave property management to well-meaning friends and relatives, as this invites disaster. Such a disaster happened next door to me. The owners of the house were relocated to Hong Kong and wanted to let their property for two years. An agent found them tenants, but the property was managed by the owner's sister. Clearly, the young owners did this to save money, but as it turned out, it cost them dear. The tenants, four young men, paid no rent, trashed the place, held noisy, smoky barbecues until four in the morning, dealt in drugs, were rude and offensive to neighbours and had drunken parties every few days. The owner's sister, whom I contacted many times, soon decided she could not manage the tenants, and washed her hands of the matter. It took the owner two months to get the place habitable once again, when the tenants had been finally evicted. Every piece of furniture in the place was ruined, and the owner had to start again from scratch.

It is not advisable to try to let your own home on the cheap, or rent it to friends or relatives to avoid having to have gas certificates, fireproof sofas and safe installations. Have an agent round and do the whole thing professionally from the start.

By far the worst problems occur in landlord–tenant relationships, according to agents, when the owner's own house is let out. Tenants find themselves accused of stealing antiques, slashing paintings and ruining priceless pieces of furniture. A common complaint from tenants is that sideboards and cupboards are so stuffed full of the owner's items that tenants have nowhere to put their own things. An owner's house is also very likely to be over-furnished, leaving no room for the tenant to add personal bits and pieces.

When letting out your own home, you should clear out all cupboards and bookcases, and put all the contents into store until you return. Don't expect tenants to be impressed by lots of ornaments, thousands of flower vases and kitchen cupboards full of years-old herbs and spices. As far as possible, your own home should be scoured of personal stuff. Remove all personal and important documents, such as birth, marriage and divorce certificates, wills, pension schemes, deeds of the house and so on and either put them in a bank vault or place them with your solicitor.

What if your home is full of priceless antiques, yet you want to let it out? What if you have fine Persian rugs on the floor, designer furniture, paintings by artists whose work is now worth thousands of pounds, then you are posted abroad for a year or two? Should you let such a home, bearing in mind that in central London you could get up to £5,000 a week for such a place?

Barry Manners, director of Chard, a London estate agent which deals with this kind of problem, advised: 'If you have a property full of expensive goods, my advice is to seek the opinion of an insurer, telling him all your circumstances.' It is important to keep up insurance cover during the letting period, especially if the value of the contents runs into six figures. The insurance company would need an extremely detailed inventory and valuations on file. With any insurance policy, you should make sure you are covered for damage by the tenant. If the unthinkable happens, and the tenant allows the bath to overflow, thus water-damaging priceless antiques, you may not have a claim unless this eventuality is specified.

But Barry Manners advises that, where possible, the most valuable goods should be put into storage and fakes substituted. 'Few tenants will be able to tell the difference between a

Matisse and a Monet, or even a Monet original and a copy,' he said, 'so do what hotels do and hang fakes.'

If by chance you do have antiques or furniture of particular value, make sure these are very specifically described on the inventory. Mike Stimpson, of the National Federation of Residential Landlords, tells the story of how one landlord put 'four dining chairs' on the inventory when in fact they were valuable antiques. The tenants sold the chairs and replaced them with cheap substitutes. When the landlord claimed back the property, he withheld the deposit on the grounds that the chairs had been replaced.

But the tenants took him to court – and won! Because the landlord had not described the chairs in any detail, it was his word against the tenants', and the court chose to believe the tenants. Any item of any value at all must be entered in precise detail on the inventory, and if possible, its value given. This should be witnessed by a third party such as a professional letting agent. There must be no room for argument when any item has actual or sentimental value or is otherwise irreplaceable.

Although it is wise to remove anything you desperately do not want ruined or stolen, this is not always possible. An antique mirror, for instance, may just be too difficult to take down and store for the length of a tenancy.

Letting to family and friends

The expert advice here is: don't! Landlords often consider letting to family and friends because then they don't have to go through all the hassle of making sure all furniture and equipment is compliant, doing reference checks and going to the expense of an agent.

But almost everybody who has let to a friend or family member comes to regret it, because it is difficult to be businesslike with people you know well. All agents I spoke to said the same: if you are considering letting your property to somebody you know, make sure you do it through an agent who will treat your friend just like any other tenant. Otherwise, it is almost always the case that the friendship will be sorely tested.

Preparing for corporate or company lets

Although by far the commonest form of tenancy agreement these days is the Assured Shorthold, which lets the property out in six-monthly renewable dollops, in some cases you may want, or be in a position, to let your home or investment property for shorter periods than this.

Short lets are becoming increasingly common in large cities, and can range from a few weeks to a few months. In some boroughs, landlords are not allowed to let properties for less than three months, as the local authority does not want a large transient population. Also, very short stay tenants can take away from the area's hotel trade.

Short lets tend to command a far higher rent than standard tenancies. They can achieve between 20 and 50 per cent more rent than standard lets, and this rent is almost always paid by a company or corporation, rarely the individual. Because of this, short-let flats must be fully furnished and decorated to a much higher standard than ordinary lets, and must be absolutely ready for the tenant to move in and start living.

Flats intended for use as short lets must have several sets of bed linen, towels, tea towels, good-quality ranges of glasses, crockery and cutlery and a full complement of cooking utensils. The flat should be welcoming, with pictures on the walls, rugs on the floor, green plants, and plenty of table lamps for subdued lighting. With short lets, it is unlikely that tenants will be wanting to add their own touches, as they are looking for a place they can already call home, without further additions.

Kitchens in such flats should have dishwashers and, always, washing-machines with tumble-dryers. Tenants of these flats are buying comfort and convenience and they, or at least their company, are prepared to pay a high rent for such convenience. In these flats, you can keep a few antiques or valuable paintings, as these tenants are usually the kind of people who would take great care of them. When accidents do happen, tenants are usually mortified, as they realize they are living in a privileged and comfortable temporary home.

The better taste you have, and the more 'designer' your flat and furniture, the higher the rent a short-let tenant is likely to be prepared to pay. Corporate tenants, which the majority of short-let tenants will be, nowadays also expect cable and satellite TV as well as terrestrial channels. The best kind of furniture for upmarket short-term tenants is very modern, very clean, very streamlined, without being too minimalist. A very minimalist flat can make tenants feel uncomfortable.

Don't put in very personal, quirky touches. An agent told me he found one particular short-term flat difficult to let, even though it was in the right location, had all the right furniture and fittings and was an ideal size and shape. 'But,' said the agent, 'in the hall there was a row of very grainy, stark black and white pictures of naked men. Many corporate clients would be embarrassed to entertain in such a place, and would feel they had to apologize for the artwork on the walls. The advice we always give is: never make very personal statements in an investment flat, but make sure your décor and pictures appeal to the widest possible range of tastes.'

Many landlords like the idea of corporate tenants as such people tend to be highly paid, they look after the property and they are unlikely to default on rent. But the relocation agents who handle such lets can drive extremely hard bargains that may disbenefit you, the owner.

For instance, they usually offer a letter of guarantee instead of a cash deposit. This means there is no ready cash for any dilapidations or breakages. Then they may want to tie you up for two years at the same rent, but insist on a get-out clause for the tenant after six months. They do this because the corporate worker may be on probation and the company does not want to commit itself for any longer than it can help. Tim Hyatt, Lettings Director of Knight Frank, says: 'Relocation agencies would insist on a break clause after three months, if they could. With corporate tenancies, the clients make all the rules and you, the landlord, take it or leave it.'

Before signing up to a corporate tenancy, make sure you understand all the terms and conditions, and that you are not agreeing to a patently unfair, one-sided contract. It is not always the case, either, that corporate lets command higher rents than ordinary lets. Very often, they will try to negotiate you right down for the dubious privilege of having a corporate tenant. And – negotiating power is strictly one-way: they have it; you don't.

Also, if considering going for short lets, with their much higher rentals, make sure this is really what you want. Many letting agents refuse to handle short lets as they say they are more trouble than they are worth, as most problems happen at the beginning of a tenancy and, by the time they are sorted out, that tenant has gone and new problems begin with the next occupier.

Short lets are not always as lucrative as they appear, as the rent has to include all bills, including council tax. These lets are very hands-on, and may in any case count as commercial or holiday lets, which puts you, the landlord, in the position of running a business with all the extra paperwork that involves. Short lets may also cause security problems in a block of flats, if nobody knows who is coming and going.

So – both of these attractive-sounding options need very careful thought.

Students

At the other end of the scale we have the dreaded students.

Ever since Chaucer's time, students have had a bad reputation. They are commonly supposed to be dirty, noisy, uncaring of other people's property, drunken, druggy louts who get up at noon (at the earliest) and leave the place in a filthy mess, with the sink perpetually piled high with washing-up. For these reasons, few landlords are happy with the idea of letting to students. It is also a common belief that students never have any money, and that any student flat will at all times be littered with 'friends' sleeping on the floor.

Because of the propensity of male students at least to turn every place into a chaotic tip, it is popularly imagined that, for students, any old accommodation will do. (And before I get accused of sexism, yes, I am aware that the female of the species can be deadlier and dirtier than the male. But as a generalization, student squalor seems a standard rite of passage for many young men.) However, nowadays, even students can be fussy.

Joel Lazarus from the Black-Katz agency, one of the few letting agencies to handle student accommodation, said: 'Nowadays students are not impressed with squalid tips. Although the standards need not be as high as when letting to professionals, kitchens should be well equipped with washing-machines and working cookers.'

All student accommodation should be furnished with the basics, although it is usual to expect students to bring their own bed linen and towels. They will most probably not take good care of those provided by the landlord.

I don't think I would put up bespoke interlined curtains in a student flat, or matching scatter cushions. But even if you are prepared to consider students, it is still the case that the better presented the accommodation when the student moves in, the better it is likely to be looked after.

Whenever letting to students, or people without a regular income, it is essential to sign up a guarantor (usually a parent) who will guarantee the rent in the event of non-payment by the tenant. It is possible to arrange a guarantor via e-letting, and a letting agent will certainly insist on such a signature for student lets.

Some landlords, feeling sorry for poverty-stricken students, waive the dilapidation deposit. This is a bad idea. The most vociferous campaigners for tenancy deposit protection have been students and students' representatives. In April 2006 they scored a comprehensive victory when the government's official Tenancy Deposit Protection Scheme was rolled out with a grand reception at the House of Commons, complete with wine and canapes. How do I know? Because I was there!

Because today's students are so active when it comes to protecting their deposits, landlords have to be extra careful that everything is done correctly. With students, as with other tenant sectors, deposits have to be protected either in the custodial scheme or the insurance-based scheme. Whichever scheme you choose, the tenant must be informed of this in writing within 14 days.

At the end of the tenancy, the landlord returns some or all of the deposit as agreed, but if there is a dispute, the landlord must hand over the disputed amount until the dispute is resolved. Where there is a dispute, the scheme provider's dispute service comes into play.

If you are interested in letting to students, all university and college accommodation departments have leaflets about the Tenancy Deposit Protection Scheme and how it affects students.

The literature states very clearly that students must return the property in the same condition as it was let, so there is now a greater onus on the students to look after the place while they are in residence. As with most things in life, the tenancy deposit scheme works both ways.

But don't forget that these days, students come in all shapes, sizes and ages and they are not all 18- to 21-year-olds enjoying their first time away from home. Nowadays, there are many mature students, students doing MBAs and similar postgraduate degrees, and university lecturers, all looking for temporary accommodation. Sometimes students are the best bet, especially if you are renting out part of your own home, or you want somebody who will not remain in the premises for ever. Mature students are usually extremely hard-working, quiet and responsible. If you have a university near you, it may be worth making enquiries about students.

If considering renting to students, of whatever age, you will now be expected to provide internet access in every bedroom, so that all may use their computers. Mature students will now expect broadband. In either case, whether you provide dial-up connections or broadband, all you have to do is put in the connections. The tenants will have to foot the bills for use of the equipment. The same goes for satellite and cable television. You may provide the connections, but the tenant pays for the package.

If you rent a house to a number of students, it is essential to keep a check on them. Here is a cautionary tale. Irish journalist Kevin O'Connor took on the task of trying to find tenants for a friend who was to be away for a year. Four student nurses took the property – and then the fun started. Rent was unpaid, the place soon became full of wine bottles, and the girls moved in their boyfriends. Now, whenever O'Connor hears the ritual whines from students about substandard accommodation and deposits mysteriously going missing, 'I slap myself vigorously on the forehead three times, bow towards Mecca and intone out loud, *mea culpa, mea culpa*. Which I loosely translate as tough shit!' (*Irish Times*, Jan 2003).

As the number of students inexorably increases, so the student sector is becoming ever more attractive to landlords. It is a specific area of the market which has its own dynamics, and certainly suits some investors. You can rent privately to students, but nowadays, all universities require houses and flats that they rent from private owners and then sublet to students. Where this happens, the university takes over the property in much the same way as a Housing Association or local authority.

In the same way, the property owner has an agreement with the university rather than the tenants. This has several advantages over letting directly to students, such as:

- guarantee of rent;
- checks made on suitable students;
- properties regularly inspected by the university staff;
- tenants being given advice on basic property care.

Such tenancies run from September to July each year – 42 weeks – and the properties must be in easy reach of the university. In most cases, properties suitable for student occupation must be able to house up to six students in single-occupancy study bedrooms, and be specifically adapted to suit student requirements.

Gas safety certificates are required, plus electrical safety certificates for new properties. Fire doors may have to be installed so that the kitchen area – usually shared – is isolated from the study bedrooms in case of fire. There must also be smoke alarms and a wall-mounted fire blanket. All locks must conform to British Standards and polystyrene ceiling tiles are not permitted. Owners must have valid buildings insurance and the insurer must be notified of, and agree to, the building's use.

Bona fide students are not required to pay council tax, so for the period of the tenancy agreement, council tax is not payable. It becomes payable again during the time the property is not let to full-time students. If there is a mortgage on the property, the lender must be informed of your intention to let your property to the university for the use of students, as with the insurance provider.

So far as tax goes, under the terms of the Income and Corporation Taxes Act 1970, the university must deduct income tax at source if the property owner is abroad. Contact HM Revenue & Customs for leaflet IR140, which explains all – allegedly. In all cases, the university must forward details of all rents paid during the financial year to HMRC. Consult the website www.hmrc.gov.uk/cnr/nr_landlords.htm or telephone 0151 647 6208 for more information on this.

Many universities issue minimum requirements regarding furnishings and equipment for student houses.

Here are the requirements of the University of Brighton:

- Each student bedroom should contain a single 3-ft bed, a clean firm mattress, cotton quilted mattress cover, wardrobe, chest of drawers, desk or table of minimum size 2.5 ft by 3 ft; a desk chair and bookcase or wall shelving.

- The kitchen must contain a four-ring cooker; fridge and freezer, plumbing for washing machine, a chopping board, rubbish bin and fire blanket, plus wall and floor units.

- The communal room must have a settee and easy chairs, table and chairs if not in the kitchen and a coffee table.

- The bathroom must have a proper shower, and not a tap attachment, washable nylon shower curtain, extractor fan if enclosed bathroom, towel rails and hooks and a toilet brush.

- In general there must be at least one working phone point and preferably one in each study bedroom for internet access. There should also be an ironing board, vacuum cleaner, dustpan and brush, mop and bucket, doormats, and space for cycle storage. Kitchen and bathroom floors should be vinyl or similar and there must also be a television point in the house.

All this is a far cry from my student days, but we all lived to tell the tale, in spite of not having a fridge, telephone or television point or even a shower or shower curtain in the bathroom. Where the university manages student housing, the property reverts to the owner during the summer. The owner can then occupy it personally, rent it out privately or refurbish. Most student landlords reckon to paint and decorate the entire property at least once a year, and usually during the long vacation.

Apart from the requirements of particular universities, you can now also invest in purpose-built student accommodation. Several developers are now building apartments aimed specifically at students in university towns, and these are normally bought off-plan and advertised heavily at property shows. If you are interested in this type of investment, look in at your nearest property show and you will find that several developers will have stands, and salespeople on hand.

As with any other Buy-to-Let investment, you would have to work out numbers very carefully to see if it makes sense financially. It has to be said that many student landlords do not actually make much money, overall, from rentals, and rely on capital gain on the property for their investment to come good eventually.

Rents are set by the university or college, whether you give your property over to the university to manage for you (there are no management costs) or rent out your property privately. You can obtain a leaflet giving rentals for particular types of property from your local university.

Postgraduate students, mature students and students from abroad doing specialist courses are a different proposition, and they are regarded more as ordinary tenants. The main concern of universities' accommodation offices are with undergraduates; young people living away from home for the first time.

The inventory (for the student market)

As we said earlier, by far the greatest number of disputes over return of deposits happen in the student market. They happen for two main reasons: 1) student accommodation tends to be grottier than other rental property; and 2) rogue landlords often enter this market, believing they can exploit students, who will never be in a position to sue them or take them to court for non-return of deposits. The introduction of tenancy deposit protection should eventually see off all the rogue landlords.

To avoid any unpleasantness over deposits, make sure the inventory is extremely detailed. It is the case that the more squalid the property, the more difficult it is to compile a useful inventory. How do you begin to describe the extent of damp on walls, the level of threadbareness of the carpet, the amount of torn-off wallpaper or 10 different kinds of tiles in the bathroom? Many students say they never get an inventory anyway, and many, away from home for the first time, don't even know about the existence of inventories.

If you, the landlord, want to cater for this market, make sure your student houses are clean, smart and well appointed. One such landlord I know carries out a maintenance programme every summer, so that by the time the new academic term starts his student properties are in top condition.

Some general points on letting

Whether you are considering letting to high-paying short-let tenants, students, young professionals, families or company executives, the following strictures apply in each case.

Electrical equipment

The more electrical and electronic equipment you have in your property, the more there is to go wrong, and the more guarantees and instructions you must provide. Unless you are concentrating on short lets, it is not a good idea to provide a television set, stereo, hairdryer or any other type of electrical equipment. These are up to the tenant to supply, if required.

In any case, you should always aim at the absolute minimum of electrical equipment necessary for modern living. Complicated kitchen gadgets (again, you can make an exception for short lets) such as food mixers, ice cream makers, cappuccino makers, sandwich makers and the like are not recommended.

An electrical safety certificate is now required for all new properties and after that, every three years. The certificate should be provided by one of the following companies: NICEIC, BRE Certification, Ltd; Elecsa Ltd or Zurich.

It is a legal requirement nowadays that landlords ensure the safety of any electrical appliances in their properties. Obviously, the more electrical equipment you provide, the more there is to worry about. It is no longer permitted for rental properties to have portable electric heaters; they must be fixed to the wall, although clearly, you cannot prevent tenants from bringing in fan heaters or other moveable heaters.

Fuse boxes should be enclosed by 30 minute fire resistant material, and all electrical installations must be carried out by a 'competent' electrician – ie these installations should not be a DIY job.

More details of the current regulations for electrical safety can be found at: www.odpm.gov.uk/electricalsafety.

All letting agents regulated by ARLA will be able to give details of what is required by law regarding electrical safety and equipment.

Are extended warranties worth it?

Nowadays, most electrical equipment comes with a so-called 'extended warranty' – an insurance policy you can buy that gives you extra peace of mind should it break down. These warranties are extremely expensive, costing perhaps 20 or 30 per cent of the purchase price. Landlords are often advised to take them out for their rental properties.

Don't forget that these warranties are optional, not compulsory aspects of the purchase, and to my mind they are a scam. I recently bought a new washing-machine for £230 and was offered an extended warranty at £73 a year – more than 30 per cent of the purchase price. But how often do electrical goods go wrong these days? Take my advice and forget about the extended warranty, however hard it is sold. Just walk away when the super-salesman comes to try to blackmail you into purchasing an extended warranty.

Inventory

Whether you are letting a furnished or unfurnished flat, you must prepare a detailed inventory. Most landlords start off with extremely amateurish inventories (I did myself) and get more professional as they go along.

You can, if you prefer, have an inventory prepared for you by a professional, and there are advantages to this. Professionals check not only the moveable items, but the condition of the walls and ceilings, noting any cracks in tiles, the number of knobs and shelves on the cooker, the condition of the bath, taps, shower and sink in the bathroom. They also test cookers, washing-machines and so on to see whether they work, and they also test the shower. Showers are frequently a bone of contention between landlord and tenant, and a professional inventory clerk will be able to assess the power and pressure capacity of the shower when the tenant moves in, in case of arguments later.

Clerks make a note of everything to do with the property's condition and equipment before the tenant moves in, and hand a completed copy to the landlord and tenant to sign. This means there can be no arguments about the number of items or the condition of the property.

Professional inventory clerk Jennifer Reigate said: 'When I check a property, the fabric is as important as the contents. Replacing a bath, for instance, can be far more expensive than getting a new sofa.'

Major things to check, advises Jennifer, are cracks in baths and sinks and whether anything is wrong with the cooker. 'I find that having a very detailed inventory makes tenants more responsible', she said. 'If they know that the condition of the walls, for example, is being taken into account, they're more careful about what they put on them. Also, having a professional inventory provides valuable distance between the tenant and the landlord. And the check-out is just as valuable as the check-in.'

As disputes about the condition of the flat and its contents can cause terrible disputes between landlords and tenants, very often ending up in bitter court battles, the more thorough the inventory, the less likely this is to occur. Here is a typical simple yet detailed inventory.

Living room
1 pr damask curtains, full length
1 large cream rug
1 large white coffee table. Condition: new
1 yellow upholstered easy chair. Condition: new
1 two-seater sofa, yellow upholstered. Condition: new
1 cream table lamp. Condition: 10 years old
3 scatter cushions, newly cleaned
Walls: newly painted. Doors, newly painted. Immaculate
1 central halogen light, new
1 dimmer switch

Bedroom
1 pine double bed. Condition: as new
1 pr Indian cotton curtains, cream. Full-length. New
1 white dining chair, Ikea
1 wicker waste paper basket
1 blue under-blanket
1 white Indian double bedspread
1 king-size duvet (not new)
2 pillows
1 set bed linen: duvet cover, sheet, pillowcases
1 table lamp, cream
2 bedside tables
1 white chest of drawers, good condition. All handles
Overall condition: newly painted

Kitchen
1 round dining table. New
2 dining chairs. New
2 fold-up chairs, aluminium
8 glass tumblers
4 white dining plates
4 white side plates
2 white soup bowls
4 mugs
5-piece cutlery set for four: teaspoons, dessert spoons, butter knives, large knives, forks; wooden handles: new
2 wooden spoons
1 wooden spatula
1 fish slice
1 colander
1 plastic bowl
1 vacuum cleaner
1 corkscrew
1 bottle opener
1 white microwave cooker: new
1 toaster
1 large cafetière
1 iron
1 ironing board
4 cream tea towels
1 brush and dustpan
1 grater
3 saucepans with lids
1 frying pan
1 milk saucepan
1 electric kettle
1 venetian blind at window
1 plastic bucket with mop
1 fridge-freezer
1 integrated dishwasher
1 integrated washing-machine
1 gas cooker, good condition. No parts missing
Condition of kitchen units: perfect. All handles present, no scratches. All drawers working

Bathroom
  1 venetian blind at window: new
  1 lavatory brush
  1 bucket
  1 mirror
  2 pine cupboards
  1 power shower: new
  Condition of bath: immaculate
  Condition of toilet: immaculate. Pine seat
  Condition of sink: immaculate
  Condition of taps: clean, working perfectly
  Wall tiles: all perfect
  Floor: no missing or cracked tiles
  Paintwork: immaculate

Hallway
  1 long mirror
  1 rag rug
  Condition of carpets: slight stain on living-room carpet near
  window: otherwise perfect

Signed:

Landlord:

Tenant:

Date:

The inventory should also contain a schedule of condition, noting overall condition and anything stained, broken or damaged.

The importance of a detailed, accurate inventory cannot be overstated. The more carefully the inventory is compiled, the less margin there is for error. Also, the more immaculate the property, the easier the inventory is to draw up.

If there are no stains on carpets or furniture, no broken tiles or window panes and everything is 100 per cent, compiling the inventory is simplicity itself. But if the place is a mess when let, how are you going to prove that the tenants ruined it even further? One tenant complained to me that his landlord withheld £100 from the deposit because the fridge door handle was broken. My tenant friend insisted the handle was broken when he took the place on. When I asked whether there was a detailed inventory, my friend looked blank. 'Inventory?' he asked. 'What's that?'

The introduction of the Tenancy Deposit Protection Scheme (TDPS) means that inventories will have to be compiled far more carefully than before, particularly as regards cleanliness and condition of the property.

Any scuffs or marks will have to be carefully detailed on the inventory and care taken that it is 100 per cent clean at the start of each new tenancy, as the overwhelming majority of disputes concern levels of cleanliness when tenancies change. In order to avoid end of tenancy disputes, tenants should have properties professionally cleaned, including windows, when the tenancy ends.

If there is a dispute, the cleanliness or otherwise of the property will be assessed by independent adjudicators, under the terms of the TDPS.

In one case, the landlord sought to retain the entire £1,500 deposit as there was a bad stain on the carpet. Here, the adjudicators felt it was reasonable to charge the tenant for the cost of a replacement carpet as the stain was impossible to remove, and the deposit was retained by the landlord in its entirety.

In another case, where cleanliness and condition were disputed, the adjudicators awarded £598.67 of the £2,910 deposit to the landlord.

Now that the TDPS is up and running, tenants will have to make extra sure that the property is spotlessly clean, in order to get their deposits returned in full. The situation can now be independently adjudicated and is no longer simply a matter for the landlord and tenant to argue out.

In simple terms, 'clean' means that all floors, curtains, windows, electrical equipment, skirting boards and picture rails must be clean. Washing machines must have soap dispensers cleaned out, and fridges and freezers must be defrosted. All cupboards, kitchen units and cabinets must be cleaned inside and out, and insides of cookers must be left free of grease. There must also be no grease marks on tiles.

In short, everything should be left as clean as you would expect to find in a five-star hotel. Remember, the Tenancy Deposit Protection Scheme cuts both ways.

All too many landlords are completely careless about inventories, and then they complain when, in their view, tenants don't look after or clean the place properly. The more detailed the inventory, the less likely the place is to be trashed, or even ruined. You are then both singing from the same hymn sheet. Also, from a psychological point of view, a good inventory proves you are a careful and caring landlord, and also looks professional. Some letting agents may insist on a professional inventory being taken, but in most cases it is easy enough to compile it yourself.

The inventory should be signed by both landlord and tenant, and each should have a copy. It is also a good idea to lodge a third copy with the agent. Personally, I do not worry about minor items such as wine glasses and cups being broken or disappearing, and never subtract these from the deposit.

A potentially contentious matter is that of cleaning the place when the tenants vacate. Here, I send them a list of what I want cleaning, and, using a 'stick and carrot' approach, say that the deposit will be returned in full on check-out if everything on the list is completed. Usually it is.

Another reason for making sure the inventory is 100 per cent accurate is that if the tenants have signed it, they will usually contact you when anything is amiss. Otherwise, you may go round on check-out to find all the tiles have fallen off the bathroom wall, for instance – and nobody ever mentioned it because it was not on the inventory.

Complying with regulations

There are many safety regulations to be borne in mind when letting property. All furniture and fittings must be covered by the 1988 Fire and Safety Regulations. This means that it is an offence to let out any property that contains furniture and fittings that do not comply with these regulations. If any property is found not to comply, the landlord could face up to six months' imprisonment or a fine of up to £5,000.

From March 1993, it became an offence to supply furniture in rented property which did not comply with standards contained in Regulation 14 of the 1988 Regulations. This only applies to furniture first supplied after 1 March 1993. Furniture manufactured before 1950 is exempt from the regulations.

These regulations apply to investment landlords, although the situation is less clear regarding owner-occupiers letting their own home. These people, letting their own home on a 'one-off short-term' basis, are less likely to be deemed as acting 'in the course of business' and may be exempt from the regulations.

Items covered by the regulations include:

- furniture intended for private use in a dwelling, including children's furniture;
- beds, headboards, mattresses;
- sofa beds, futons and other convertibles;
- nursery furniture;
- scatter cushions and seat pads;
- pillows;
- loose and stretch covers for furniture.

These items are exempt:

- sleeping bags;
- bedlinen;
- loose covers for mattresses;
- pillowcases;
- curtains;
- carpets;

- furniture made before 1950 and reupholstered furniture made before that date.

Most furniture purchases since March 1990 should automatically comply.
Other regulations include:

- *The Gas Safety (Installation and Use) Regulations 1994.* Under these regulations, all landlords have a duty to maintain gas appliances in their property through annual inspections and safety checks. These must be carried out by a registered CORGI engineer. Failure to comply with these regulations could result in a fine or imprisonment.

- *The Electrical Equipment (Safety) Regulations 1994.* These regulations require that electrical equipment between 50 and 100 volts a/c should be safe and tested regularly.

- *Smoke Detectors Act 1991.* Any building built after June 1992 must have smoke detectors installed on each floor.

It should be said that the details on décor outlined in this chapter apply to smart self-contained properties on which you are seeking an optimum rent. Cheaper flats and rooms that are advertised in local papers and in newsagents' windows, for instance, may not conform to all these regulations, and are unlikely to be nicely equipped with sparkling, shining cookers, washing-machines and fridges.

We are talking here about a gold standard of rental properties, and one to which not all landlords, unfortunately, conform. But to my mind, everybody benefits from a chic, harmonious interior – including the landlord, who gets a better class of tenant and more rent. The thing is, as always, to bear in mind the needs and pocket of the market you are hoping to attract.

The gas safety certificate

In recent years there have been a few stories about people in tenanted properties dying from carbon monoxide poisoning as a result of the landlord failing to carry out the annual gas safety check. As a consequence of these stories, it is now a criminal offence not to have a valid gas safety certificate. Landlords can be prosecuted for not having a current gas certificate, in much the same way that people can be prosecuted for not having a current television licence.

This ruling, however sensible it seems, has had an unfortunate effect in that landlords who rent out very many properties are deciding to abandon gas in favour of other forms of heating. Although gas is generally acknowledged to be the best fuel for heating purposes, landlords find it too much trouble to arrange for 50 or 60 gas checks to be made by a registered CORGI engineer. Mike Stimpson, who rents out around 250 properties, says: 'The dangers of carbon monoxide poisoning have been greatly exaggerated, and have led to many landlords taking out the gas central heating and installing storage heaters instead. This is a shame, as storage heaters look dreadful and are far less efficient.'

The electrical safety certificate

It is not yet law to have an annual electrical safety check, as with the gas safety check, but it is increasingly advised, and will most likely become law eventually. In any case, since January 2005, any new electrical installation must be carried out by a qualified electrician, who will issue an appropriate certificate.

For instance, a new shower must have a certificate from the approved body for electricians, and it is the landlord's or agent's responsibility – where the property is fully managed – to make sure all appropriate electrical certificates are in place. This applies to installations rather than appliances and is intended to put an end to cheapskate DIY jobs on rental properties.

Energy efficiency

Rented properties must now have a valid energy performance certificate (yet another certificate!). The Home Information

Pack will also provide an assessment of the energy efficiency rating of any property put up for sale.

The 10 per cent wear and tear allowance claimable on furnished properties will in future be conditional on rented properties meeting a certain level of energy efficiency. The National Federation of Residential Landlords (NFRL) works in partnership with the Energy Saving Trust to implement allowances for energy improvements made by landlords.

More information on energy-efficient measures can be obtained from the Energy Saving Trust, www.est.org.uk or by phoning 0845 727 7200.

5 Finding suitable tenants

All landlords, without exception, want clean, smart, tidy tenants who will pay the rent on time, never bother them, never have any complaints, and will leave the property in exactly the same condition as they found it. Ideal tenants never have noisy parties, never sublet, never bother the neighbours and never cause any trouble of any kind whatsoever.

But how do you find such paragons? There is no guaranteed way of finding perfect tenants, but there are a number of safeguards you can take to minimize the risk.

In their *Lettings Handbook*, Hamptons estate agents admit: 'Letting out a property can be an anxious time for a landlord. There will naturally be concerns that will arise and fears that need allaying.'

One way of minimizing the risk is to make sure that the property is absolutely immaculate and in the right location to attract professionals in high-paying jobs. If you as the landlord feel proud of the flat, and know that the location is good, there will be that much more confidence about the place, a confidence that will be instantly relayed to the tenant.

Advertising

If you decide to go it alone rather than using a lettings agency, once the flat is ready the next thing to do is to advertise the property in the places that your ideal kind of tenant is likely to look. E-letting has been described in Chapter 3.

As most of my rental flats in London have been near White City, where the BBC studios are, I have often advertised in *Ariel,* the BBC staff magazine, and this has produced several

Finding suitable tenants quickly and minimising your void periods is an essential part of the road map to success for your rental investment. In today's internet age the process in which tenants are found has dramatically changed for the better, as Landlords and Agents are now able to tap into a fast internet resource when looking for the right tenant. Landlords can attract prospective tenants without the tenant ever having to leave their home. Gone are the days of tenants walking up and down the high street knocking on the doors of agent after agent. 85% of home searchers now simply visit the larger property websites such as Rightmove.co.uk, Findaproperty.com, Propertyfinder.com, Primelocation.co.uk, Fish4.co.uk and others to search through 1000's of rental properties across the UK. Discount Letting is a UK wide letting agent who offers landlords this service and more.

Discount Letting offer the landlord a unique £59 Tenant Find Service, which allows the landlord to manage their own rental property whilst benefiting from the maximum exposure provided by a UK wide letting agent who advertises their property on the UK's largest property portals which attract millions of potential tenants. The Discount Letting Tenant Find Service is tailor made for the landlord who wishes to reach millions of potential tenants and manage his/her own rental property.

If you are a landlord on the move and require a management service Discount Letting can provide a full management service throughout England and Wales for just 6%. Both of the services offered by Discount Letting are carried out by professional staff in conjunction with an easy to use website **www.discountletting.co.uk**

Discount Letting is offering all readers a special 17% discount on their Tenant Find Service, valid until 30/09/09. To take advantage of this discount please use the following discount code **udny36vt** when visiting **www.discountletting.co.uk**

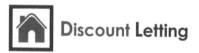

excellent tenants. You could also try local gyms and health clubs, language schools, personnel departments of large companies and supermarket noticeboards, for example. Local newspapers can be a good idea, although you are very likely to get calls from agents, even when stipulating 'No Agents'. Advertising in national newspapers can be very expensive, and I have never had a good response by this means. Newspapers such as *Loot* can work, but again you are very liable to get calls from agents. One flat I advertised in *Loot* produced nothing but calls from agents.

Advertising in magazines such as *The Lady* and *The Spectator* will usually guarantee an upmarket tenant, and often produce a good response. Shop window ads can also work well, although response is not guaranteed. The advantage here is that this type of advertising is very cheap. The disadvantage is that it is very local indeed.

Deciding on the sort of tenant you want

Most landlords, myself included, are paranoid about rent not being paid. The Hamptons booklet states: 'Whilst all landlords will have worries specific to their own circumstances, there is a concern and fear common to the majority – that the tenant may default on their rental payments.'

There is no absolute way of preventing this, whatever checks are carried out, but it's possible to reduce the risk greatly by choosing your tenants with care. If ever you decide to rent out your property to a freelance or self-employed person, it is essential to have a guarantor, who must be a homeowner, and who will be in a position to guarantee the rent in case of default. Very often the guarantor will be a parent, and if there are rent arrears these must be paid by the guarantor. It is also essential to have a letter from the previous landlord confirming that the rent was paid in full and on time. This landlord must be contactable and a bona fide landlord, not just a friend of the applicant.

Although, of course, one is not allowed to discriminate on racial grounds, I'm afraid I discriminate against would-be tenants who can't be bothered to turn up for appointments on time, or who are always cancelling at the last minute. Such sloppiness does not augur well for good tenancies. I like my tenants to look clean, neat and tidy, and I use my gut reaction here. I always ask myself: would I want this person to live in my house? After all, your investment property is the next thing to your own home.

I also discriminate against children and pets, as my particular flats are not suitable for either. Some landlords don't mind these, and it certainly does widen the scope of the tenant pool to choose from.

I do not discriminate on grounds of gender or race. Experience has taught me that there is no automatic difference between male and female tenants. They are equally likely to be neat or slobby, equally likely to pay rent on time or try to wriggle out of their obligations. The many male tenants I have had have all been immaculately clean and tidy, and one female tenant, although otherwise fine, turned out to be the world's untidiest woman.

These days, very many tenants come from abroad, and can present their own problems, such as unfamiliarity with the language and how appliances and fixtures work in the United Kingdom compared to their own country. Also, foreign tenants may not understand the instructions you have carefully left in the neat and tidy tenant's file.

In my time as a landlord, I have had French, Spanish, Japanese, US, Australian, Canadian, Swiss, Russian and Indian tenants. These days, the lettings market is very international – but be prepared for more questions and more problems with tenants from another country.

If going it alone, which I often do, I never, ever bargain with the tenant over the rent. If they offer less, they can look else-where. I would rather wait for a full-paying tenant than grab at somebody who wants to negotiate me down. Some agencies advise against this, saying that it is better to have a lower-paying tenant than no tenant. But in my experience agencies want, above all, 'bums on seats', and are inclined to grab to get their commission. Allowing yourself to be bargained down just causes resentment against the tenant later, and feelings that if you'd waited just that bit longer, you could have got the full asking price.

When looking for suitable tenants, there is one absolute, unbreakable rule to bear in mind: *never, ever let your property to friends or relatives* – at least, not if your main concern is to run a business. One friend of mine has a tenant in a beautiful flat she owns who is not paying the full rent. 'She simply can't afford it', my friend explains – but underneath the pity for the poverty-stricken tenant, there is seething resentment. In fact, friends and relatives rarely do pay the full rent, in my experience.

Although it can be tempting to let to somebody you know rather than a complete stranger, the arrangement is almost guaranteed to break up the friendship or relationship, and will virtually always end in tears. My next-door neighbours, a young couple, had a loft room with bathroom at the top of their house. It was not self-contained, but surplus to their immediate requirements. They kindly let a friend crash there for four weeks while she found herself somewhere to live. Ten months later, the friend was still in residence (she was fast becoming an ex-friend) and my neighbours were tearing their hair out wondering how on earth to get rid of her.

Although she was paying the market rent and there was no problem with this, she also expected to join them every night for supper, and at weekends. When she finally left, my neighbours celebrated by buying a very expensive sofa and chairs with the rent money. In this way, they felt at least that they had something to show for all the months they had endured in purgatory.

Another acquaintance once let a couple of rooms in her house to a friend who lived in the country, but who was doing a course in London and wanted somewhere to bed down during the week. Everything went fine and she was a perfect tenant, paying her rent on time, leaving the bathroom and kitchen immaculate, and being away every weekend. In the evenings, she was very careful to keep herself to herself. But then the owner decided to put her house on the market, and the tenant went spare. 'Where does that leave me?' she asked. The tenant had come to expect that her friend would provide a cheap, comfortable roof over her head for the whole three years of her course, although there had been no agreement that this would be the case. The owner duly sold her house, and lost a friend. They have not spoken since she moved out, now several years ago.

I hope the moral is now clear. Don't let to friends or relatives or, I might add, to student or 20-something children of friends. This can also ruin a long-standing friendship.

Before they move in

Once you believe you have found a suitable tenant – and if the property, the price and the location are good, it shouldn't take more than two weeks, at most – the next thing is to ask for, and take up, references. Typical references are from the current place of employment, the bank and the previous landlord. Or you can use a professional referencing agency such as Taylor Trent Management, which will reference potential tenants exhaustively, including making checks for County Court judgements (CCJs).

Once these references have been received, the next thing is to check them out as far as possible.

Once you are satisfied that the references are genuine, you must take one month's rent at least and one month's deposit in full before handing over the keys. Make sure any cheques are cleared first. At the same time as taking the rent, you and the tenant should sign the tenancy agreement – legal forms for this purpose are available from most stationers and from all landlord organizations – and set up a standing order whereby future rents will be paid directly into your account.

If there are any problems over this, or if the potential tenant wants to pay a smaller deposit, be on your guard. If the tenant does not have the deposit ready, then there is every likelihood you will have problems with the rent, or difficulties with the tenant in other ways.

It is easy enough to instruct the bank to stop a standing order, and dishonest tenants know this. One potential tenant of mine really loved the flat: she loved it to death and wanted it like crazy. The only thing was, she didn't have the full deposit. She would have it next week, she assured me, once she had received her salary. I was suspicious. She might have been completely genuine, but I decided against her anyway. It seemed to me too much like starting out on the wrong foot. My own belief is that you should make it an absolute rule that you do not let the tenant in unless and until the entire deposit is paid, and in your or your agent's account, or in the custodial protection scheme.

Next, you and the tenant should go over the inventory together, and both sign it as correct. You give a copy of the rental agreement and the signed inventory to your tenant to keep in a file along with instructions and guarantees for electrical goods, central heating and so on.

Finally, you must make sure all utilities such as gas, electricity and water are now in the tenant's name. The tenant is also responsible for paying council tax, and for organizing the telephone and television licence. All you as the landlord have to do here is to provide a telephone point and television point. It is then up to the tenant whether she wants to reconnect the telephone, or have a television. Some tenants don't watch TV and just use a mobile phone.

It cannot be said too often that you must never, ever allow a new tenant into your property until all these preliminaries have been completed. One landlord friend, Mike, did this, with disastrous results. He had just spent over £10,000 on refurbishing his one-bedroom flat and on completion of the renovation, advertised it in a local paper. Instantly, a potential tenant came along. Mike let him in without going through the proper checks, for two reasons. One was that he was desperate for the flat to be let after a void of several months during the refurbishment period, and the other was that he was about to go on holiday.

The incoming tenant assured Mike that the deposit and rent would be paid into his bank without delay, and he took possession of the property. But when Mike returned from his holiday, no rent or deposit had been paid. When the tenant was questioned, he started to wriggle and shift and say that he'd had a bit of bad luck lately, and some money he was expecting had been delayed, but he would pay as soon as possible. The tenant asked Mike to understand his position and to be patient. The weeks went by and yes, you've guessed it, no rent appeared. In the end, Mike took direct action and, when his tenant was out one day, changed the locks.

It has long been a feeling throughout the landlord community that some letting agents across the UK have been getting away with daylight robbery by charging extortionate fees for what is often felt as a second rate service. When choosing a letting agent the landlord has many considerations to take into account, one of which is "am I getting value for money?", and a second "how quickly will a suitable tenant will be found for my property?" Both of these considerations are important to the success of your rental investment and warrant careful and calculated judgements on the landlords' part.

Discount Letting offer a full management service set at 6% throughout England and Wales whilst showcasing landlords rental properties on the largest property portals including Rightmove.co.uk, Findaproperty.com, Propertyfinder.com, Fish4.co.uk, Primelocation.co.uk and others. At present the collective partner sites associated with Discount Letting achieve over 36 million views per month, so you can be sure that when using Discount Letting your property will be placed in front of millions of potential tenants which means the chances of a landlord's rental property staying vacant are greatly reduced and assists in making void periods a thing of the past.

Discount Letting also offer the landlord a unique £59 Tenant Find Service, which allows landlords to manage their own rental property whilst benefiting from the maximum exposure provided by a UK wide letting agent. The Discount Letting Tenant Find Service is tailor made for the landlord who wishes to reach millions of potential tenants whilst managing his/her own rental property.

Discount Letting is offering all readers a special 17% discount on their Tenant Find Service, valid until 30/09/09. To take advantage of this discount please use the following discount code **udny36vt** when visiting **www.discountletting.co.uk**

Whether it's a Tenant Find Service or a Full Management service you can be sure to find the right rental product at Discount Letting. Simply visit the easy to use website **www.discountletting.co.uk** and choose the right product for you.

An understandable action, you might think, but a crime, and so completely against the law. The tenant sued the landlord – *and won*! Mike had put himself completely in the wrong by locking his tenant out, and emerged from this terrible experience a sadder and wiser (and much poorer) man. He never did get any rent or any deposit. But such an eventuality could happen to any of us. It is easy to become desperate for a tenant when you have spent months, maybe, on redecoration of your property. 'If I'd carried out the proper checks and insisted on one month's deposit and one month's rent, this would never have happened', Mike said. 'I learnt a very hard lesson, one which I will never repeat.'

One letting agency told me: 'We've all heard about terrible landlords, but in our experience, it's usually the tenants, if anything, who are terrible.' There is a very good reason why this is so. Tenants, by their nature, are transient creatures, living in the same property for perhaps six months, perhaps a year, but rarely longer. They move on and have no involvement with the property other than paying the rent, nor do they particularly care about the property, as they have no sense of responsibility towards it. The landlord, by contrast, has invested many thousands of pounds in the property, sometimes hundreds of thousands of pounds. He is responsible for it, and he is the one who stands to lose serious money if he has a bad tenant. The most that the tenant will lose, if she is unlucky enough to sign up with a bad landlord, is a few hundred pounds' deposit.

The landlord is also the one who has to carry out repairs, pay tax, pay service charges and buy furniture and fittings. So there is more onus, these days at least, to be a good landlord than to be a good tenant.

Using an agency

If you find tenants by yourself, you will keep all the rent they pay you. But if you go to a lettings agency, they will take at least 10 per cent, plus VAT, of the agreed rental in commission.

Most lettings agencies, although not all, will only agree to handle self-contained flats. If you wish to let a room or rooms in your house, then you may find that you have no choice but to go it alone. Any worries about the legality of the arrangement, though, can be solved by having agreements drawn up by a solicitor. This will incur a one-off fee, but not commission as such.

The major advantages of using a lettings agency are:

1. They put some distance between yourself and your tenant.
2. They handle references, inventories, deposits, standing orders, every single working day, so are well geared up to it.
3. They can intervene on your behalf if disputes arise.

The disadvantages are that they take away some of your hard-earned rent, and that they will not take your property onto their books unless it meets every one of the current fire and safety regulations.

Also, it must be said that no agent can magically produce a suitable tenant for you. I have sometimes had flats with agents for three or four weeks before a tenant has appeared. Sometimes a potential tenant seems very keen and then changes her mind – as when you are going it alone. Agencies can do their best, but they cannot create tenants for you where a market does not exist. They cannot guarantee that there will be no void periods, or that your property will be let for 365 days of the year, every year.

Choose your agent with care

If you do decide to use an agency, it is imperative to do some homework first. Although they may all seem much the same, in fact they vary widely. You should always use an agency that is a member of ARLA. Although some non-ARLA agencies may be perfectly reputable, there have been stories of lettings agencies using clients' money to pay their staff. Any lettings agency you use should have a separate client account that can't be raided to keep the business going. In fact, one agency that went bankrupt and was discovered to be raiding client accounts *was* a member of ARLA. So, there are never any absolute guarantees.

In addition, I would always recommend using a specialist lettings agency, rather than an estate agent that buys and sells property as well. If you do go to a general estate agent, make sure they have a separate well-established lettings department. The advantage of specialist agencies is that where lettings are their only concern, they have to work harder on your behalf, otherwise they have no business.

I once asked a major high street estate agent to find a tenant for one of my flats. I was unable to keep a check on them as I was going away for three weeks. On my return, I was extremely disappointed to discover that they had failed to let the property. I immediately went to a specialist lettings agency a few yards up the road, and within hours they had found an ideal tenant. I now don't think the big agents could be bothered – there wasn't enough money in it for them.

Always make sure you match the agency to the type of property you are letting. So, if you want to let to students, use an agency that specializes in this type of letting. If you are interested in short lets to corporate clients, choose a market leader for this kind of rental. Upmarket properties need upmarket agencies and vice versa. No agency is all things to all people, so look in the windows first, to discover the speciality of a particular agent.

It makes sense to use an agency if you live a long way from your property, if you are very busy, if you are away a lot, and if your property is likely to command a very high rental.

Understanding terms and conditions

Because the lettings industry remains unregulated, you will find that agents vary considerably in what they offer and what they charge. So, make sure you fully understand all their terms before signing up. Some agencies charge an 'introduction only' fee – usually three weeks of the monthly rental – while others take commission on a sliding scale for every year the same tenant is *in situ*.

Unless you opt for full management, the agency will take no further interest in your property once it is let, and they will not hold keys. They may like to hold the deposit, but unless they are collecting rent, I would not agree to this. How difficult is it for the deposit to stay in your bank account? If the agency is collecting rents and holding deposits, it must have a separate client account; otherwise the temptation is to raid these monies for their own use. It happens, I'm afraid.

Most agencies take the entire commission up front, for the length of the tenancy agreement. So, if the tenancy is for a year, they will take their 10 per cent plus VAT. Make sure there is a 'clawback' agreement if the tenancy ends before this time. This means that, if a year's commission is taken up front and the tenants leave after six months, you should get those six months' fees, plus VAT, paid back immediately, in full, with no questions asked.

How to pick a good agent

As the popularity of Buy-to-Let increases, lettings agencies are proliferating as never before. If you are new to the lettings game, how do you pick a reputable agency, remembering that the industry remains unregulated and anybody at all can set up as a letting agent?

First of all, offices should look professional. They should open by 9 am at the latest, and look busy. Beware agencies that have ever-changing staff.

Second, do not touch agencies that offer cut-price rates. Although all agents are in competition with each other, cutting prices means cutting the service. All agents are on commission, and it they cut their rates to the customer, this means they cut their rates to their staff, which inevitably means they cannot attract quality staff.

It is rarely, in my view, worth going for 'full management' at another 5 per cent. Statistically, problems happen extremely rarely, and if they do, the agent will have to come on to you anyway, before going ahead with a repair or replacement. Kitchen appliances can nowadays be replaced easily using the Internet, and for minor repairs there is no reason why tenants should not take some initiative in calling out plumbers, electricians and so on, and sending you the bill.

If you use an agency, you will have to keep paying that agency for the entire length of the tenancy. This will be the case even if the same tenants are there for 10 years or more. The agents' argument is that they found the tenant for you and it is your good luck that the same tenant has remained in place for so long. Most operate a sliding scale of fees as the years go by, but you still have to pay them a yearly commission. The tenant will also have to pay for the tenancy agreement to be renewed. You may believe this is money for old rope, but it is the way they all operate.

The best way to choose a reputable agent is by word of mouth recommendation. If the office looks pleasant and welcoming, that is also a recommendation. Around 35 per cent of new agency business comes from people walking in off the street, so the more the agency can do to attract new business in this way, the more professional its services are likely to be.

The National Approved Lettings Scheme (NALS)

The National Approved Lettings Scheme is a government initiative, set up by the now defunct Office of the Deputy Prime Minister, whereby letting agents are expected to meet certain standards, and it also gives advice to the general public on what you should expect from a good agent. Hugh Dunsmore-Hardy, chairman of NALS, offers this advice to get the very best from your letting agent:

First of all, ask which professional bodies your agent belongs to, and what these professional bodies mean. Visit the agent to see what sort of reception you get, as there is a potential for a long-term relationship, by contrast with a sales agent, where the relationship may be intense but is of necessity brief. With lettings, by contrast, you may have an ongoing relationship with your agent for many years. I have been with the same agent since 1997, for example.

Your agent should discuss the likely tenant profile for your particular property, and also let you know what, if anything, needs doing to the property before it can be successfully let. You should get proper advice on current market rents, and also be given advice on what kind of tenancy agreement is suitable for your situation.

The agent should also carry out all the proper reference checks, including on the guarantor, where applicable. The agent is responsible for conducting all viewings and reporting back to you.

If you go for full management, the agent must carry out regular property checks and it is not your job to chase them up. With management, the agent deals with all tenant enquiries.

It is the case, added Dunsmore-Hardy, that 75 per cent of lettings agents do not belong to any professional body whatever:

This does not mean they are no good, but it does mean there is no complaints procedure if clients are not happy with the service. The majority of lettings firms are small businesses and there are very few big players in the industry. Most offer a reasonable enough service but mixed in with them are a number of rogues. So often, the consumer doesn't know which is which as they all look superficially the same.

Landlords – and tenants – can log on to www.nalscheme.co.uk and download current service standards expected by reputable agents.

Company lets

Where the tenant is a company rather than an individual, the tenancy agreement will be similar to an Assured Shorthold, but will not be bound by the six-month rule. (See Chapter 6 for details of Assured Shorthold agreements.) Company lets can be for any length of time, from a week to several years, or as long as you like.

The major difference between contracts and standard AS agreements is that the contract will be tailored to individual needs, and the agreement is bound by the provisions of contract law. Company tenancies are governed by contract law and are not regulated by the Housing Act 1988. Note: if you are considering letting to a company, you *must* use a letting agent or solicitor. In fact, most companies will insist on it.

The advantages to the landlord of letting to a company are:

- A company or embassy has no security of tenure and therefore cannot become a sitting tenant.

- A company tenant cannot seek to reduce the rent by statutory interventions.

- Rental payments are often made quarterly or six-monthly in advance.

- The financial status of a company is usually more secure than that of an individual.

- Company tenants often require long-term lets to accommodate staff relocating on contracts of between one and five years.

The main disadvantages of company lets are:

- A company tenancy can only be to a *bona fide* company or embassy, not to a private individual.

- A tenancy to a partnership would not count as a company let and may have some security of tenure.

- If the tenant is a foreign government, the diplomatic status of the occupant must be ascertained, as courts cannot enforce breaches of contract with somebody who possesses diplomatic immunity.

- A tenancy to a foreign company not registered in the United Kingdom might prove time-consuming and costly if it became necessary to pursue claims for unpaid rent or damage through foreign courts.

Short lets

Although company lets can be of any length, it is becoming increasingly popular for companies to rent flats from private landlords on short lets.

A short let is any let of less than six months. But here it is essential to check the rules with the borough concerned. Some boroughs will not allow lets of less than three months as they do not want to encourage transient people in the neighbourhood.

Generally speaking, short lets are only applicable in large cities where there is a substantial shifting population. Business executives on temporary relocation, actors and others involved in film or TV production, contract workers and visiting academics are examples of people who might require a short let.

From a landlord's point of view, short lets are an excellent idea if you have to leave your own home for seven or eight months, say, and do not want to leave it empty for that time. Short-let tenants provide useful extra income as well as keeping an eye on the place. Or, if you are buying a new property and have not yet sold the old one, it can make good business and financial sense to let it to a short-term tenant.

Short-let tenants are usually, from a landlord's point of view, excellent, blue-chip occupants. They are busy professionals, high earners, out all day and used to high standards. You may also get a celebrity tenant, as these people also provide a big market here. You could have Leonardo Di Caprio or Sharon Stone staying in your flat, while they are filming on location.

As the rent is paid by the company, there are no worries for the landlord on this score, either. Sometimes the company pays the deposit, but very often the deposit is paid by the tenant, as a safeguard for the landlord. The thinking is that if the tenant pays the returnable deposit, there will be that much more incentive to keep the place in pristine condition. Also, a large company may not want dollops of deposit money sitting doing nothing in other people's accounts.

If a company has a hundred employees in short-term accommodation, this could mean that at any one time £100,000 is out of use. To counteract this, some firms offer 'letters of guarantee' rather than cash deposits to the landlords, where they guarantee to replace any lost, stolen or damaged goods. In practice, this does not always work out as planned, and landlords are strongly advised not to accept letters of guarantee instead of deposits. There have been several cases where companies have simply refused to pay up where goods are damaged.

A major plus of short lets is that they command between 20 and 50 per cent more than the optimum market rent for that type of property. The greatest demand is for studios and one-bed flats, as mostly, short-let tenants are single people rather than families. The days when whole families were relocated from one country to another are fading fast.

The one downside of short lets from the landlord's point of view is that no agency can guarantee permanent occupancy. Most agencies operate on a 75 per cent average occupancy in a year. The tenants are great when you've got them, but you may not always have them.

Upmarket estate agents Foxtons have pioneered short lets in central London. A director said: 'We started when there was a need for short-term accommodation for the entire cast of *Riverdance*. They wanted accommodation for four-and-a-half months, and there was nothing available. It was felt there was a huge gap in the market, and since 1993 we have tried to fill it. The demand is fantastic, and increasing all the time. In one sense, short-term accommodation is similar to a hotel, but there are very many pluses. For the company which is paying, private flats are much cheaper than hotels, and better too, as few people like living in hotels for months on end.

'Multinational companies have multinational staff and it's a nightmare to try to put 15 important employees in hotels or serviced accommodation when working out budgets. Also, with a hotel, you are paying for services you may not require, such as room service, reception, restaurants. There are so many outside costs, yet in a self-contained flat, the tenant can feel much more a part of the city. It's more tranquil than a hotel.'

Although a number of short-let landlords are people letting their own property temporarily, by far the biggest number of owners are investment landlords, owning perhaps whole blocks of flats. 'Very often, investment landlords buy show flats for this purpose. They buy the entire stock – furniture, curtains, kitchen appliances, the lot.

'The short lets that go fastest are those where the landlord is prepared to go that bit further than the absolute basics, and provide magazines, coffee makers, a few touches of luxury which will be appreciated by the tenants.'

Gavin Dawson, who works for Channel Four, needed to rent out his immaculate three-bed, two-bath maisonette in Chiswick, west London. He went to three agents who were offering a short-let service, to find they were offering very different market appraisals.

Foxtons offered a complete service for 26 per cent, and valued the property at £650 a week. Andrew Nunn, in the same high street, valued the property at £600 a week, with 20 per cent commission. Featherstone-Leigh, just a few yards away, valued the flat at £350 a week, at 8 per cent commission. Then Gavin had to work out which of these deals was the best one, all things considered.

Many people imagine that a property has to be extremely high-spec to attract short-let tenants. In fact, this type of let operates at all levels of the market. Foxtons, who pioneered the idea of short lets, said: 'Although most of the tenants are high-end corporate, we also let to people coming to the UK for hospital treatment, to look after a relative, or as mature students doing short courses. Such people do not necessarily want to pay a lot of money, but they need a place for a shorter time than the six-month AST tenancy.'

Foxtons have recently improved their short-let service and offer 'gold' and 'platinum' services to their short-let tenants whereby they will pick them up from the airport, arrange to have bread, milk, water and other basics in the property when they arrive, and will also arrange regular cleaning, if required. It all helps to make the short-let tenant feel looked after – and of course if arranging the short let yourself, you could also provide these nice little extra touches. As Foxtons said, there is nothing worse than arriving at your new place after a long journey, only to find you have to locate the nearest corner shop for basic foods.

Housing Benefit

In the last few years, the entire Housing Benefit (HB) scene has changed out of all recognition. HB is now known as the Local Housing Allowance in some parts of the country and is to be paid directly to the tenant. The days of paying HB straight to the landlord – which most landlords and their agents insisted on anyway – are over. The new scheme, known as the 'Pathfinder', was introduced in Brighton and Hove in February 2004, and is gradually spreading all over the country, so that in time all direct payments to the landlord will cease.

The government is hoping that the new scheme will result in 'fairness, transparency, responsibility, increased work incentives and simplicity'. Weasel words? We shall see.

The idea behind this scheme, which has caused most social landlords to quake in their shoes, is to increase the self-esteem of social tenants and make them feel more responsible and in charge of their own destiny. The idea also is that they will be given an incentive to handle their own finances and to budget sensibly. There is also the estimable aim of treating these tenants in exactly the same way as tenants not claiming benefit, to enable them to retain a sense of dignity and self-worth.

By receiving payments directly, tenants become consumers, and are thus able to shop around, choosing the price and quality of their accommodation. It is expected that between 50 and 60 per cent of social tenants will be better off under the new scheme. Such tenants are being strongly encouraged to set up 'basic bank accounts' whereby they can pay their rent by cheque or standing order. At present, most social tenants do not have a bank account as they have no cash reserves or resources and so have nothing to put in a bank account. Such people operate entirely by the old-fashioned method of cash.

If, however, tenants are considered to be 'vulnerable', then the rent can be paid directly to the landlord, as before, but only after eight weeks. The two months' arrears will put tenants straight into the 'vulnerable' category, but they have to be given the benefit of the doubt first, except in very special circumstances. They must not be assumed to be 'vulnerable' before they have had a chance to prove themselves not to be. The exact definition of 'vulnerable' remains unclear, but in practice any tenant who is eight weeks in arrears will be deemed unable to cope with paying rent, and will forfeit the right to be paid directly in future.

Well, that's the theory, all sounding very nice and egalitarian. But how does it work out in practice? Mike Stimpson, a Brighton landlord who rents out around 250 properties, and who also sits on many official committees dealing with housing matters, offers the following experience:

I have a total of 65 tenants in receipt of Housing Benefit, of whom 21 are already established as being unlikely to pay, or vulnerable. The money for these 21 tenants comes directly to me.

Of the other 44, three are paying by standing order, and a few are paying by cheque. But most are paying by cash as they have no access to a bank account or cheque book.

This means that I, as their landlord, am in the position of receiving large quantities of cash each fortnight, when the Local Housing Allowance is paid. At least I am receiving rent from these tenants, even if collection is somewhat difficult.

So far, so good. But when I spoke to Mike, he had a total of £4,399.52 outstanding from the non-paying tenants. Ten tenants altogether had not paid any rent since the money intended for rent was paid directly to them.

> Three tenants have informed me that they have spent their Local Housing Allowance on themselves, so have nothing left over for the rent. This leaves me with £1,010 I am very unlikely to recover. Another three tenants are gradually paying what they have received and spent on themselves.
>
> The remainder are unknown as they have neither replied to my letters nor have they paid any rent. I have so far served three notices to quit and applied for County Court eviction in one case.

Mike has, he says, been very active in notifying tenants of the new situation and has kept them informed of everything. 'This means that my management time has doubled from 20 hours to 40 hours a week – for no more money. For less, in fact, owing to the 10 tenants who still owe rent.'

Looking on the bright side, Mike says that the number of non-paying tenants is much lower than he feared, and he will take action to recover lost rent though he doubts that he will ever recover it all. If tenants have no money, and no means of getting any, they cannot ever pay their arrears.

Mike Stimpson is a major player in the lettings industry, the chairman of at least two landlord associations, and extremely vociferous, speaking at many conferences and seminars. He is a 'professional landlord' and very knowledgeable. But small-time, amateur landlords who find their social tenants get into serious arrears may wonder what they can possibly do to recover lost rent from such tenants.

Local authorities say they are keen for landlords to report any cases where the LHA has not been paid, and they will start to pay the landlord directly in these situations. Only time will tell how this new situation will work out in practice and it may be that the terror of social landlords that they will not be paid turns out to be misplaced. But it will not exactly encourage new landlords to enter this market, and could mean that the number of homeowners willing to rent to social tenants steadily diminishes, thus worsening the housing problem.

As a social landlord you may not be able to take a deposit from your tenant, especially if the tenant has no financial resources whatoever, which is often the case. The rent is normally paid to the tenant four weeks in arrears, and in order for it to be paid directly to the landlord both of you would need to sign a declaration agreeing to this.

The HB or LHA may not cover the entire rent. Before a social tenant can rent a property, there must be a pre-tenancy determination whereby the Rent Officer Service will come and value the property. Housing Benefit will only meet full rents when they are average for the area, and there are strict guidelines for the type of property a particular tenant can take. For instance, a single person will only be able to take a studio or one-bedroom property.

Housing associations

Increasingly, landlords are allowing housing associations to take over the letting of their properties, and there are many advantages to this. Mostly, such tenants are on Housing Benefit and some may be asylum seekers.

Housing associations are now the main providers of social housing, and there are over 2,000 such associations in England, managing a total of 1.45 million homes.

People housed by housing associations are defined as being 'in housing need' – does that mean the rest of us aren't, and can live in a hole in the ground or on the street? Be that as it may, most tenants are taken from local authority housing lists, as council housing as such is more or less a thing of the past. Housing associations are non-profit making and are designed to help the most disadvantaged in society.

Where a housing association takes over your property, rent is guaranteed, repairs are carried out, there is no commission, and on top of all this, there is often an upfront cash incentive for the landlord. Mark Nathwani now only lets to housing associations, as he feels that private tenants are too much trouble, and that in any case you get a better rental yield with the housing association.

This is a typical example of how it works. The London Notting Hill Housing Group offers a cash incentive of between £2,000 and £5,000 to landlords, in return for which you make over your property to the association. From then on, the association takes care of everything, offering you a lease of between three and five years.

There are no management fees, no commission to pay and no maintenance bills. In return for all this largesse, you will be housing society's poorest and most vulnerable members.

Madeleine Jeffrey, director of temporary housing at Notting Hill, says: 'When landlords enter into an arrangement with us, rent is not an issue. We pay every month whether or not we have received HB from the relevant local authority. We guarantee 52 weeks' rent paid directly to the landlord, and we also have powers to evict unsatisfactory tenants. We take over all the risks and remove worry from the landlords.' Most 'temporary tenants' are homeless people moving into second-stage accommodation from B & Bs. They are people whom the local authority has a duty to house, but this does not mean housing associations will accept any rundown dump.

Before an association will accept your property, it sends a surveyor round to inspect, then prepares a report. There is a fee for this which you will have to pay. Then you, the owner, must pay for any upgrading the surveyor deems necessary, such as safety precautions, smoke detectors, window locks and fire-resistant doors in kitchens. Once works are completed, a final inspection is made, and if the property is accepted, its condition is recorded in detail.

Then a lease is signed with the housing association and you can forget all about it until the expiry date, after which the property is returned to you in its original condition and with full vacant possession.

Although this all sounds relatively foolproof, there is much margin for error when buying properties with housing association lets in mind. You might buy the wrong property in the wrong area, or spend more on renovation than you can recoup in rent.

In any case, if you are interested in leasing your property to a housing association rather than taking the risk of the private market, talk to a number of local associations first, to discover exactly how they operate. And do not buy a property with a housing association let in mind, only to find they turn up their noses at it. Find out what they want, what kind of property is most in demand, and which locations are popular.

Problems with social tenants

Social tenants are not at all the same animals as private tenants paying their own rent. In the first place, references are not taken as these tenants are housed according to 'need' rather than their suitability as rental occupiers. This does not necessarily mean they are all bad people, but clearly there is far more of a risk with such tenants than others.

Nor can they be easily evicted, as then they would be made homeless, and possibly cause even more bother to the authorities responsible for housing them. Such tenants are, though, issued with a tenancy agreement when they are housed in a property, as with any other tenancy, and they must abide by its terms.

If they then cause problems by their bad behaviour, complaints must be made to the relevant housing authority in writing. The authority will then write to the tenants in question – although those determined to behave badly usually deny ever receiving any letters – and caution them. Further complaints will cause the matter to be brought to court, at which time they can be evicted instantly, if the judge determines that they have violated the terms of their tenancy agreement. But however bad their behaviour, it is difficult to evict them before they have been in the property for six months.

Any landlord owning a leasehold property must get permission from the freeholder, managing agents or directors beforehand, to lease his property to a local authority or Housing Association. The freeholder or agents must be provided with details of the Housing Association and the name of somebody to contact when problems arise.

Personal note: in the building where I live, there is one flat on lease to a local authority. Most of the tenants have been absolutely fine, but one, a young mother with a two-year old child, caused immense problems with horrendous noise, drugs, music being played into the small hours, police being called out, windows being smashed and violent boyfriends. We eventually managed to get her evicted after three official letters and numerous telephone complaints.

Ordinary tenants can cause these problems too, of course, but landlords, managing agents and others must be aware that social tenants can be loose cannons. After all, without wishing to prejudge, there is a reason why these people have become homeless in the first place. Also, although Housing Associations and local authorities undertake to keep properties they lease in good repair, in practice this often does not occur, and such properties can be a disgrace to surrounding houses or flats.

Holiday lets

Before the Housing Act of 1988 became law, many landlords advertised their properties as 'holiday lets' to bypass the then rules regarding security of tenure. Strictly speaking, a 'holiday let' is a property let to one tenant for no more than a month. If the same tenant renews for another month, the landlord is breaking the law. Nowadays holiday lets must be just that – let for a genuine holiday.

If you have a flat or cottage that you wish to let for holiday purposes, whether or not you live in it yourself for part of the year, you are entering quite another type of landlord–tenant arrangement.

Holiday lets are not covered by the Housing Act. The contract is finalized by exchange of letters with the tenants where they place a deposit and the owner confirms the booking. If the let is not for a genuine holiday, you may have problems in evicting the tenant as the whole point of a holiday let is that it is for a fixed period of no more than a month.

Generally speaking, certain services must be provided for the property to count as a holiday let. Cleaning services and changes of bed linen are examples. The amount paid by the holidaymaker will normally include utilities such as gas, electricity, water and council tax, but would exclude use of telephone, internet and so on.

Magazines such as *The Lady* have dozens of pages of holiday lets, but you can if you like go through an agency specializing in holiday cottages, which undertakes to find you suitable tenants. But beware – some holiday cottage companies are extremely fussy, and insist on gas, electricity and furniture safety regulations being met. If the equipment and fittings are not 'compliant', the company may refuse to take your cottage onto its books.

Increasingly, ordinary estate agents are now embracing the holiday cottage industry and many landlords are deciding to go for holiday lets rather than Assured Shorthold Tenancies. The main difference with a holiday let is that you are not providing a home, just a service, and so do not enter into the complicated laws of landlord and tenant.

Sarah Wood, who founded Mulberry Cottages, an offshoot of Humberts Estate Agents in Kent, says: 'For the investor, holiday lets can be great once they get going. But to succeed, a holiday cottage has to be pretty and in a place where people want to visit.'

At one time holiday cottages were simply summer lets, but now they can be let all year round. 'The short break market is increasing,' says Sarah, 'and in winter you can still fill a holiday cottage. People are starting to take holidays in the UK again, so this business is taking off.'

Neil Collins wished to let his idyllic cottage on the South Downs. He contacted a well-known agency, but soon found himself hemmed in by red tape. A representative of the agency called and inspected the place. She told him that the carpet would have to go, she demanded a washing-machine, a heated towel rail in the bathroom and redecoration of the kitchen. She also suggested redecoration of the hall and landing and replacement of the cooker. Two of the beds were deemed 'non-compliant', and the wiring appeared suspect. A stair gate should be put at the top of the stairs in case of small children falling down, Mr Collins was advised.

Tenants eventually arrived and paid a very high rent, a quarter of which was deducted by the agency. But there were yet more inspections and regulations, so Neil Collins decided to pull out of the country cottage scheme. 'Full compliance is virtually impossible for any normal mortal who is trying to let a home that is not built and equipped specifically for the task', he wrote. 'Like your beds, your house is bound to be non-compliant: look round at that slightly frayed carpet, that cup with the handle stuck back on, that dodgy banister you always meant to fix...'

Increasingly, though, landlords are buying properties specifically for letting as holiday cottages, rather than letting out a cottage which they use themselves.

The term 'cottage' does not always refer to an actual cottage: a holiday cottage could be a flat, a mansion, a manor house or even a modern property, but characterful, quaint properties are always the most popular with this market.

Robert Brew, who recently converted all his former Assured Shorthold Tenancy flats into holiday lets, said: 'Holiday lets bring you in three times the money of six-monthly rentals, but for six times the work. You have to clean the place completely before each tenant arrives, and they may be only there a week. Also, you have to change the sheets and have everything ready for occupation – literally down to the last teaspoon.'

Holiday lets, it goes without saying – or should do – will only be popular in holiday resorts. As such, the demand may be seasonal, although some holiday-let landlords report that even in resort towns, there are often people coming for conferences or on short-term jobs who prefer a fully equipped 'home' to a hotel.

Letting rooms in your home

Lodgers, paying guests, tenants, call them what you will – from earliest times homeowners have let rooms or bedsits in their own houses, for which they receive rent. If you are currently living in a house that has become too large for your needs, but are reluctant to sell it and move to a smaller one, then letting out rooms could be a good way of generating extra income.

There are special laws relating to running a bed and breakfast business, but generally speaking there are very few laws relating to letting out rooms in your own home. Be careful to heed the warning above: do not be tempted to rent out rooms in your own home to friends or relatives, as it may not be such an easy matter to obtain a proper rent, or to get rid of them when you've had enough of them.

If you have a house with spare rooms and are considering letting some of them out for extra cash, make sure you embark on a business arrangement right away so that both of you know where you stand as regards use of the bathroom and kitchen, having guests in, access to your living room, television, telephone, washing-machine and so on.

Also bear in mind that having other people living in your house and sharing facilities is an intimate arrangement, and subtly alters the atmosphere in your home. At various times when I have had temporary lodgers in my home, I could always sense whether they were in residence. Although the vibes may be difficult to pin down, they are always there.

It is a far better idea, if at all possible, to create a self-contained unit where lodgers and tenants can have the place all to themselves. For this you will need planning permission. It may not be feasible to create a separate entrance, but if tenants have their own bathroom and kitchen facilities, and a separate telephone and television point, you are less likely to get on each other's nerves.

Some homeowners create a granny flat out of their basement or other part of their home. There are special rules relating to dependent relatives, and if you are interested in letting out part of your home in this way, you should contact a council tax official and ask for advice on whether the let part constitutes a separate entity or not. There are many grey areas here and it is not always easy to decide, but generally speaking a flatlet or bedsit may count as a separate self-contained entity if it has a proper cooker point. 'The provision of a microwave oven does not constitute a kitchen', I was told by one council tax officer. If, however, a part of your house is designated a separate self-contained flat, you may be eligible for a different council tax banding.

Bedsits

Bedsits, or bedsitting rooms, to give them their proper name, were created in large numbers just after the Second World War, when many soldiers and others returning from service found themselves homeless. The idea of the bedsit was to give some privacy to both the tenant, or lodger, and the resident landlord. Very few, if any, letting agencies handle bedsits as they do not constitute self-contained accommodation, and for the novice or potential landlord, they are best left alone.

For many years, the trend has been towards creating self-contained accommodation that will be subject to the Assured Shorthold Tenancy agreement. The days of the seedy landlord presiding over an assorted jumble of bedsits and ever-complaining tenants, like Rigsby in the TV sitcom *Rising Damp*, are numbered.

Now that even students require self-contained accommodation, there seems little future, at least for the private landlord, in providing non-self-contained bedsits.

Adapting your own home

Very many people nowadays are creating loft rooms, basement rooms, garden rooms and annexes with a view to renting them out for extra income if the need arises. This needs a great deal of thought, as very often there will not be a separate entrance or separate utilities.

One friend, Sue, converted her attic to a tiny self-contained flat, but her tenant had to go through the main house to get to it. Because of this, Sue, a single parent with a young daughter, decided that she would have only females, and they had to be students, otherwise she would have to pay more council tax.

Sue said: 'When I went to letting agencies, my flat was at the very bottom of what they would consider, as it was not really self-contained. Eventually one agency found me a mature Japanese student, and she was brilliant. But my particular circumstances very much restrict the type of tenant I can have.'

Before going ahead with an expensive renovation, consider how you would cope if some of the facilities had to be shared. With basement conversions, for instance, you might lose the garden. Or you may lose privacy because the occupant of the basement can see into your windows. Obviously the more self-contained the apartment is, the better, as this widens the potential tenant pool, but in your own home all the problems with noise, loud music, visitors, or boyfriends or girlfriends staying overnight will be right on your doorstep.

Houses in Multiple Occupation (HMOs)

The Housing Act 2004 has completely altered the previous definition of HMOs, or Houses in Multiple Occupation, and has introduced mandatory licensing, to be carried out by the appropriate local authority, for certain types of rented property. This came into force in April 2006 and landlords and local authorities were given three months' grace to implement the new laws.

It is now a criminal offence, punishable by a fine of up to £20,000, for those HMOs which require a mandatory licence not to have one.

The definition of a 'household' has also changed. In simple terms, a 'household' can now consist of any one person living in a house, such as an au pair, who is not related to the others living in the house.

The new laws mean that houses in multiple occupation where there are five or more residents comprising two or more 'households' (that is, not related to each other) and where the property is three or more storeys high, will require a mandatory licence.

In order to be granted a licence, you have to be a fit and proper person to be a landlord – that is, not have any criminal convictions – and the local authority must be satisfied with the management of the place. The property must also be suitable for the number of people living there. Licences last for five years and can only be granted when the requisite gas and electrical safety certificates are in place. If you believe you have an HMO which requires a mandatory licence, you need to get an application form from your local authority. The forms are very long and, some consider, extremely intrusive. Already, some landlords have put 'mind your own business' as answers to some of the questions.

Mandatory licensing also means that your property must be inspected by the local authority as to its health and safety provisions. The cost of running this service is to be met by the licensing fees, not council tax and each local authority sets its own rate. The rate for Wandsworth, for instance, in London, is £1,100 for mandatory licences; with other authorities, it is around £600.

In Scotland, this kind of mandatory licensing has been in place for some time. The aim in England and Wales is to upgrade accommodation occupied by unrelated people, and as well as the mandatory licensing, local authorities have discretionary powers to extend licensing to smaller HMOs if they see fit.

Although the idea of this discretionary licensing is to improve smaller units, such as two-storey houses occupied by unrelated people, this could also mean that perfectly decent homes occupied by professional sharers could also come in for licensing, although the aim of these new laws is to clamp down on slum landlords and try to combat anti-social behaviour of certain tenants.

But if local authorities want to increase their income, they could insist on these smaller units being licensed. In any case, any rented unit where three or more unrelated people are sharing, of whatever size, is now deemed an HMO. Three separate self-contained studio flats would not count as an HMO as there has to be a certain amount of shared provisions, as in an old-fashioned rooming house.

There are certain exceptions, however. An owner-occupied house where there are, say, two lodgers, is not deemed an HMO.

A building occupied by two sharers only is not an HMO, either. If the property is managed by the local authority, it is not an HMO.

The new laws have implications for those buying at auction, as you need to consider whether you would be creating an HMO and whether it might need a licence.

In drawing up these new regulations, the government and local authorities are all too painfully aware that they have to be careful they are not cutting off the supply of rented accommodation, especially to those who need it most, or putting off potential landlords and investors who might consider buying up such a property. The fear is that all too many owners will now sell their HMOs, so as to avoid the expensive and intrusive licensing process.

Traditionally, HMOs have been occupied by the poorest and most vulnerable sections of the community and many investor landlords have never wanted to consider housing such people.

Buying a property with existing occupants

If you buy a property already tenanted, in a sense the search for tenants will be unnecessary. Mostly, existing tenants in an upmarket property being sold as a rental investment will be corporate or professional tenants who should not create problems.

Properties sold with protected or regulated tenants paying perhaps £10 a week rent are virtually non-existent nowadays. In any case, these cannot be considered as an investment as the sitting tenant is a liability, not an asset. Some seaside properties, for instance, are sold with existing tenants, and these are most often houses that have been divided up into four or more units, where the freeholder wants to offload the property. Very often, such properties are extremely run down and suitable only for the serious property developer.

Your relationship with your tenant(s)

Whether or not you decide to use a letting agency or e-letting, you will still have to decide on what kind of relationship, if any, to have with your tenants. Agencies are acting on your behalf and will take their instructions from you. If you stipulate that you do not want children or pets, then agencies must abide by this.

Mostly, children and pets are looked upon with horror by landlords, but not all landlords object. Greg Shackleton, for instance, is quite happy to have tenants with either, and says that in some flats he has even provided a cat-flap. The main objection to children and pets, especially in blocks of flats, is that they disturb the other residents. Also, there may be a clause in the lease excluding domestic animals.

Unless you opt for full management from a letting agency, you will have at least some relationship with your tenant. I have discovered that the best kind of relationship is one where you remain friendly and polite but never interfere, and you do not mix your tenant with your social life. Once my tenants are in place, I leave them completely alone to get on with their own lives. They leave me alone as well. However, if we meet in the street, or by chance, we have a friendly chat. We emphatically do not socialize together, though. It is simply not appropriate when you are taking money off people, and can make the relationship unclear. Agents and inventory clerks always throw their hands up in horror when either the tenant or the landlord says they have become great friends. 'The friendlier they are, the greater the problems at the end of the tenancy', said inventory clerk Jennifer Reigate. 'Just about all the legal disputes happen when landlord and tenant have got too friendly with each other.'

Nowadays, first-name terms are indicated. My tenants refer to me as 'Liz' and I call them by their first names. So do all other landlords and tenants I know. Estate agents long ago stopped using surnames, and will always introduce your potential tenant to you as 'Clare' or 'Alex' or whatever.

If a tenant contacts you with a problem, it must be attended to right away. A good landlord is one who sends out a plumber, or electrician, or washing-machine engineer, on the same day as the complaint is received, when at all possible.

One difficult problem with a good, long-standing tenant is when or whether to put the rent up. Although you are legally allowed to put the rent up every year, some landlords waive this for an exceptional tenant. A landlord friend, with a single tenant of three years' standing, put it like this: 'When my tenant last renewed, I wondered about putting up the rent, especially as the agents mentioned it. I thought about it, but decided that although the increase would mean little to me, it might make a lot of difference to her.

'When I contacted her about renewing the agreement, I said that I would not put up the rent and she was profoundly grateful. She would have found the extra money, I'm sure, but I felt that three years without a single void was a good record, and also the agent's commission had been reduced after that length of time. Even one month's void during that time would have cancelled out the extra rent I might have got.' When this tenant leaves and a new one takes her place, then this landlord will of course put up the rent.

As to whether couples or single people make better tenants, I don't think you can generalize. Some landlords prefer single occupants on the grounds that one against one is better than two against one, but I have never had any problems with the couples who have rented my properties.

As with any business, establishing exactly the right relationship with your tenant is a matter of trial and error, and we all make mistakes. The thing is, though, not to make the same mistake twice, if you can help it.

There are few resentments stronger, or greater feelings of hate, than when a once-good landlord and tenant relationship goes sour. It can be compared to a once-loving couple squabbling bitterly over their divorce. And, as with a bitter divorce, the ill-feeling can remain for very many years, on either side.

The longer the same tenants stay in your property, the more likely it is that repairs and renovations will be necessary. How do you handle this? The usual thing is for the landlord to foot all bills, but in these days when tenants often negotiate rents down and down – it is not even unusual for tenants to renegotiate the rent down when renewing the tenancy – there should be room for negotiation.

For instance, if the tenant wants a room painted, there is no reason why she should not do this herself, or arrange for it to be done at her own cost. The same with minor repairs. If the tenant has secured a good deal, she should be more than willing to do this.

One friend had the same tenant in his property for six years. In that time he only put the rent up once, in return for which the tenant replaced the fridge, carried out a number of minor repairs and repainted the flat, all arranged by herself and at her own expense.

One tenant, Australian businessman Brian Bacon, went even further and rented a rundown property near Oxford which the previous tenant had occupied for the past 42 years. He negotiated a low rent in return for which he completely renovated the property, including putting in a new kitchen, bathroom, carpets, curtains, central heating and electricals. As a result, he has the house of his dreams and reckons it will actually work out cheaper than the cost of buying and selling somewhere, as he is unlikely to remain in the house for more than three years.

As the Buy-to-Let market matures, there is ever more room for landlord–tenant negotiation. Nothing – except what is stated in the tenancy agreement, of course – need be set in stone for ever.

Nor is it necessarily the case that the landlord has to pay for everything. If tenants want to redecorate, want a microwave or a power shower – or anything that is not on the inventory and is not provided – they can always offer to pay for it themselves, or share costs with the landlord. The longer the same tenant remains in a property, the more this is likely to happen.

Some landlords these days even take new tenants with them when choosing new carpet or curtains – so that the tenant's choice is taken into account.

That said, any tenant who wishes to make even a minor improvement, such as redecorating a room, must consult with the landlord first and have the colour or design approved. It is not on for tenants to undertake redecoration without consultation, as the property does not ultimately belong to them.

Checklist for assessing the suitability of tenants

1. Have a clear idea of your ideal type of tenant.
2. Is your prospective tenant clean, tidy and punctual?
3. Make sure the deposit is paid in full upfront.
4. Be on your guard if your tenant withholds necessary information, such as previous employer, previous landlord, etc.
5. Make sure they are in a financial position to pay the rent.
6. Be clear about whether you will accept pets or children and be firm about your decision.
7. Never panic over possible voids to such an extent that you accept a tenant about whom you have misgivings.
8. As with any other business transaction, use logic and common sense – and then go with your gut reaction. If there seems something odd about a potential tenant you can't quite determine, follow your intuition. You will rarely be wrong.

In most cases, good relations between landlord and tenant come down to a simple matter of communication. You can't expect your tenants to be mind-readers, so write a letter to them if there is anything they need to know, or if they are infringing their tenancy agreement, or the terms of the lease, in any way. Very often, a timely letter will do the trick. But you need to know that any letter you write is legally valid, even if it is not exactly a legal letter.

A useful book (with background legal information) is: *Landlords' Letters: Plugging the Communication Gap* (Lawpack, £12.99). This contains ready-drafted letters for landlords in businesslike but non-emotional language to use in common situations where misunderstandings can easily occur.

All you have to do, says author Adam Church, is pick a letter in the book which most suits the circumstances. As the Buy-to-Let market grows, and ever more ordinary people start to accumulate impressive property portfolios, it is important to be able to communicate to your tenants without rancour, ill-feeling, anger or resentment.

The importance of good communication cannot be over-estimated and if there is one overriding problem with the new breed of landlords, it is that they hate communicating with their tenants. All they want is to see the money rolling in, but it ain't that simple. Tenants are human beings too, and they appreciate being treated as such. After all, they are paying what they consider to be a very large sum of money for the privilege of living in your property.

In the end it all comes down to this: treat your tenant in the way you would like to be treated yourself. The vast majority of tenants are perfectly decent people who should not be regarded with suspicion or treated as an alien species.

6 Rights and obligations

The main fear of landlords is that tenants won't pay the rent, and the main fear of tenants is that they won't get their deposit back. In theory, these twin financial fears, integral to all residential letting arrangements, should cancel each other out and make sure both sides are on their best behaviour at all times. However, it doesn't always work out like that, and in order to protect both parties, there exists a huge amount of legislation relating to landlord and tenant.

The Landlord and Tenant Acts 1985 and 1987 are the main pieces of extant legislation governing the rights and obligations of landlord and tenant. They are extremely complicated documents, not readily understood by the layperson. Also, when disputes arise, there are many grey areas that often only a solicitor or judge can decide, taking all aspects of the dispute into consideration. No piece of legislation, however comprehensive, can foresee all eventualities.

Most of the basics covering the majority of eventualities are set out in the modern Assured Shorthold Tenancy agreement. (The main points of the tenancy agreement are set out below.) When the first Housing Act came into force on 15 January 1989, there were two distinct types of tenancy covered by the Act: Assured, and Assured Shorthold. The terms of each were similar, but the Assured Tenancy gave more security of tenure, as it was not for a fixed contractual term. Since 28 February 1997, however, all tenancies for self-contained properties are automatically Assured Shorthold, unless both parties wish to enter into an Assured Tenancy, for a longer term, or if the Assured Shorthold type of tenancy does not apply, as with a company let or where the annual rent exceeds £25,000.

Assured Shorthold Tenancy agreements state that, basically, the landlord has a duty to maintain the property in good repair and not to hassle or otherwise annoy the tenant. The law also recognizes that while the tenant is paying rent, she is entitled to the same amount of peace and privacy that she would have if she owned the property. The 1988 Housing Act states:

> Once a tenant has a market rent tenancy and is occupying the property as his or her home it is right that he or she should have a reasonable degree of security of tenure.

The tenant's main obligation is to pay the agreed rent on time and in full. So long as the landlord is fulfilling his part of the bargain there can be no deviation from this. Even if the landlord does not instantly carry out repairs, the tenant is not allowed to withhold rent. No part of the tenancy agreement makes any provision for withholding rent, and if a tenant does so, she automatically puts herself in the wrong.

All landlords should remember this if and when a dispute arises. But even here there are grey areas, as in the following case. A landlord wrote to a newspaper legal advice column:

> I have let out a flat at a rental of £700 a month on a 12-month lease. The tenants have now decided to withhold £100 rent every month until I fix a so-called faulty shower. Two plumbers have looked at it and both say it's not faulty. The tenants also want a new washing machine because they claim that the present one does not work to their satisfaction. My tenancy agreement says that I can end the tenancy if they have not paid rent 14 days after it is due. Does withholding £100 a month constitute not paying rent?

The answer to this query by former *Evening Standard* lawyer, the late Fenton Bresler, went thus:

> Withholding a part of the total rent because of a genuine dispute is not the same as the non-payment of rent that entitles a landlord to end a tenancy legally. In fact, at times it can be a tenant's only weapon with which to force a landlord to honour his obligations, especially where the tenant has spent his own money in doing repairs which the landlord should have undertaken.
>
> You would not, in my mind, be justified in ending this tenancy merely because one-seventh of the monthly rent is withheld. Indeed, your letter in its entirety indicates such a tense situation that I think you should discuss it calmly with a solicitor.

In this case, I can understand how the landlord feels, as in my own experience showers are a very common cause of complaint, and an easy one with which to berate the landlord. Hamptons' *Lettings Handbook* addresses the vexed issue of the shower, pointing out that although modern investment properties require power showers, water pressure varies and in the United Kingdom, what passes for a perfectly working shower may not be as powerful as one in the United States or in Australia, for instance.

Although it may seem trivial, I would say that around 90 per cent of tenants' complaints are about showers. In one of my present flats, two tenants have rung to complain about the shower. In the first instance, the complaint was justified – the shower had broken down. In the other, the tenant, an Australian, had just not worked out how to use it. 'These showers are different from the ones at home', she said, after the manufacturers had carefully explained its workings to her.

Some wily tenants use the excuse of a non-working shower to withhold all or part of the rent. Every landlord I know has had a complaint at some time about the shower, but as it is essential to have one, it's difficult to see how this can be addressed in advance. My advice would be the same as Fenton Bresler's: where a dispute seems incapable of settlement by ordinary means, seek the advice of a solicitor.

For most of the time, the rules and regulations set out in the tenancy agreement are upheld by both parties, as both have a vested interest in the arrangement working smoothly. However, as in all human endeavours, things (even apart from the shower!) do sometimes go wrong, and it may not always be obvious what the landlord or the tenant should do. If in doubt, go to your nearest Citizens' Advice Bureau, check with your lettings agency, if using one, or ask your solicitor.

Tenancy agreements

The usual type of tenancy agreement these days is the Assured Shorthold. This was originally devised in 1988 and amended by the Housing Act 1996. It was designed to make the letting of property to private individuals more attractive by making it easier to let property at a market rent, and to recover possession. Originally, these proposals were made to encourage the growth of the private rented sector, and in this the Assured Shorthold Tenancy has been extremely successful.

Assured Shorthold Tenancies are designed to last for six months at a time (although a longer one can be drawn up), and apply to all dwellings rented since January 1989, with certain exceptions. Nowadays, the Assured Shorthold is a standardized form, and all lettings agencies have these as a matter of course. These agreements are legally binding between landlord and tenant, although, like most contracts, they can be difficult to enforce if one or other party is determined not to abide by their strictures.

This is a fairly standard tenancy agreement under the Assured Shorthold legislation:

The agreement is called ASSURED SHORTHOLD TENANCY AGREEMENT for letting a residential dwelling house.

On the first page, the agreement contains this caveat:

This tenancy agreement is for letting furnished or unfurnished residential accommodation on an assured shorthold tenancy within the provisions of the Housing Act 1988 as amended by Part III of the Housing Act 1996. As such, this is a legal document and should not be used without adequate knowledge of the law of landlord and tenant.

The next page of the agreement sets out all relevant dates, the name of the tenant, address of the flat, term of tenancy, the monthly rental paid, and the amount of the deposit.

The rest of the agreement, every page of which should be signed or initialled by both landlord and tenant, sets out the terms of the tenancy. Again, they are standard items.

Here are the main points of the tenancy agreement, couched in appropriate legalese:

The Tenant agrees with the Landlord

To Pay the Rent on the days and in the manner specified to the Landlord.

To pay promptly to the authorities to whom they are due, council tax and outgoings (including gas, electricity, water, light and telephone if any relating to the Property, including any which are imposed after the date of this Agreement), and to pay the total cost of any reconnection fee relating to the supply of gas, electricity and telephone if the same is disconnected.

Not to damage or injure the Property or make any alteration or addition to it. Any redecoration is to be made only with the prior written consent of the Landlord.

Not to leave the Property vacant for more than 30 consecutive days and to properly secure all locks and bolts to the doors, windows and other openings when leaving the Property unattended.

To keep the interior of the Property and the Contents in good and clean condition and complete repair (damage by accidental fire and reasonable wear and tear excepted) and to keep property at all times well and sufficiently aired and warmed during the tenancy.

To immediately pay the Landlord the value of replacement of any furniture or effects lost, damaged or destroyed or at the option of the Landlord, replace immediately any furniture or effects lost, damaged or destroyed, and not to remove or permit to remove any furniture or effects from the property.

To yield up the Property and Contents at the expiration or sooner determination of the tenancy in the same clean state or condition as they shall be at the commencement of the tenancy.

To pay for any cleaning services that may be required to reinstate the Property to the same order that it was provided at the commencement of the tenancy, including the washing and cleaning of all linen, bedding, carpets and curtains which shall have been soiled during the tenancy.

To leave the Contents at the end of the tenancy in the same places in which they were positioned at the commencement of the tenancy.

That the Landlord or any person authorized by the Landlord may at reasonable times of the day on giving 24 hours' notice (unless in the case of an emergency) enter the Property for the purpose of viewing, inspecting its condition and state of repair or for the purpose of repair or repainting.

Not to assign, or sublet, part with possession of the Property, or let any other person live at the Property.

To use the Property as a single private dwelling and not to use it or any part of it for any other purpose or allow anyone else to do so.

Not to receive paying guests or carry on or permit to be carried on any business, trade or profession on or from the Property.

Not to permit or suffer to be done in or on the Property any act or thing which may be a nuisance, damage or annoyance to the Landlord or to the occupiers of the neighbouring premises, or which may void any insurance of the Property or cause the premiums to increase.

Not to keep any animals or birds on the Property without the Landlord's written consent, such consent if granted to be revocable at will by the Landlord.

To keep the gardens if any neat and tidy at all times and not to remove any trees or plants.

The Landlord agrees with the Tenant that provided the Tenant shall pay the Rent and perform the agreements on his part already referred to, the Landlord shall permit the Tenant to have quiet enjoyment of the Property without interruption by the Landlord.

The Landlord may re-enter the Property and immediately thereupon the tenancy shall absolutely determine without prejudice to the other rights and remedies of the Landlord if the Tenant has not complied with any obligation in this Agreement, or should the rent be in arrears by more than 14 days whether formally demanded or not.

The Landlord agrees to carry out any repairing obligations as required by sections 11–16 of the Landlord and Tenant Act 1985.

The agreement should also include a definition of what is meant by a landlord, what is meant by a tenant, and on what grounds a tenancy may be brought to an end. It should also state the notice period necessary to be served by either party (one month by the tenant; two months by the landlord) and state that the tenancy must run for at least six months.

The tenant(s) and landlord must then sign the agreement, preferably in the presence of witnesses, and the contract then becomes legally binding on both sides.

The Assured Shorthold (AS) has become a user-friendly agreement, and the one most often used. The Assured Tenancy, originally designed for people who wanted longer tenancies, and offering more protection, and the AS became one and the same thing on 28 February 1997. The 1997 Housing Act amendment also stated that all tenancies should be AS unless otherwise stated.

In order to create an AST, the following points have to be addressed:

● The tenant must be an individual, not a company.

● The tenant must occupy the property as his or her own home, or main home. It is not possible to do an AS tenancy for a pied-à-terre, or a second home.

● The yearly rent must not exceed £25,000 a year or £480 a week. If it does, the tenant is a non-Housing Act tenant, and the law of contract applies.

● The landlord must not be resident. If a property was built as one house and has been divided up, with the landlord occupying a part, then an AS cannot be created. However, most agencies say that where all flats are self-contained and the landlord, say, lives in the basement with a separate entrance and front door, then AS tenancies can be created, as with any other self-contained flat.

Note: the terms of the tenancy under the law of contract may be the same as with Housing Act tenants, but the agreement must be covered by contract law. In practice, this may not make all that much difference, but if you are renting out a property that comes outside these categories, legal advice must be sought. Letting agencies are geared up to deal with these eventualities.

New Model Tenancy Agreement

In late 2002, ARLA got together with the Office of Fair Trading (OFT) to produce a new model tenancy agreement. Although its clauses are basically the same as in existing agreements, as no significant laws have changed, the new agreement puts a slightly different emphasis on the contractual relationship between landlord and tenant. Under the terms of the Unfair Terms in Consumer Contracts Regulations, issued by the OFT in May 2001, landlords are treated as suppliers and tenants as consumers.

The new tenancy agreement seeks to put an end to any 'unfair' terms and conditions that might be contested by a tenant wishing to lower the rent, or wriggle out of the agreement should they want to end the tenancy early. Although ultimately any contested clause would have to be decided by the courts, there are four tests against which standard tenancy agreements can now be measured.

These tests are: Is the agreement written in plain, intelligible English? Is it misleading, or does it have the potential to mislead the tenant over legal rights? Does it impose disproportionate or unfair financial penalties on the tenant? Does it create a significant imbalance in rights and obligations to the detriment of the tenant?

On the new agreement, small print is banned and the agreement is written in plain English rather than convoluted legalese.

The new ARLA model Assured Shorthold Tenancy Agreement has been available to agents and individuals from September 2002, and can be ordered by calling the ARLA hotline: 01923 896555, or by visiting www.arla.co.uk and downloading the order form.

As the new agreements are aimed mainly at agencies, they are available only in bulk and cost £49.35 for a pack of 12 –

rather expensive for an individual with only one property but useful perhaps for portfolio landlords who prefer to go it alone. You can also purchase a CD for £91.06, which allows you to print out any number of agreements. A pack of 25 agreements costs £102.88. At the time of writing, it is not possible to obtain these agreements singly.

Clauses forbidding tenants to hang washing in the garden, to play music after 10.30 pm or to clean the windows once a month (all usually flagrantly ignored and probably completely unenforceable anyway) could constitute 'unfairness', even if the tenant has signed, and therefore agreed, such clauses before moving in.

Common problems

Here are the answers to the most vexing and frequent landlord and tenant problems.

Q: There appears to be a leak in the bathroom of one of my flats, and as a consequence the ceiling of the flat downstairs has fallen down. The owner threatens to sue me for damage. Meanwhile, the other tenant (not mine) is refusing to pay rent. There is no damage to my flat. What should I do?

A: Water damage occurs frequently in blocks of flats. Before admitting any liability, get a plumber to check the source of the leak; in blocks of flats, water can travel from all kinds of places. If the leak is traced to your bathroom, your first job, after getting in a plumber to repair the damage, is to check with the freeholder or managing agent of the block to see whether you are covered by buildings insurance. You should be. If this is the case, the insurance company will pick up the bill for the damage to the downstairs flat. You should also make sure your tenant is not using the bathroom in such a way as to damage the downstairs flat.

If you do everything possible, the owner of the downstairs flat would have no grounds to sue you. The downstairs tenant must not withhold rent and, in any case, this is a matter for the downstairs owner and tenant to sort out between themselves. For all you know, there may be long-running problems on other issues between these two people.

The most important thing to do in such cases is to check what your block building insurance covers, the amount of excess and who pays. Most block policies cover for accidental damage and then it is often a matter of negotiation as to whether you pay the excess or whether the managing agents agree to meet it from the sinking fund – assuming there is one.

While we are on the subject, it is always worth checking the terms of the block insurance policy, and what may be met by contents cover taken out either by the tenant or by the landlord.

Q: My tenant is going away for two months and wants to sublet her flat in the meantime. Can she do this?

A: The person (or people) named in the tenancy agreement is the only one allowed to occupy the premises. If your tenant wishes to sublet she should ask you first. Should you agree, the new tenant's name can be added to the tenancy agreement, with the amount of time she will be staying there. Never let in a new person, though, without first checking references and taking a deposit. Do not ever admit somebody into your property on the say-so of the existing tenant, but always make sure all the same checks are applied as with the original tenant. All references must come from the previous landlord or employer, and not be provided by the tenant, as she could easily have faked them.

A common variation of this situation is that your tenant wishes to move in a boyfriend or girlfriend – permanently. Again, the same thing applies. If you are happy in principle with having another person on the premises, take references and a deposit and increase the rent slightly, to accommodate the other person. There will be extra wear and tear on the property, and if damage is caused by a person not named on the agreement, you could be in trouble.

Lettings agencies say that the decision to grant permission to include another person rests with the landlord. If your tenant sublets or brings in another person without your permission, this is grounds for eviction, as they have broken the tenancy agreement. Many landlords do not mind having an extra tenant, but permission must always be obtained first.

One of my own tenants wished to move in his girlfriend. I checked with the lettings agency, and they took up references, an extra deposit and extra rent. My tenant was happy with this, the girlfriend proved no trouble at all, and the arrangement worked out perfectly well. It's where tenants sneak in other people, and you just happen to find out, that you should be on your guard.

However, if you take more than two months' deposit upfront your tenant may legally be allowed to sublet, as this amount can be considered a 'premium'. Landlords and agents these days tend to be taking ever-larger deposits, and you must check with your solicitor or nearest Citizens' Advice Bureau that the level of deposit you wish to take does not constitute a premium, and give the incoming tenant automatic extra rights.

Q: I have let my three-bedroom house with garden to young professionals sharing. Although they have looked after the house fairly well, they have let the garden – my pride and joy – go. It looks terrible, and I am bitterly disappointed, as gardening is my hobby. Do I have any redress?

A: This depends on what was stated in the tenancy agreement. If the tenants agreed specifically to look after the garden, then they are liable. But in general terms, you cannot expect tenants to be keen gardeners. The usual advice given where you are letting a house with a garden is that the tenants agree to keep it neat and tidy, mow the lawn and so on, but if you as the landlord want it kept as a wonderful garden, it's up to you to arrange to have a gardener.

Similarly, you cannot expect tenants to have green fingers when it comes to window boxes, houseplants and so on. If plants form part of the inventory, you should expect that they are in the same condition as when you left the property, either by the tenants looking after them or buying new ones, but in general, it's safest not to have loads of plants and window boxes. Leave it up to the tenants as to whether they want to be bothered. The best advice is to have any lawn paved over and a few low-maintenance shrubs.

In one case, a tenant had taken a property with attractive plants in pots on the roof terrace. He had ignored them and let them die, to the fury of the landlord at the end of the tenancy. The upshot was that the landlord asked a garden firm to estimate the cost of replacing the plants. The total came to £1,600 and the tenant had to pay, even though he made an almighty fuss – because the tenancy agreement contained a clause saying the tenant would look after the plants, and this tenant had blithely signed, probably without even reading the agreement.

Q: My long-term tenants have redecorated the flat in colours that I hate. Can I do anything about it?

A: Most tenancy agreements specifically state that tenants are not allowed to redecorate. If they wish to do this, they must get your written permission. Otherwise, you could make them decorate the flat back in the original colours.

Q: My tenant wants to leave after six weeks as her mother has become seriously ill, and she says she is needed at home. Yet she signed a six-month agreement. Can she just break the agreement like this?

A: Strictly speaking, she has broken the terms of her tenancy agreement, and is liable for the six months, whether she is there or not. However, unforeseen circumstances do arise, and you have to decide how flexible or rigid to be. Most decent landlords will let a tenant leave after a shorter length of time if (a) the tenant finds another suitable tenant or (b) the landlord or agency manages to find another tenant.

If this cannot be done immediately, you may be able to come to an arrangement whereby she agrees to pay you until a tenant is found. Then you can both sign off when the new tenant moves in.

Q: I hate smoking, and have a clause written into my tenancy agreements that only non-smokers will be considered as tenants. My current tenants signed the agreement, but they are smokers. I know this for a fact because my investment flat is just below my own flat. Can I turn them out?

A: If you hate smoking so much, and it's certainly up to you to decide whether or not to let smokers in, then yes, you can. To some, smoking seems a trivial reason for eviction, but allowing smokers in can be very expensive, as it means the property needs constant redecoration. In one flat of mine inhabited by smokers, the walls and ceiling needed repainting each year. Also, with heavy smokers, it is difficult to get the smell out of curtains and carpets. As smoking can be a serious addiction, it may not be feasible to order your tenants to stop, so you may have no option but to bring the tenancy to the speediest legal conclusion. If your tenants are smokers, it is in order to increase the deposit.

Q: My tenant, who has been in residence for a year, wants to extend her tenancy for another year. Can I put up the rent?

A: Yes. Most tenancy agreements state that the rent will remain the same for a year. You are perfectly entitled to ask for more rent after a year, though not before. When extending tenancies, always make sure a new agreement, duly signed and witnessed, is drawn up. Never, ever leave anything to chance.

If your tenant wishes to extend her tenancy for another few months, this can be done under an arrangement known as a 'periodic tenancy', whereby the tenant continues to reside in the property from month to month, with a month's notice given by the tenant and two months' notice (in writing) by the landlord. But the tenant may ask for the rent to be *decreased* instead.

Q: Although Assured Shorthold Tenancies seem to work quite well, six months is an awfully short time to live in a place. Surely longer tenancies are a better bet, for both sides?

A: It is true that some lettings experts are beginning to chafe at the restrictions of the Assured Shorthold Tenancy agreement. Frances Burkinshaw, former chairman of the Association of Residential Lettings Agents, said: 'Agents should stop dribbling out rental agreements in six-month doses, like Scrooge in a counting house. It suits everyone to arrange tenancies for as long as possible.'

Yet the experience of some landlords is that long lets can actually increase the problems, particularly when tenants prove unsatisfactory. One landlord let out his two-bedroom house to a childless couple who seemed perfect. All went well for a year, then the tenants asked for a three-year tenancy, during which time they agreed to replace the kitchen units. The landlord complied with this arrangement. But soon, neighbours complained about dogs barking, even though the agreement had a 'no pets' clause. Before long, there were 9 dogs and 18 cats on the premises, and rent payments became erratic. Eventually, the rent stopped altogether, and the landlord subsequently obtained a possession order from the County Court. Still the tenants did not move out. Finally, a bailiff appeared, but by this time the tenants had disappeared, leaving the place filthy and uninhabitable. None of this would have happened, he said, if he had stuck to six-month agreements. 'My advice to other landlords is to insist on six-monthly terms with options for extensions. As it was, it took me two years to get the tenants out, and I had to employ industrial cleaners in the place.'

Although this story may seem extreme, something similar happened in the three-bedroom terrace house next to me. Non-paying tenants stayed in the place for several years, terrifying the neighbours, trashing the place and allowing all kinds of people to stay there.

From a letting agent's point of view, the longer the let, the greater the commission. Often, the whole of the commission is taken upfront, and the agent does not have to bother to find new tenants.

The best advice is to stick to the six-monthly agreements, and extend them if the tenant proves to be good.

Q: My outgoing tenant has left the place very untidy and dirty, although nothing has actually been broken or stolen. The fridge and cooker, for instance, have not been cleaned. Can I withhold the deposit?

A: The Tenancy Deposit Protection Scheme now regulates such behaviour. You cannot now withhold the deposit, or part of the deposit, unless the tenant agrees to this. Otherwise, there will be a dispute that must be adjudicated by an independent adjudicator appointed by the TDPS operators.

To avoid this kind of situation occurring, you must make sure the property is absolutely immaculate when first let, and get your tenant to sign the inventory agreeing to its condition. Then you will have documentary evidence at the start of the tenancy and will be able to claim the cost of the cleaning from the deposit.

Don't forget that if there is a dispute, it will take the outgoing tenant longer to get back the deposit, or part of the deposit, so it is in the tenant's interests to make sure the place is clean and tidy when vacated.

My own solution to this potential problem is as follows. Three weeks before checkout, I send the outgoing tenant a list of what has to be cleaned, and ask him or her to tick off each job as completed. This is a simple solution which almost always produces the desired result.

Here is a common problem relating to owner-occupiers living in the same building as tenanted flats:

Q: We live in a well-maintained and very pleasant block where, until last year, all the flats were owner-occupied. We residents are mainly middle-aged or retired, but the owner of the flat adjoining ours moved out last year. The new owner rents it out to a succession of young foreign students, who presumably pay him a high rent, but are the most appalling neighbours. They seem to change every two months, but our leases all contain a clause saying that the minimum sublet is six months. We have complained to the managing agents, but they seem strangely unconcerned. Is there anything we can do about it?

A: Clauses limiting the length of permitted subletting are quite common. They are meant to ensure that good-class residential blocks retain their individual character, and it is in everyone's interest – including managing agents and free-holders – to do all they can to achieve this.

There are two ways of dealing with the problem. One is to remind the managing agents of the landmark 1997 Appeal Court decision in *Chartered Trust plc v Davies*. In that case, Lord Justice Henry ruled that the freeholder himself can be sued by an unhappy flat owner, where the freeholder's failure to enforce the terms of another flat owner's lease in the same block had materially damaged his enjoyment of his own flat. Lawyers are still working out all the ramifications of this judgment.

Secondly, all residential leases say that flat owners must not allow their property to become a nuisance or annoyance to the other residents. So you should ask the managing agents to enforce this clause. If they refuse, you can threaten, as a last resort, to report them to their clients, the freeholder, or apply direct to the local leasehold valuation tribunal to have them removed as managing agents. It would help you considerably in this to obtain support from the other flat owners in the block. (Advice given by Fenton Bresler in the *Evening Standard*.)

Q: The tenancy agreement states quite clearly that the landlord is responsible for repairs of appliances. But what happens when damage has been caused by the tenant's misuse? My last tenant ruined the microwave, which now won't work but which was in perfect order when she started the tenancy. It was an accident, and she is very sorry, but surely she is liable?

A: If damage is caused by the tenant misusing an appliance, then the tenant is responsible. Tenants can get insurance cover for this kind of eventuality, obtainable from most agents. I would deduct the cost of providing a new microwave from her deposit. Microwaves are now very cheap anyway – not something to worry about.

Q: If a tenant breaks a few cups and glasses, should I make her pay for them?

A: My inclination here is not to worry about such low-cost items, and not to deduct them from the deposit if you are otherwise happy with your tenant's occupancy.

Q: My tenant has Blu-tacked and Sellotaped pictures on the walls, even though this went expressly against the agreement, and now there are nasty gaps in the emulsion. Can I ask her to pay for redecoration?

A: Technically, yes. But bearing in mind that most tenants will want to put up pictures, why not hammer in picture hooks (the white ones with three nails in them) to prevent this possibility? Then tell them they can only put up pictures on these hooks. If a tenant leaves gashes in the walls where her pictures have been, and you did not provide masonry-type picture hooks, I think you have only yourself to blame. Unless, of course, this is only one example of wider desecration, in which case you should withhold enough deposit to pay for redecoration of the affected areas.

Q: My tenant, although otherwise satisfactory, has just become pregnant. I do not want a baby or child in my flat. Should I give her notice?

A: If you have stipulated no children or pets, then yes of course, as the presence of a child alters the tenancy agreement.

Q: My tenant is impeccably clean and tidy, always pays the rent on time and I have no complaints about her except that she appears to have moved her mother in. How can I find out whether her mother is a permanent fixture, or only a temporary guest?

A: It seems, for some strange reason I have not been able to fathom, extremely common for tenants' mothers to move in. If the situation bothers you, you should confront your tenant and ask whether she would like her mother's name added to the tenancy agreement. You could point out that only one person has signed the agreement and that technically her mother cannot move in permanently. My own inclination, however, is to leave well alone. Mothers, in my experience, rarely cause trouble and often ensure the place is extremely clean and tidy.

Q: If I wish to put the rent up for my current tenant, what is the best way to do it? And by how much can I increase the amount?

A: There is a standard procedure for this. Renewal clauses in tenancy agreements usually link increases to the Retail Price Index (RPI). If there is no such clause, you should not increase the rent beyond this limit, or beyond the current market rate. To do so would inevitably sour the relationship between you and your tenant. Whenever rents are increased, paperwork is involved, and plenty of time should be left to give your tenant notice of an increase, and to complete the paperwork.

Q: What if it all goes wrong and my tenant will neither pay rent owed, nor leave?

A: It must be said that, thankfully, these situations are extremely rare. When they do happen, though, you must abide by the law. You are not allowed to evict your tenant yourself, change the locks or use force to get her out – however sorely you may be tempted to do this.

Here is a true story. A landlord in my building wanted her tenant out – and evicted her forcibly at eight o'clock in the evening, bringing in a couple of heavies in black leather jackets and a couple of Rottweiler dogs. The heavies turned out all the furniture and effects into the corridor.

The tenant took the landlord to court and was awarded £7,500 costs. However badly a tenant behaves – and this particular tenant did not behave badly at all – you are simply not allowed to take the law into your own hands in this manner.

Laws on eviction are always subject to change, but the present law (2007) states that non-paying or otherwise unsatisfactory tenants can be evicted after eight weeks of behaviour that directly contravenes the agreement. In order to evict a tenant, solicitors must be instructed. You can instruct your own solicitor, or your agent's solicitor can be instructed. Either way, you will have to pay, and you may not recover this money.

The solicitor will serve an eviction notice on your tenant, and make arrangements to hand this to her in person. If she does not leave or pay up of her own accord, the next thing is to take her to court, if you consider it worthwhile.

There is now what is called an 'accelerated possession procedure' whereby tenants can be evicted without the need for a court hearing. This particular procedure does not include a claim for arrears of rent – it is simply a means whereby bad tenants can be speedily evicted. You can use this procedure directly where the tenancy is an Assured Shorthold, and you claim possession under Section 21 of the Housing Act 1998, or where there is an Assured Tenancy dating back to before 1997, under Section 8 of the Housing Act. In this case, 'grounds', or reasons, must be supplied. Under Section 21, accelerated possession can be claimed if:

- the tenancy was for a fixed period and that period has expired;

- the existing tenancy, and any agreement covering it, is for an unspecified period;

- you as the landlord have given at least two months' written notice under Section 21, saying that possession is required.

Making a claim under Section 8 of the Housing Act 1988 is more complicated. 'Grounds' include: the property is your main home and you wish to reclaim it; you intend to live in it as your main home; the tenancy was a holiday let, let to students, or is now needed as a residence by a minister of religion. Where these grounds apply, you must have given your tenant notice at least four months before the end of the tenancy.

After you have filed your application to the court, and given the court all the papers required, including a copy of the tenancy agreement, the defendant has 14 days to reply. If an order for possession is made, the defendant will normally be told to leave the property within 14 days. Should the defendant be able to show that this will cause exceptional hardship, the court can extend this period for up to six weeks, but not longer.

Note: the best thing to do, if you think you may be able to use this procedure, is to go to your nearest County Court and ask to see an official. Nowadays, court officials are extremely helpful and will explain everything to you in person. They are not allowed to give actual legal advice, but can certainly explain what the procedure is all about.

Once rent gets into arrears, you should waste no time, but write to your tenant immediately, saying that this month's rent does not appear to have shown up in your account. It may be that there has been an oversight of some kind, so tenants should be given the benefit of the doubt initially. If the money still does not show up, or if the tenant does not reply to your original polite letter, you should write again, saying that if the money is not paid in full within 14 days, court proceedings will be instigated without delay. Then act on that threat immediately. If tenants know that there is no substance to your threats, they will just bin the letter and carry on.

Where it comes to getting rent paid, you should write out the amount owed in arrears, plus any damage to the property or goods stolen, on a form available from the County Court. You will also have to pay a court fee on a sliding scale, depending on the amount owed. This is recoverable from the defendant, should you win your case. The court will send this form to the defendant, who will either pay up there and then, counterclaim, or let the judge decide the matter at a court hearing.

The procedure is now quick, simple and straightforward, and you should never be nervous of taking anybody to court when you are owed money. A High Court judge friend of mine pointed out when I was dithering over whether to take a bad tenant to court: 'You owe it to future landlords' – and he's right. Bad tenants should be stopped in their tracks as quickly as possible – and taught that they can't hope to get away with it.

I have taken two people to court for non-payment of rent. The first action was not successful, not because the claim was disputed, but because I was unable to serve papers on the defendant. She had left her job by the time the court summons was received, as she had been sent to prison for other offences. By the time I knew this, and had sent the papers to the prison, she had served her sentence and gone. I never did catch up with her, and she got away with owing two months' rent.

However, when she eventually left my flat, taking the vacuum cleaner and some other items, I reported the theft to the police and managed to get the items returned.

On the second occasion, I got a form from the County Court and wrote out the amounts owed. The defendant counter-claimed, alleging that only some of the amount was owed. Eventually the case came to court and, before a district judge, we settled for the full amount minus interest.

In many cases, the threat of court action is enough to make the defaulter pay up, if for no other reason than the fact that if the judgement goes against them, they will find it extremely difficult ever to rent another flat. Also, with a County Court judgment (CCJ) it can be extremely difficult to get any kind of credit. Defaulting tenants will usually do all they can to avoid a CCJ, although it must be said that some are so far gone that they no longer care.

But all relevant court leaflets make the point that there is little purpose in taking somebody to court if they absolutely do not have the money to pay you. Although the judge can order the money to be paid, it is up to you to enforce this. Leaflets advising plaintiffs on ways to enforce CCJs are freely available from County Courts, and many have been awarded a Crystal Mark for being written in plain English.

Lettings agents can now access a form of referencing whereby CCJs show up on the checking system, and no reputable agency will take such a tenant onto their books. The referencing system cuts down the risk of non-payment to almost nil, but there will always be determined fraudsters who slip through the net.

You may be in a difficult position, however, where your tenant is a visitor from abroad and simply vanishes into the ether without paying. To avoid such an eventuality you can, if you think it is worth it, take out insurance cover. As with any insurance cover, only you can decide whether it is money down the drain or money well spent, bearing in mind that all insurance covers you against things that are extremely unlikely to happen.

If you are in the process of taking a defaulter to court, a word of advice: never, ever discuss the matter with them either in person or on the telephone. If they have not paid and they have ignored your reminder, you have nothing further to say to them. In my experience, non-payers fall into two main categories: those who bully and blackmail, and those who have a sob story. Very often, a defaulter will try both tactics. Don't be browbeaten and don't be swayed by hard luck stories. There is nothing personal involved: you are simply doing your utmost to recover money promised and owed to you, but not paid.

All you have to do if a non-paying tenant tries emotional or other blackmail is to repeat 'Let the court decide.' This is known as the 'broken record' technique and is extremely effective. But never enter into any justification, argument or discussion directly. You could be putting yourself in the wrong. Also, there is no need to justify your action. Non-payers have to be taken to court. If they cannot afford to pay the rent, they should not have taken the property in the first place.

Money Claims Online

It is now possible to take a non-paying tenant to a virtual court and do the whole thing online. Landlord Jane Caught used Money Claims Online when her tenant stopped paying rent, and found it quick, easy, cheap and successful. She said: 'First of all I tried to negotiate with him but he refused to answer the phone. He finally wrote me a letter saying he'd had cash-flow problems, so I contacted him at work to see whether his circumstances had changed at all. Then he became very aggressive and accused me of harassment.'

At this point Jane became nervous and contacted a solicitor, at the same time as issuing the tenant with a Section 8 notice to quit. Then she logged on to the online court service. Here, you pay £80 upfront and are given an ID and a password. Notice of the claim was sent to the tenant by post. Jane Caught requested judgment using Form N225, which went in her favour.

She was given three options for payment: sending in the bailiffs, making an order to stop the defendant emptying his bank account, or an Attachment of Earnings Order (A of EO).

She chose the third option. The judge directed that it should be served on the defendant's employer, which meant the money came out of his wages before he was paid. This ensures there is no possibility of defaulting. The tenant paid off his arrears at £100 a month, and it took Jane eight months to get all the money back. Much of the money was for costs, which the defendant also had to pay. He cannot wriggle out of paying because if he changes his job, the order automatically goes to his next employer.

The cyber court service for debt recovery was introduced in February 2002 and is administered by the Department for Constitutional Affairs, formerly the Lord Chancellor's Office. It can be used for claims up to £100,000 and any defence can also be conducted online.

Claims are sent electronically to the County Court Bulk Centre in Northampton, and claimants are issued with a claim number so that they can check progress online. Defendants receive claims by post and have 14 days to respond.

As most landlords these days have to service mortgages, they can't afford to write off debts. This new service avoids all the bother of going to an actual court, and, of course, it can be done out of office hours.

Visit www.courtservice.gov.uk/mcol.

Where there is genuine hardship

It may be that your tenant, while having perfectly good intentions, has lost her job, been made redundant, or become ill and simply cannot pay the rent that she was perfectly well able to do at the start of the tenancy. In this case, if she is otherwise a good tenant, she will let you know her position, and ask what you are prepared to do. Then you can decide either to let her go before the end of the tenancy, waive the rent until her Housing Benefit is payable, or demand the full rent as agreed.

A tenant under an Assured Tenancy cannot be made to leave until after the court has made an order saying that the plaintiff can have possession of the property. If the tenant disagrees with anything said in the affidavit, she may be able to get help with legal costs via legal aid. A parallel leaflet for tenants to the one produced for landlords, available free from County Courts, advises tenants to act quickly once a court order is received.

You as the plaintiff will have to produce written evidence that the tenancy was an Assured or Assured Shorthold made on or after 15 January 1989, when the Housing Act came into force.

If the judge decides that the tenant must leave, she will be sent a form saying when. If the tenant does not leave when told to, the plaintiff can ask a court bailiff to evict her. Should the matter proceed to a court hearing, both parties should be present to put their side of the story. Tenants who are unsuccessful in asking the court to set aside the eviction order may have to pay the plaintiff's costs. If ordered to pay, the defendant must pay the plaintiff directly, and not through the court.

It has to be said, though, that only the most determined tenants will go this far. It goes without saying – or should do, at any rate – that landlords should not go to court unless they are absolutely sure of their ground. It is unlikely that a court will issue an eviction order for, say, a friend who you took in out of the kindness of your heart, who did not sign an agreement and who now insists on staying put.

The possibility of non-payment or other unsatisfactory behaviour on the part of tenants should encourage you as a landlord to protect your investment by making sure any arrangement to let out your property to others is executed according to current laws on the matter. It cannot be said too often: *never have an ad hoc or open-ended arrangement.*

Remember: a bad tenant is a bad tenant is a bad tenant, and a good tenant is a good tenant is a good tenant. In other words, a bad tenant is a bad tenant all the way through: not only will she not pay the rent, she will also not take care of the place and will return the flat to you in bad condition. When I finally regained possession of a flat inhabited by a tenant from hell, not only was the bathroom clogged up with hairs, there were cigarette burns and worse on the sofas and chairs, and the fridge and cooker were filthy.

Good tenants – ie those who pay rent on time and who are polite and courteous – always, in my experience, leave the place impeccably clean and tidy, and have a list of anything soiled or broken.

Mostly, I must say, tenants are a decent species, and it's only the occasional one who turns out to be terrible. Usually, I find, they are terrible in all other aspects of their life as well. My own hellish tenant was, I discovered later, undergoing psychiatric treatment, although she carefully concealed this when her references were being checked.

If your tenant dies

There are tenants who don't pay their rent. Tenants who outstay their welcome. Tenants who bring in their pets. But what about the ultimate horror – a tenant who actually dies in your property?

Surprising as it sounds, this is not as uncommon as it might seem. Most lettings agents have experienced a situation where a tenant has died while in the rental home.

Letting agent Mary Hennigan-Lawson said: 'Once I had let a flat where the tenant died just a month later. The landlord in the case pointed out that the deceased tenant had signed a contract for six months and he would hold him – or at least his estate – to that.

'In the event, we quickly found another tenant, but the landlord held the deceased's estate responsible for fees, inventories and cleaning, even so.'

Although most tenancy agreements do not make provision for a death, there are clear legal rules to follow when this happens. The landlord can demand full rent until the tenancy officially ends, although this might be contested by the deceased's solicitor. It may be possible for the tenant's representative to give two months' notice to the landlord, but normally this cannot be done within the first six months of an agreement.

Landlords who take out rent guarantee insurance should ensure that it covers this possibility. One friend of mine whose tenant died while in her property had taken out, on her agent's advice, a cheaper form of insurance that did not cover death. Also, as luck would have it, her tenant died on the very day that his tenancy agreement ended.

My friend takes up the story. 'I got a call from the police one night. The tenants in the flat above, which I also own, had rung the police to say the television in the flat below had been on all day and all night.

'The tenants upstairs had rung the bell but could get no reply. The police took a key from me and went in, finding my tenant unconscious on the floor. He was taken to hospital and recovered.

'But then a fortnight later I got a call at eight in the morning from my tenant's girlfriend, who also had a key, although she did not live with him. She said she had gone in to find him dead in a pool of blood. She was, not unnaturally, in a terrible state.

'By the time I arrived, the police were there, and confirmed that my tenant was dead. They said that nothing must be touched as we had to wait until they had ruled out any suspicious circumstances.

'It was the most horrific sight imaginable. There was blood everywhere, pools of blood at the side of the bed, and a trail of blood to the bathroom. It looked as though he had vomited at the side of the bed and then haemorrhaged to death. The social worker gave the cause of death as heart attack, and the coroner later ruled out any suspicious circumstances.'

The question was, what to do next? My friend contacted the deceased's ex-wife, who didn't want to know, and was unable to get in touch with any other relatives. The flat also had to remain as it was until the coroner released it, a month after the death.

The tenant's belongings then had to be dealt with. There was a large bed, lots of hi-fi equipment, CDs and so on that nobody would claim. In the end, the police had to clear it away.

The tenant, in his forties, had lived in the property for six years and there had never been any problem over the rent. He was known to suffer from ill health, although death was not expected.

Lettings agent Jane Salthouse, of Lane Fox, advises: 'In the case of somebody living alone, look for work numbers and next-of-kin details. Otherwise, contact the person who supplied the character reference and take it from there. As a last resort, search the flat for address books, credit details and so on.'

As it was, my friend had to replace all the carpets and redecorate completely, at her own expense, before the flat could be re-let. It is not advisable to tell an incoming tenant that the previous person died in the property, as this may put them off taking the place.

Although over 80 per cent of tenants are absolutely fine, and don't die or commit any other horrors in your property, it's as well to remember, as a landlord, that all human life is likely to be there eventually, and no weirdness can be completely ruled out.

Stressed out?

You may like to know that counselling and therapy are now available for stressed-out landlords.

Deborah Morley, a trained counsellor, is also a landlord. She said:

> I was not prepared for the intensity of the stress that can hit you when something goes wrong. At one time I had two tenants who were not paying rent and, on another occasion, the roof came off one of my properties during exceptionally high winds. The tenants rang to say you could see the sky through the roof, and also it was raining hard. Whatever was I going to do?
>
> I called a contractor I knew and, although they were coping with other work caused by the extreme weather, they fixed up a temporary covering until they could do the job properly. Most landlords, at least when they are new to the game, imagine that everything is going to go smoothly and there will never be any problems.
>
> But because of my own experience, I am now offering crisis intervention and also longer-term psychotherapy for landlords who find themselves being hit by stresses and traumas they never imagined – and then discover they do not have any coping strategies.

7 Becoming a portfolio landlord

Be warned: investing in property can become so addictive that no sooner have you got one flat up and running than you are looking for another to buy, with a view to renovating and letting that one out as well.

I admit that I have become such an addict. Every week I scour through property magazines and newspapers, asking myself: would that one let? What would be my gross yield on that one? I then get out my calculator and do quick sums to determine whether, in theory, this or that particular property would be a good investment buy. In this respect, I am rather like a racing fanatic who is always studying form, whether or not he actually places a bet.

Mostly, I'm glad to say, I can control the addiction, especially where it comes to paying out £100,000 or more. I am prevented from indulging my habit to the full by the simple fact that I have very few chunks of one hundred grand plus to play around with, and also because I have an emotional aversion to borrowing large sums on which I have to pay interest. But every now and again, the urge to buy, renovate and rent out an apartment becomes irresistible.

I believe most investment landlords are like this. What begins as a little hobby, an interesting way of making some money (with any luck), can soon turn into a way of life and, as with most enjoyable pursuits, the income received from rents is only part of the fun. There is the excitement of the chase, the possibility that you are hunting down a bargain, the adrenalin rush when you make an offer, and the thrill combined with the intense stab of fear when your offer is actually accepted and it

finally sinks in that you now have to go through with it and buy the damned thing.

I went through such a scenario a few years ago. On seeing a property that I felt I absolutely had to have, whatever, I first of all took down the name of the estate agent, thinking to myself: oh well, no harm in asking the price. On discovering the price, I arranged to view, telling myself that there was no harm in viewing, and that viewing didn't commit me to buying the place. On viewing, I made an offer, telling myself now that there was no harm in making an offer, and that making an offer didn't constitute any form of commitment. The offer was rejected and I heaved an immense sigh of relief. My money was safe after all.

But then the estate agents came back with a lower price. I haggled and bargained a bit, and in the end the owners said yes. Damn! I had to have it now; there was no getting out of the deal. Thankfully, time has proved that this particular property was a good buy, but I have now recognized the danger signs, the times when I am in the grip of a house-buying addiction.

Once the many fears involved in actually buying a place and parting with the money have been allayed, there is the tremendous excitement involved in doing the property up. But even that is mixed with fear as you keep asking yourself whether you are overspending, whether you could have done better by going somewhere cheaper, or not taking quite so much trouble.

You may be torn between charity-shop curtains that are nearly, but not quite right, and going to the expense of having curtains made specially. These, you know, will add greatly to the look and appeal of the place, but at the same time there is a risk that you will go over budget. I know I always worry when I edge dangerously near the 5 to 6 per cent of the purchase price that I allow myself on renovation. I start to panic if I go over 6 per cent, especially when I have yet to buy a sofa, a washing-machine, a fridge-freezer...

There may be some investment landlords for whom these fears, these lurches of alternate terror and excitement, stress and peace of mind, do not exist, but I don't know of any. Perhaps ice-cool Hong Kong businessmen can buy investment properties without a trace of emotion, but most people aren't like that.

When I bought my first investment flat, a small studio in a 1930s block, and had overcome my initial terrors of being a landlord and spending huge sums of money to induce a paying tenant into my lair, I was soon looking for a similar flat to buy. Nothing to this property-buying lark, I thought. Within a few months, I was the proud owner of an identical flat just below my first one and, as with the first, I soon found an ideal tenant who appreciated the place very much. I was very fond of my two little flats, both done up simply but effectively, I thought. So, as soon as I had some spare funds again, I was looking for a third. I was well on the way, in my mind at least, to becoming a property magnate.

I discovered that buying properties to rent out was so much more fun than any other type of investment I might be able to make. OK, it wasn't entirely risk-free, and it was certainly not without effort, but here I was, creating lovely little homes for people, and making some money into the bargain. When, a couple of years later, I sold my two studio flats to buy other properties (the service charges on the studios had gone through the roof, and meant they were no longer a good investment), I made a useful profit on resale, even after the dreaded Capital Gains Tax had been levied.

Yes, there are heart-stopping, anxious moments, but there are also wonderful long periods of calm as well, where you do nothing but watch the money come in. Although the money I receive in rents is a useful bonus, buying investment properties is certainly not a way to get rich quick. Although now a 'portfolio' landlord on a small scale, I still regard myself as an amateur, doing it as a hobby-plus rather than as a means of becoming a 'Rachwoman'.

The multiple landlord

Most portfolio landlords, even those with many more properties than I possess, still regard the business as a more or less lucrative sideline rather than anything else. They do it because they enjoy it, get a buzz out of it, and although of course the books must balance, most people are not, contrary to the view of certain tenants, making vast amounts of money out of being a multiple landlord.

Multiple landlord Greg Shackleton, the owner of around 50 rental properties in Brighton, who has it all down to a fine art, became a 'reluctant landlord' when he acquired a property from a client. His day job is as a loss assessor, and this particular client offered him the property, a former shop that had been gutted by fire, instead of his fee. Greg took possession of the property and turned it into a smart one-bedroom flat. The flat let instantly and, within a few months, Greg decided he had enjoyed the process so much that he started looking round for another property to buy.

As he does not have the funds to buy his properties for cash, he calls in a bank official to value a potential new property. If the loan is approved, Greg buys the property, usually in dilapidated condition, and sets about renovation. Then the bank official returns and revalues the property.

Greg made the point that if you own 31 properties, you can receive a cheque for every day of the year – 365 cheques a year, provided every tenant pays up on time, of course.

On average, Greg reckons to have bought one property a month in this way since becoming a super-landlord, and he lets out all his flats unfurnished. Otherwise, as he said, he would own 40 washing-machines, 40 sofas, 40 dining tables and so on – rather an encumbrance for anybody. When you operate on that sort of scale, it becomes impossible to furnish the properties. Greg just puts in a new kitchen (often without washing-machine, as the tenants can hire these) and a new bathroom, carpets the place and rewires if necessary. Because of the need for a yearly gas certificate, Greg makes sure the heating and all appliances run on electricity.

All his flats are let through Leaders letting agents in Brighton, and Greg is constantly adding to his portfolio. He is on the books of all local estate agents, who now know just what he is looking for, and contact him when a flat that may be suitable comes onto the market.

Greg is very clear on what he's looking for: a dilapidated flat in a conversion, rather than a purpose-built block, near to public transport and shops, and going at a cheap price. He does not buy into purpose-built blocks because of the high service charges and the propensity of freeholders to add extra levies all the time, which just take away from profits if you're a landlord.

As Greg goes for high rents rather than capital appreciation, he does not expect his properties to increase greatly in value. Therefore, the bulk of the return on his investment will come from rents rather than resale. Also, as Greg keeps buying more properties, he is constantly ploughing money back rather than resting on his laurels and watching the rents come in.

A point to bear in mind if you are collecting up properties: you must keep a beady eye on the length of the lease. Although the general trend of properties is to rise in value, this is not the case when leases get progressively shorter. This is why, unless the lease is extremely long, it is important to have a definite timescale in mind for the properties to pay for themselves in rent. If you bought a couple of flats with 80-year leases and kept them for 20 years, you might find it hard to sell properties with only a 60-year lease on them. This, of course, is not the case in central London, where leases of 60 years can be considered long. But it does apply in the rest of the country.

Most portfolio landlords acquire their investments by the process known as 'gearing up' described on page 97. Gearing up is rather like making yoghurt: you have to have something to start the process off. In other words, you must have some money to start with – you cannot gear up from nothing.

Greg Shackleton was able to gear up because he owned his first investment property outright. Then he released some of the equity in his first flat to buy another. Mark Nathwani, another enthusiastic supporter of the gearing-up process, also released equity from some of his early buys to finance later purchases.

If you want to start from scratch, you must have some actual money from somewhere. If you do not already own an investment property, you may be able to release some equity in your main home. Or you may have been left some money, or have savings or other investments you can cash in. The more you gear up, the more you are mortgaged, until eventually you can get into a situation where you are mortgaged up to the hilt. This can be a high-risk operation, especially if interest rates rise, or the value of your property goes down, or both. Also, it is never possible to guarantee full occupancy of rental properties.

Mortgage lenders sometimes offer fabulous introductory rates, but remember that the good deals on mortgages only last for a certain length of time. Discounts are typically for a two-year period, after which the interest rate will rise. No cut-price mortgage deals will last for the entire length of the mortgage.

Gearing up requires a strong head and a strong stomach. If you are, in the current phraseology, 'debt-averse' and are liable to lie awake in bed at night worrying about mortgage repayments, gearing up is better avoided. It is, though, the only way to amass a property portfolio quickly, and it is certainly exciting. But before you even embark on this process, intensive research is required to determine the likely rental yields. Most financial experts believe you can only make money if the rental yield is 8 per cent or above. If it is 6 per cent or less, you are likely to lose, as there is too little margin for error.

Another good tip is to avoid sales talk from estate agents when gearing up. Their job is to sell you property, and that is what they are good at. Instead, take advice from a lettings agent as to whether this or that property represents a good buy from a rental point of view.

And do not on any account rely on capital growth. This is Las Vegas land or gambling on a horse. With Buy-to-Let, you must go on as many certainties as possible, and the most certain aspect is rental yield in percentage terms.

Money

If you are interested in becoming a multiple landlord, the first thing to do is to work out the figures. Otherwise, you could easily find yourself paying out far more in costs than you have coming in in rents. As I only ever buy rental properties for cash, obviously I proceed very slowly compared to some. I have passed the age and stage where I can calmly contemplate having long-term mortgages and loans. By nature I am not a great risk-taker with money, maybe because I don't really understand money, or at least, high finance. And although I will take a calculated risk, I would not like to be burdened down with huge loans.

Going into partnership

As I don't have the nerve to buy a large dilapidated building or to borrow to buy a block of flats, I used another method of acquiring more properties than I could readily afford in cash, and that was to go into partnership with a friend who was of a similar turn of mind.

My friend had already employed this method, some years previously, of buying a place he could not afford on his own. He had his eye on a house which cost more than he could raise, and approached a friend of his to put in a proportion of the price with some spare funds he, the friend, had at the time. (This was, of course, how The Body Shop International started out. Anita and Gordon Roddick were quite unable to raise a bank loan to start their business, and in the end managed to borrow £4,000 from a friend. The rest is history.)

The whole thing with my friend and his co-purchaser was drawn up legally and some years later the property was sold for a handsome profit. Both my friend and his co-purchaser made a useful sum of money from the sale, and were well pleased with the result.

It was this method of property buying that Labour MP Peter Mandelson used with such disastrous and public results, when he borrowed over £350,000 from fellow socialist Geoffrey Robinson. Although, as Mandelson continually pointed out, he had 'done nothing wrong', in his case the whole thing smacked of naked capitalism and a desire to beat the system, rather than the socialism the two men supposedly espoused. Where my friend and I were concerned, however, nobody was likely to report us to the papers if we put our financial assets together in this way.

We sat down one night and worked out the figures. We discovered that if we joined forces, we could just afford two more cheap properties without having to resort to borrowing. We drew up a Deed of Covenant with a solicitor, and bought them. We set up a separate bank account to deal with money relating to these properties, and the enterprise, embarked on so tentatively and nervously a few years ago worked out.

The advantages of joining with a friend in this way are that you don't have to borrow money from a bank at punitive interest rates which has to be paid back, whatever, and you are both able to share the worry and the rewards. When things go wrong, it is not anything like so bad if you don't have to shoulder the whole burden yourself. There is also the distinct advantage that you can have another perspective on the property when buying, and so can make a more informed and objective decision. Where somebody else's money is at stake, you are less likely to make a purchase you later regret.

The friend with whom I have been buying properties has a good eye for building defects, which I do not possess. I, on the other hand, can look at a flat and visualize how it could look. He does not have this kind of imagination or colour sense. So, by buying together, we are doubling our expertise quotient. In fact, we are more than doubling it as the whole is often greater than the sum of the parts.

My friend and I have also discovered that we can save a lot of money on refurbishment by doing it together. My heart tends to sink when I contemplate redecorating a room by myself, and the prospect of getting out brushes, paints, newspapers, white spirit, ladders and so on fills me with despair. But if I am doing this same task with a friend, it can even be enjoyable. The other advantage is that with two of you working away, the time spent on redecoration is halved. Also, I find that I take more care when somebody else is involved. I paint more painstakingly, and try to do a much more professional job than I could probably be bothered to do entirely on my own.

Is it a good idea to join forces with your spouse or intimate partner? That depends on the kind of relationship you have. It can work, but in so many ways spouses are hardly considered separate people. To my mind, the situation works best in a relationship where not everything is joint, but where a certain amount of your life is kept separate from each other. If you're too close all the time, investment properties can easily become just another area of friction, and cause immense trouble to apportion fairly when and if you split up.

Of course, you must choose your co-investor wisely. It must be somebody who you can trust absolutely and about whom you have no misgivings. The friend should also be somebody who can put in an equal amount of time and effort. Otherwise, if one partner feels they are doing more than the other, resentment can set in.

Buying a property jointly with a friend can be the quickest way to ruin a beautiful friendship. But if it works, it can work wonderfully well. One reason that many immigrant Indians, for instance, have done so well in host countries is that they work together and stick together. Instead of borrowing money from a bank, they will try to borrow from family members or those within their own community. By keeping business transactions private, and by not using banks, they have been able to expand without paying crippling interest rates, or being ripped off by outsiders.

When everybody concerned has a stake in the enterprise, it is more likely to be successful than when you are using outsiders who don't care and who are only interested in their wages or repayment of the loan.

Being a multiple landlord can be a lonely business, especially when a tenant rings with a serious problem in the middle of the night (as they tend to do). But if you join up with somebody else equally enthusiastic, it can become exciting and challenging.

According to the Law of Property Act 1925, the maximum number of people who can buy a property together is four. The best way to secure the position legally is to draw up a Deed of Covenant with a solicitor whereby all the parties become Tenants in Common. The percentage of the purchase price provided by each partner is entered, and they own an equivalent share in the property. For instance, if one partner provided 75 per cent of the purchase price, he would have a 75 per cent share.

With a Tenancy in Common, there is provision for one partner to get out of the deal, should they wish to. If one partner wishes to sell his share, he must offer it to the other partner at the current market price, or find another partner. If another partner cannot be found, the property can be sold within three months. If one partner dies, the other share passes to the survivor, unless arrangements are made for somebody else to inherit that share.

If you do not have the full purchase price, you may be able to get a mortgage between you. NatWest, for instance, will lend on a maximum of three gross annual incomes. The amount borrowed can be up to three times the main income, and one times the second and third incomes. In some cases, two-and-a-half times the joint incomes of two people and one times the third may be allowed.

Whenever you are buying property with somebody else, whether a close friend or a business partner, the legal agreement must be drawn up very carefully. Even then, the arrangement can come to grief. Problems tend to arise when the property drops in value and partners risk losing their stake.

The friend with whom I bought several properties has now died, which brings us on to another very important matter when buying investment properties. As soon as you buy your first property, you must make a will, and then renew or add to the will with each new acquisition, stating very clearly what you want done with each property when you die.

If you have a portfolio of six or more properties, it may be worth creating a company, which can carry on trading after your death. A company can be set up for less than £400 online, but it does involve a lot of extra paperwork, and means you have to submit accurate accounts to Companies House every year.

In any case, all bank accounts are frozen on death until probate is granted, and the hideous prospect of Inheritance Tax means that properties may have to be sold to pay the IHT – which must be paid before anything can be sold. These days, almost anybody who has a Buy-to-Let property will have an estate large enough to attract IHT.

Working with agencies

Yet another way of becoming a multiple landlord is to contact a company that specializes in this type of investment property. A number of estate agents are now turning their attention towards this, and some have put together a very professional-looking package aimed at the investment landlord.

Hamptons International, for instance, have a dedicated Investment Lettings Consultancy, which will advise clients on every aspect of rental investment. They will, among other things, advise on suitable rental investment properties and prospective rental levels, report on tenant profiles and prepare rental investment appraisal reports. All at a cost, of course. They can also provide an independent rental investment service, and advise on newly built and newly refurbished properties and all aspects of design and specification of the development.

This type of service is aimed mostly at the big-time investment landlord with a lot of money to spare, rather than the person interested in just one or two properties. It is a sophisticated service for very professional landlords, but you never know – even the biggest landlords started off small.

Andrew Reeves Property Investments is a company specializing in acquiring and managing residential property portfolios for clients. Founder Andrew Reeves, a former accountant, believes it is better to borrow to buy three investment properties rather than buying one outright, as within five years you stand to make far more money by borrowing.

Against this, for the crucial five years you will have neither usable capital nor income as all rents will go on servicing the Buy-to-Let mortgage. Andrew Reeves points out: 'Assuming property prices go up 10 per cent per annum, if you buy one property outright with £80,000 capital, in five years you will have achieved capital growth of £39,178, or 49 per cent. Plus you will be getting a useful income over that time as well.

'But if you use that same capital to buy three properties, your net capital growth will be £117,534, or 147 per cent, in the same timescale.'

Of course, by the time you've paid the mortgage, letting and running costs, you can say goodbye to any income, as this will amount to no more than four pounds for each property.

Taking everything into account, Andrew Reeves, who was responsible for launching Buy-to-Let for ARLA, advises: 'If you absolutely need to get an immediate income from your property, then you should not consider borrowing. It is not easy to get a usable income from Buy-to-Let properties when you borrow.

'On the other hand, if you don't need the income and can tie the money up for five years, you will see a substantial return on your investment that nothing else can match.'

These calculations assume property will necessarily rise in value, but this cannot ever be guaranteed.

It is true that those who have long since paid off the mortgages on their own homes are often extremely reluctant to take on another one voluntarily, but you have to view it, says Reeves, as a mortgage on the investment property, not on your own home. Then, if disaster strikes, you can sell the rental properties without losing or risking your own home.

Becoming a portfolio landlord is a matter of jam today if you don't borrow, or jam, cream and butter in five years' time (with any luck) if you do.

Other things to bear in mind

If you are interested in becoming a multiple landlord, there are some other factors you should bear in mind.

Flats or houses?

One is to have a very clear idea indeed of the kind of property you are looking for, and how much you are prepared to spend on the purchase and renovation. Never let your heart rule your head.

Generally speaking, if one property in a block of flats lets well, then another property in that same block will also let well. For this reason, it is very common for portfolio landlords to buy up more than one property in the same block. Once you get to know a block and its ways, it can be a case of the devil you know. Against this, there is something to be said for not having all your eggs in one basket.

If you have all your properties in one block, any problems arising with the block can adversely affect your entire investment. One friend, who has three flats in the same building, found himself with a bill totalling £8,000 as his contribution to the exterior decoration. As he was unable to put the rents up any more, this amount made a severe dent in his profits. In fact, the £8,000 knocked them out altogether.

Another idea is to buy investment properties in a building where you are already resident. Then you have a greater interest in the place and benefit from any general improvements – unlike my friend above who paid out £8,000 on a property he did not occupy and in which he had no personal interest. A 'living flat' and a 'letting flat' in the same building can make good sense.

It's important to bear in mind, if buying leasehold properties in blocks, that few blocks seem to run well for any length of time. Also, the older the block, the more acute the problems are likely to be, as elderly blocks suffer a similar fate to all elderly institutions and people, in that they tend to get set in their ways and become resistant to change. Also, they start to become extremely decrepit and need expensive medication. The older the block, the more you are likely to have to fork out in repairs and renovation. And if it is a listed building, your problems are compounded, as you have to get listed building consent before embarking on any repair work. That can take ages.

It took over two years to get planning permission for essential repair work on a listed building I once owned. The council was quite happy to let the place go to rack and ruin, which it had been in the process of doing for very many years, but when it came to trying to improve it, this was a different matter altogether. If you do try to improve a listed building without consent, you can find yourself ordered to undo the good work and start again in the proper fashion. So, although listed buildings are attractive, they may not be the best places to build up a property portfolio.

Anything in a block of flats can change at any time. The freeholder may decide to sell, the managing agents may change, or there may be problems with long-standing debtors or planning permission.

In some ways, it may be better to concentrate on freehold houses. These do not attract the problems of blocks of flats, and of course there are no service charges, no overwhelming problems of maintenance and no risk of high extra charges from the freeholder or head lessee. In a block of flats, charges for lift maintenance alone can add up to several hundred pounds a year – for each resident.

Against this, it has to be remembered that houses on the whole let less well than small flats and tend to have longer void periods. On the plus side, houses are more likely than flats to increase in value, especially as with a flat you can run into problems when the lease starts to run down.

The rental return, percentage-wise, is usually greater on a flat than a house, and flats tend to be more secure than houses, especially in blocks where there is a resident porter. So, there are many pros and cons with, perhaps, no outstandingly 'best buys'.

If you are considering letting to students, it might make more sense to buy houses than flats, as students almost always want to share, and in a three-bedroom house a downstairs room can double up as an extra bedroom. Investors in student accommodation tend to buy new, rather than old, houses, as the new ones tend to need less maintenance. If you are interested in the student market, it is worth looking at new developments being built close to colleges and universities.

The student market, although large, is also specialized and needs very careful research. Students like to be near other students, so buy only where there is already much student accommodation. Most students will only pay full rent from the end of September to the end of June, so you may not get a full 12 months' rent. They may pay a summer retainer worth half the rent, at most.

The best properties for students are houses with lots of rooms of equal size. Through living rooms are not a good idea, as a separate dining room can become another bedroom. Also, nobody wants the tiny box room, so aim for houses with rooms of roughly equal size. All rooms used as bedrooms should be able to take a double bed.

The best time to start looking for student houses is just after Christmas, so you will be ready for the new academic term the following October.

Some agents believe that in the right areas, student lets can yield around 2 per cent more than conventional lets. But as with all popular investment products, the student market is rapidly becoming overheated, with a distinct danger of more eager parents buying houses for their student children than the market will stand.

Anybody seriously wishing to build up a property investment portfolio should probably go for a mixture of types of properties in much the same way that investors in stocks and shares are advised to build up a mixed portfolio.

Watch the market

A very important aspect, as with all investments, is to keep an eagle eye on the market. If you find you are getting long voids, or cannot seem to command the same rents as a few years ago, it may be time to consider cutting your losses and selling up. Don't think that, because it's property, it has to be on your books for all time. It may be that in order to acquire three or four properties that are a genuine bargain, you have to sell existing ones that, for you, have passed their 'let by' date. Always be prepared to do this, and never become sentimental over your existing properties, however attractive they may be. Properties, like anything else in life, can outlive their usefulness.

It is vital to become a friend of all the local estate agents. Get onto their mailing lists, tell them what you are looking for and keep reminding them that you are still looking. Otherwise, with many other people on their books, they will tend to forget about you. Professional property developers are always badgering estate agents, and you must start doing the same. Make sure they remember you, and know precisely what market you are in. Also, keep a close eye on the many property websites.

Many estate agents now advertise properties on the internet, so do get into the habit of checking the net daily, as very often properties are put on the net which are not advertised in brochures or windows.

House auctions are good places to look for bargains and, if you are a novice, get your hand in by attending a number of auctions before you intend to make an offer.

It goes without saying, or should do, that you should never buy any property or properties, however cheap and however much a bargain they seem, without first checking that they will let well. The nearer to shops and transport links, the better they will let – always. Properties right in the centre of town, where shops and facilities are, make the best rental propositions.

Two voices of experience

Here are views from two multiple landlords of very long standing. Jean, a friend who has let out several properties for many years, said: 'I've discovered that being a landlord doesn't really make you a lot of money. If you sold the flat and put the money in a building society, you would probably be making as much as you take in rent, by the time all expenses have been taken into account.'

But, she added: 'The huge plus is that the money you invest in property is going up in value all the time. To my mind, the gross yields quoted by agents and others trying to sell you investment schemes mean nothing whatever because if the roof collapses, that could be your year's yield completely wiped out. Having said that, property is a good investment as it goes up in value faster than anything else and is relatively low risk. If you just put the money into the building society your capital sum never increases, but the value of my flats is enormous compared to what it was when I bought them.

'I think that if you are to be a landlord, you must have a fairly tolerant outlook, and you have to be able to smile at the vagaries of tenants. I would also say that although I always use agents, you can never expect them to do everything or to be there all the time. Full management is hugely expensive and wipes out just about all your profit, so I never go for this option. In the end, something always comes down to you, especially when tenants ring you to ask you to come to change a light bulb. Tenants tend to contact you with the most trivial enquiries, and you have to be able to cope with them.'

Geoff, who owns a number of letting properties on the south coast, said: 'The more properties you have, the more lucrative the business becomes. If you have 400 properties, you are bound to make money. I think that in order for the business to be genuinely profitable, you need a great deal of properties. Otherwise, it's vital to take the possible capital increase into consideration. Properties bought on a short lease will almost certainly not increase in value, and it is difficult to make a killing on rents alone as so many things can go wrong.'

If you talk to estate agents, you will discover that very many of them are investment landlords themselves. One estate agent I know owns properties all over London. All of them are small one-bed flats or studios. Some agents have 20 or more properties they let out, and while they are showing you round a property, they may well be wondering whether they might be better off buying it themselves instead.

My hunch is that if estate agents, as true professionals in all aspects of the house business, are becoming investment landlords, there must be some advantage in it.

8 Buying and letting property abroad

It has long been a dream of many Britons to buy a place in the sun in which to rest and relax, and maybe retire. And a potent part of that dream can be the prospect of making the place pay for itself by letting it to others when you are not there yourself.

For most people, the starting point of buying a holiday villa in a favoured foreign spot is the experience of a blissful holiday there, or maybe several blissful holidays there. When you never want the holiday to end, you can fantasize about how wonderful it might be to return there at any time you like, to your very own villa or apartment, your very own place in the sun.

Beware!

Those who have actually turned their dream into reality warn that, although the perfect holiday may be the trigger to buying a home in the locality, your judgement, lulled by warm sunshine and local wine, may be temporarily clouded.

Buying a place in the sun can be rather like trying to make a holiday romance permanent. What works wonderfully well for two weeks, when you are relaxed, happy, stress-free and optimistic, may not look so good when you try to turn it into a lasting relationship. As with romantic holiday lovers, the defects of romantic holiday villas can soon start to show up once you realize that you are saddled with them year in, year out, and cannot just go home and forget about them once the heady excitement has worn off.

George East, author of *Home and Dry in France: A Year in Purgatory,* believes that many people start to suffer from what he calls 'French Property Brain Loss Syndrome'. His advice, based on his own bitter experience is: don't buy in the dark, or after you've been drinking.

But the brain-loss syndrome doesn't just happen in France. It can happen in any country where you have just had a wonderful holiday. You naturally want to hold on to the dream by making the temporary situation permanent. Some people even buy properties while they are on holiday, before it all fades away.

One friend went to Canada for a holiday and loved it so much that while she was there she bought a log cabin by a lake. That must be the impulse buy to beat all impulse buys, especially as whatever the reality eventually turns out to be, she will not be able to pop over at a minute's notice and keep an eye on it. And though it may be wonderful in summer, what will it be like in the middle of a typical Canadian winter, with snow up to the roof?

Although such gestures are romantic and make life exciting, it is most probably a good idea to wait until you're home and back to your normal routine before taking the plunge. Then ask yourself whether that wonderful holiday home is, in fact, such a good idea:

- Do you have the finances not just to buy the place, but to run it?

- How often would you actually use it? For two weeks, four weeks in a year, or more?

- For how many weeks in the year, realistically speaking, would it be let to paying customers?

- What about getting there? How cheap or expensive are the air fares or train fares? How much is petrol?

- What considerations have to be taken into account if you are interested in letting it out for part of the year?

- What, if any, is its letting potential?

Of course, the opening of the Channel Tunnel has made 'abroad' seem far less distant and intimidating than it used to be. When you can board a train at St Pancras and be painlessly deposited in the middle of Paris not long afterwards, with no fuss and no discomfort, the prospect of owning a holiday home in a country that can actually guarantee some sun becomes ever more appealing.

The main thing that tends to go wrong when buying property abroad is that you purchase a picturesque tumbledown farmhouse or chateau, say, only to discover that renovation is way beyond your means. Either that, or you get hopelessly bogged down in the bureaucracy of the country as you try to get planning permission and satisfy all the requirements of the building regulations in that area. It is all too easy to become entangled in the red tape of another country, and if you are not conversant with the laws, or do not speak the language fluently, you can end up in a hopeless impasse.

There can also be endless bills not anticipated when the property was bought in that first fine careless rapture. One former owner of a French holiday home said: 'We found we were sitting outside in the sun with a bottle of wine – paying bills.' In fact, some sound advice when contemplating buying *any* holiday home, wherever situated, is to add up all the costs you expect, and then double them. When I bought a holiday home, I estimated the yearly running costs (without letting the place) at £1,500, which I thought a generous estimate. In fact, the place costs over £3,000 a year to run, whether occupied or not. I had forgotten about council tax, the enormity of the water rates, the cost of transport, repair bills. Even something as apparently minor as replacing light bulbs in a second home can add up.

There is also the question of who looks after the place while you are not there. Some owners of holiday apartments outside the United Kingdom retain friendly locals to keep an eye on the place and make sure, for instance, that pipes do not freeze up in the winter. Some properties may need annual refurbishment to make them suitable for letting, so this has to be taken into account as well.

Buying to let

Estate agents are reporting that second-home buyers are now representing a considerable chunk of the Buy-to-Let market, and that this is increasing all the time. But what about the property you buy? Many people who have enthusiastically bought abroad have sobering tales of buying a wonderful-seeming flat or villa only to discover later that the block or estate had been built without the permission of the landowner, or was in a protected area. When this happens, for instance in Spain, the deed, the *escrita de compraventa*, is either non-existent or meaningless, and the entire investment is wiped out.

Because of the capital cost of buying a second home abroad, the possibility that you may not use it as much as anticipated, and the fact that bills don't go away simply because you are not there, you may wonder whether you can make the place pay for itself by letting it out to paying tenants, at least for part of the year.

In fact, such is the propensity for second-home owners to let their properties that in some countries it is actually assumed, if you are a British buyer of a holiday villa, that you will be letting it. One British owner of a Spanish villa said: 'The Spanish authorities assume that I will be letting my villa, even though in actual fact I don't.' This particular owner, who is retired, finds he spends at least six months of the year in Spain, and at the times when it would be a good letting proposition, he wants to be there himself. So, for the moment, he does not feel he can bear to let it, even though he might make some useful extra cash by doing so.

This certainly is yet another of the many problems besetting those who would buy a place in the sun. They buy with a view to letting the place out, and then discover that they can't bear to have strangers in when they are not there themselves.

In the main, though, owners of holiday homes abroad *do* want to let their property out to others. Or, even if they don't exactly *want* to let it, they often find they have to, simply so that they can afford to keep it on. So, if you buy with a view to letting, either temporarily or permanently, it is essential to make sure that you are buying in an area where you are actually allowed to let for profit.

Making your choice

Do your homework first. For instance, in some areas of France you may not be allowed to rent your home out as a holiday let. You may be classified as a 'professional' landlord if you are letting out property in certain areas, and under the French Planning Code you are not allowed to let out property in some places if you are deemed to be such a 'professional'.

It's a good idea, before signing on any dotted lines, to contact the tourist board of the relevant country, so that you can avoid falling foul of any restrictions well in advance. Estate agents in your chosen locality or country can also help you to decide on a property that has letting potential, as well as being a place that you want to inhabit yourself.

If you are interested in buying a property in another country with letting in mind, what factors should you consider? One very important aspect, according to Stephen Smith and Charles Parkinson, authors of *Letting French Property Successfully*, is that a place that appeals to you because it is beautiful, tumbledown and remote may not seem so attractive to paying tenants.

You must make sure that the place you buy has good rail and air links, and that potential tenants do not have horrific journeys to make before reaching their destination. There should be nearby shops and other facilities. Climate should also be taken into account, as places will not let easily when it's freezing cold, there are biting winds or other extremes of weather. It can be very cold in the winter in many European countries and this could mean either a lengthy void period or a lengthy period when you as the owner don't want to be there either.

The competition

It seems that when it comes to letting holiday properties abroad, there are often two stark choices to face:

1. If you buy a remote, hard-to-reach property you may find it difficult to let.
2. If you buy a property in an already popular tourist area you stand to face intense competition from other holiday apartments.

In the latter case, your property will be hard to let if it is vastly more expensive or less well equipped than similar holiday properties in the area. In extremely popular tourist areas, you will also face competition from international holiday companies that may be in a position to offer huge discounts on holiday packages.

An Englishman I met while on holiday in the South of France had bought an apartment in a holiday village some years previously. The idea was that he would live there for some months of the year, then let to holidaymakers at other times. In this way, he would have an ideal retirement, as he would be getting income from his apartment as well as having it for his own use, as he thought.

Theoretically this was fine. The only problem was that there were four or five big holiday companies also operating there, in intense competition with each other. While this was good news for the holidaymaker, as huge discounts were being offered on apartments, it meant that my new friend could make nothing whatever from letting his own property. In fact, he soon decided it was not worth the bother of even trying to let it, and so just kept it for his own use.

It was one reason, he realized with hindsight, why the apartment had been suspiciously cheap. There was just no money to be made from letting it out in the season, even though it was in a prime holiday spot. And out of season, nobody would want to be there anyway, as this place was suitable only for seaside holidays.

You must make sure that your apartment or villa is not inferior in any way to others in the same area. For instance, if all the villas in your area have private swimming pools, yours may not attract many paying customers if it is without one. But if you want to put in a swimming pool or make other structural alterations, you may have to get planning permission and satisfy the authorities that the planned construction conforms to local building regulations.

When thinking about letting property in another country, more or less the same considerations must be taken into account as when buying investment property in your own country. The numbers must add up, and at the end of the day you should not be out of pocket from your investment. The additional factor is that the market for holiday lets in popular tourist destinations is extremely competitive, and you may well be up against many properties that are very similar or even identical to your own, but much cheaper.

Local customs and practice

Don't forget also that you will be dealing with customs, laws and traditions that may be very different from those you are used to. If your property needs alterations or renovations (and these may be essential if you are to appeal to the lettings market), you will have to deal with French, Spanish or Italian workmen, for instance, who have their own methods of doing things, as we learnt when reading Peter Mayle's *A Year in Provence*. Then you have to ask yourself whether you will be on hand to supervise all refurbishment work. Most owners of property in other countries maintain that it is not a good idea to engage local workmen and then disappear for months on end while the builders work on their own initiative. So, large amounts of time have to be made available for supervision of the workforce if your property needs adaptation for letting purposes.

In most countries, public liability insurance is compulsory, and you may have to have fire insurance as well. If you are letting, your insurance may have to be extended to include third parties such as tenants temporarily staying in the place. Your insurance company must also be notified if you are using the property for holiday lettings.

With holiday lets in other countries, there is usually not the choice of letting furnished or unfurnished. A holiday apartment must be fully furnished and include linen, kitchen equipment, tea towels, crockery and cutlery.

Fitting out the property

As with letting properties in the United Kingdom, you can get away with any standard of furnishings, provided somebody is willing to pay you rent, if you let privately. But if you let through an agency, certain standards regarding equipment, fire and safety regulations and so on must be honoured, again in the same way as letting through agencies in the United Kingdom. In France, for instance, you may not be allowed to let on a commercial basis if the property or equipment falls below a certain standard. That said, in my experience the standards must be pretty low, as I have stayed in some truly terrible 'commercial' apartments in France that presumably met legal requirements.

If you want your property to be attractive to paying tenants, then the furniture and fittings should be of good quality and, above all, *comfortable*. In very cheap apartments, the beds tend to be uncomfortable and flimsy, and the utensils may be all but useless. In fact, the two commonest complaints concerning holiday apartments are the discomfort of the beds and the poor quality of the kitchen equipment. Another common complaint is the lack of easy chairs. Of course, beds, easy chairs and good-quality utensils are all expensive to provide, which is why they are frequently not found in cut-price apartments.

If the apartment is equipped too cheaply and nastily it may not encourage repeat bookings. Some experts advise not providing linen, as it is 'not unreasonable' to expect tenants to provide their own. Well, I don't know about you, but I don't want to travel to another country with my suitcase full of bed linen. I believe that it is absolutely essential for landlords to provide plenty of linen for tenants. The bed(s) should be already made up when visitors arrive, as they are often exhausted after their journey, and there should be at least one change of linen for each bed in the apartment.

In recent years, I have stayed in two holiday apartments in Spain and one in the South of France. Although all were in idyllic settings, in each apartment the beds were absolutely terrible, the cheapest possible sleeping arrangements, and the kitchen utensils so bad that I had to go to the local supermarket and buy knives, can openers and so on. Although the climate, the scenery and the ambience at each of these places were wonderful, the furniture in the apartments was so gimcrack that I would not want to book those particular places again. A fortnight of sleeping on a bed that kept coming apart and collapsing is an experience I do not wish to repeat. Also, the sheets were so skimpy that they would not tuck in the bed, with the result that each morning I woke up mummified, tightly wound up in a sheet that refused to stay in its proper place during the night.

If you are letting out a place which is essentially a holiday home for yourself as well, you also have to make sure that there are not too many personal items lying around. This is not so much for fear of burglaries, but simply because personal possessions tend to clutter up apartments so that the tenants have nowhere to put their own stuff.

The problem of how to have a holiday home that you can happily live in yourself at the same time as being lettable to others is not one that is easily solved, as in a home you naturally tend to collect favourite objects around you, and few people want to live in a completely sterile minimalist environment.

I have a holiday home that I originally bought with letting in mind, but almost imperceptibly it has filled up with personal objects, so much so that it is now unlettable unless a massive cull were made of the contents. Objects, paintings, ornaments have somehow appeared which now have no other home, and the bookcases are full of my books. The wardrobes have also filled up with my clothes and shoes, the bathroom has my toiletries in it and the kitchen is full of my spices, herbs, pasta, rice and so on. I soon realized that I could not keep the place in a permanently lettable condition as well as living in it myself, as to do so would severely truncate the quality of my life while I inhabited my own place.

But tenants will not be impressed by a lot of your personal objects being around, not just because these take up space, but because it makes the tenants feel like intruders, and uncomfortable. A place which is suitable for letting should look exactly like a hotel room: spotlessly clean, with a few bland pictures on the walls, maybe one or two books in the bookcases but with absolutely no personal items of any kind lying around. The kitchen should be completely clear of old herbs, spices and jars of salad dressing, tomato ketchup and so on, and there should be no personal papers in the place.

It is an effort to keep a holiday home in this condition, so if you want to let it as well as live in it yourself, you yourself may have to live in it like a tenant – in which case, much of the fun of having your own holiday apartment is lost.

Marketing your property

After you have satisfied all the building, insurance and maintenance regulations, and fitted out the property ready to let, the next matter to address is the marketing of your holiday property. You may, as in the United Kingdom, decide to use a specialist agency for this, and this will in a sense take care of your problems, provided that a reputable agency is prepared to take on your property. As with UK rented property, lettings agencies that handle foreign properties will not take you onto their books unless the property satisfies local regulations and conditions. Also, of course, they will take their percentage, although in high season they may be able to achieve a higher rent than you could do on your own.

Most lettings agencies in Europe require your written authority to let the property (as in the UK), and have their own standard form for you to sign. This is very similar to a short-let or holiday-let contract in the UK, although there may be some local differences, as there may be slightly different laws and regulations in the particular country.

There are of course many UK lettings agencies that handle foreign properties and usually there is a sliding scale of services and charges. Some offer a complete marketing and fully insured management service, while others simply find tenants for you but do not provide any local service in the country concerned. In this case, you will retain responsibility for cleaning, maintenance and repairs. A usual fee for a complete management service is 20 per cent, plus the local equivalent of VAT, as in the UK.

In most European countries, similar laws to those in the UK govern holiday lets. Those to whom you let on this basis must have a permanent home elsewhere, and the letting period must not extend beyond the 'official' holiday season. In most countries the property must be let purely for holiday purposes. Tenants are not allowed to carry on any kind of business in a property designated a holiday apartment. Otherwise, the standard terms are very similar to those found in the UK Assured Shorthold Tenancy agreement.

Should you wish to let your property to somebody for six months or so, then you have to enter into a different kind of agreement. An extended agreement of this kind must be drawn up by lawyers and usually has to be in the language of the country concerned. Otherwise, you may not be able to get your tenant out when you want to reclaim the property. There may also be difficulties over obtaining rent without a legally binding agreement.

If you are going it alone, proper marketing is extremely important. You can get your hand in by reading a publication such as *The Lady*, which advertises dozens of holiday properties to let every week. Advertising in newspapers and magazines can be expensive, though, and it may actually work out cheaper for you to use an agency.

The authors of *Letting French Property Successfully* advise that foreign advertising is risky for the inexperienced, and suggest instead contacting the English Tourist Board's offices in Europe. In any case, if you are very new to letting property in another country, it is probably safest and best to go through an agency, at least at first. If you find you are getting repeat bookings from the same people, you may decide you can go it alone without any problems. What you must never do is let your precious property to friends and hope for the best. As with letting property in the UK, proper, legally binding agreements detailing when and how the rent is to be paid, what is to happen to the deposit and what happens if a tenant refuses to pay rent or to leave the property when the agreed time is up must all be sorted out before you hand over the keys.

Never, ever allow yourself to take in friends who 'need a holiday' or who are in poor circumstances, just because you are lucky enough to own a property in another country.

The best way to market your overseas property is to have an explanatory, up-to-date and well-designed website which will give potential customers all the information they need. A photo is essential as well.

Increasingly, investors are buying offplan properties abroad purely to let out. These are people who are in it solely for the money and who do not ever intend to use the villas or apartments themselves. There are now many property seminars, many websites, which promise untold riches if you buy offplan in a foreign country. The fact is that you need to proceed with extreme care and ensure that there is a ready holiday rentals market that will cover your running costs and more. New and inexperienced landlords are being lured into this market with promised discounts, guaranteed rents and other incentives. Make sure you fully understand all the figures and legal requirements before entering this potential minefield.

One friend bought two offplan properties in Bulgaria only to be told a year later, when the next instalments were due, that the market had 'changed' and that the apparently guaranteed flood of holidaymakers and tourists was not guaranteed after all.

Finance

If you want to buy a holiday property in another country and do not have the ready cash, there are a number of ways of financing the purchase. In many European countries prices have not shot up as much as in the UK, and standard mortgage providers might well be prepared to lend you money to buy property in another country. You can take out a mortgage in the currency of the country concerned, where there may be lower interest rates. But, as with buying a property in the UK, interest rates and exchange rates can change, and monthly repayment costs can go up after you have bought.

Abbey, for instance, offers foreign currency mortgages to people buying properties in France and Italy, and loans in sterling for those interested in buying in Spain and Portugal. In order to secure one of these mortgages, you will have to provide at least 20 per cent of the purchase price.

You will also have to inform the mortgage provider if the property is going to be available for letting for at least some of the year. Some people may decide to buy a holiday home in another country for their future retirement, and in the meantime make it pay for itself through lettings. If the property is going to be available for letting for at least 140 days a year, and perhaps actually let for 70 days in the year, tax relief can be obtained on mortgage interest payments and other expenses related to the upkeep of the property. If you are looking to buy a holiday home for your future retirement, you can also avoid Capital Gains Tax through 'retirement relief'. If this is your plan, ask about this when you talk to your mortgage provider.

If you let out property in another country for profit, however small, you will of course be liable for tax, both in the UK and in the country where the property is situated. In France, for instance, a UK resident who lets out a property in France will have a UK liability to income tax under Schedule D, and will be entitled to credit against his UK tax bill for the French tax which he has paid on his French rental income.

Income from letting property must be declared to the authorities of the country concerned each year, even if neither the owner nor the tenant(s) of the property resides in the country. Under self-assessment or self-declaration rules, the onus is on the taxpayer, and not his letting or other agent, to make a complete and accurate return of profits and expenses from furnished lettings.

Many UK non-resident landlords do not declare their rental income to the local tax authorities, and although the country may take some time to catch up with you (or may never do so), there are penalties for non-declaration. In France, the tax office can assess up to three years in arrears, so you could be landed with a heavy tax bill plus interest, for trying to get away with it.

Of course, as with UK properties, there are very many deductions that can be taken into account with rental properties. Because the laws on taxation vary from country to country, it is worth discussing the situation with your accountant, or with somebody well versed in the tax situation of rental properties in other countries, before you make a decision on buying. If you have already retired, for instance, your tax position will in any case be very different from that of a working, or earning, person.

If the property being let out from time to time is your main residence, then you may be exempt from paying any tax on rental income. If the annual income is extremely small, again you may qualify for exemption. There will also be differences in the tax position according to whether you are treating the property as a business proposition or as a personal asset. This will normally be assessed on the amount of rental income achieved over a year.

Once you have declared your rental income in the country concerned and paid any taxes due, you must then declare your rental income to HM Revenue & Customs. You can claim a credit for tax paid to another country, and your total liability will be determined by your liability to UK income tax.

Before the 1995 Finance Act came into force, the UK Inland Revenue was reluctant to accept that the letting of a holiday home in another country qualified as a business for UK tax purposes. Therefore, there was no relief available for any interest on money borrowed to purchase the property. Section 41 of the Finance Act changed the whole basis of taxation of rental income from overseas properties. This income is still assessed under Schedule D, but now, income on one property may be relieved against losses on another, and interest relief is available as on any other genuine expense. For instance, relief may be available for interest on loans taken out to repair a non-UK property.

As this subject can be hugely complicated, and depend on your tax liability in the UK, it is best to discuss the matter with a financial expert so that the extent of any liability and the relief available are known in advance.

A few tips for buying overseas: always buy through a qualified and licensed agent. By law, agents in most European countries must be licensed, but if you buy through an unlicensed agent there may be no comeback if things go wrong.

Don't sign any document until you are sure you understand it; property buying can happen much more quickly in some countries than in the United Kingdom. Make sure you hire an English-speaking solicitor if you are not fluent in the language, as it's important to ensure that there are no debts attaching to the property and that planning regulations are in place.

9 Mostly for tenants

Although this guide is aimed mainly at prospective and actual landlords, we must not forget the tenant, who makes rental investments possible. Without paying tenants, the letting market would not exist, so landlords must do all they can to keep their tenants happy. So, this book ends with some advice and information aimed at tenants. Landlords will also find it useful as a checklist when contemplating renting out properties.

Very often, tenants and landlords are one and the same people, at different stages of their lives. Or even, sometimes, they are both landlord and tenant at the same time. It is not at all uncommon for owners to let out their own property at the same time as renting somewhere else. This can happen if you move to another part of the country, for instance, and for one reason or another do not wish to sell your home. One friend decided to rent out her flat in Brighton when she landed a job in London, and to rent, rather than buy, a property in London.

Another common situation is where an owner moves in with a partner, then rents out his or her own property while sharing costs with the partner. Most people will have had at least some experience of being both landlord and tenant, in much the same way that most adults will have had experience of being both child and parent. So, theoretically at least, people wishing to become landlords should be able to see the picture from the tenant's point of view as well as their own.

Who are the tenants and what do they want?

In a survey carried out by Leaders, the largest dedicated lettings agents in the UK with 16 branches, the following facts emerged:

- 71 per cent of today's tenants are aged under 30;

- 51 per cent of tenants are single, 26 per cent are living with a partner, 13 per cent are married and 9 per cent are divorced or separated;

- 78 per cent of today's renters have no children.

As to what modern tenants want, the most important factor by far was location: 72.5 per cent of those surveyed put location above every other consideration. Next on the list were quality fittings and fixtures (38 per cent), and about the same number (37 per cent) felt easy parking was important. Then 35 per cent wanted large rooms, and a good kitchen was seen as more important than a good bathroom, if they had to choose between the two. Less than 5 per cent were interested in a garage, and only 21 per cent felt that outside space was important.

The great majority of tenants viewed three or fewer properties before coming to a decision, indicating that most tenants quickly make up their mind. Around 35 per cent mentioned cheap rent, not surprisingly, but no further information emerged as to what constituted cheap rent.

As to why they chose to rent, most respondents said it was because they could not afford to buy a home. Some, though, liked the flexibility and lack of maintenance of renting, but mentioned as a negative consideration the fact they were not allowed to decorate and present the property as they choose.

A very real fear was that of not getting the deposit back, or being adversely affected by the bad credit history of previous tenants.

The inventory

If you are a tenant viewing prospective apartments, it is important to understand that the property, unless otherwise stated, is being let 'as seen'. You cannot demand a microwave, for instance, if one is not present or not listed on the inventory.

Generally speaking, items that are not included and not listed are not available to the tenant. If the place does not include an iron and ironing board, for instance, you cannot demand one, though there is nothing wrong with making a request, as the landlord might have spare equipment and utensils lying around for all you know.

If you wish to rent a fully furnished and fully equipped property, it is up to you as the tenant to make sure that linen, crockery and so on are included in the inventory. You cannot sign the inventory and then complain later that there was no duvet, for example. (As a landlord, I always keep a spare duvet and set of bed linen in my home for tenants' emergencies, but not all landlords do this and it cannot be expected.)

References

Once you have chosen the property that you are interested in renting, the next step is to provide the landlord or agent with satisfactory references. Most agencies require separate references from your bank, a previous landlord or agent and a personal reference, usually from an employer. Your agent will apply for these directly; you cannot supply them yourself, as they could be faked.

Some agencies use a credit reference agency for this purpose, and you as the tenant may be charged for this. Once the references have been checked and found to be satisfactory, they will be presented to the landlord. Don't forget that the landlord has the final say on whether or not he decides to accept you as a tenant, and there is not much you can do about it. If your prospective landlord has an aversion, based on previous negative experiences, of letting to somebody of your profession or appearance, you may be refused, even though you are otherwise a perfect tenant. There is little you can do about this. The property remains that of the landlord and he has a perfect right to refuse admission, with no reasons being given.

The tenancy agreement

Provided both you and the references are acceptable, the next step will be to draw up a tenancy agreement. You should read this through very thoroughly, including the small print.

Embedded in the document will be break clauses and renewal options. Do not sign unless you are happy – your signature means that you agree to the terms. Once it has been signed and witnessed it should be returned to the landlord or lettings agent. If an agent is being used, it is standard to ask for a holding deposit of £200 or so to secure the tenancy. This amount is deducted from the final amount you hand over.

Before the tenancy can commence, you will receive an invoice detailing all monies to be paid over before you can take possession. These will include:

- The initial rent, usually for one month or one quarter, depending on the terms of the agreement. For short lets of less than six months, you may be asked to pay the entire rent up front, as when booking a holiday.

- The deposit, which will be not less than one month's rent, and could be the equivalent of six weeks' rent. This deposit covers dilapidations, breaches of contract that may arise, and repairs. It cannot be used as rent payment during the tenancy, and is refundable in full at the end of the tenancy if there are no deductions. If you use the deposit as the last month's rent, the landlord could take you to court.

- The inventory contribution fee. Usually, unless the tenant is a company, the landlord will pay for the inventory.

- The credit reference fee, if applicable.

- The tenancy agreement fee. This is non-refundable should you, for any reason, decide not to proceed with the tenancy. Most agencies will only charge the tenants for the agreement if it deviates in important ways from the Assured Shorthold agreement, ie if the tenancy is for a short let, if it is a company let, or if the rent exceeds the current £25,000 per annum ceiling, which puts it outside the terms of the Assured Shorthold. This fee is usually around £100.

Before you move in, the deposit, initial rent and any other fees payable must have cleared into the landlord's or agent's bank. A standing order for subsequent payment of rent, directly payable to the landlord or agent, must also have been set up.

Moving in

On the day the tenancy commences, but not before, your landlord or his agent will check you into the property. Sometimes this check-in will be carried out by an independent inventory clerk. You will be asked to sign a document detailing the furniture and equipment and also the condition of the property. Factors such as missing tiles, stains on carpets and so on should be noted, in case of disputes later.

Once the check-in has been completed and you are satisfied as to the inventory contents, the keys will be handed over to you. Now the place is yours, until the tenancy agreement ends.

Meter readings will be taken at the check-in, and the landlord or agent will notify the companies concerned of the new account holder and make arrangements for the utilities to be changed into your name. From the day you move into your property you will be liable for all gas, electricity and water used and also any standing charges levied.

You will be responsible for organizing the telephone reconnection. Sometimes this is done by the inventory clerk or agent, but you remain responsible for all telephone use. All the landlord has to provide is a telephone point. There is no law that says a telephone itself has to be provided, although usually there is one. Even if the landlord or agent has contacted the telephone company, it is still up to you to contact them to confirm the start of your tenancy.

Now you're a tenant

You will, in most cases, be responsible for council tax. There may be exemptions where you are renting a bedsit in the owner's house, where you rent a flatlet that includes payment of council tax or where you are on a short let where the rent covers all bills. This tax is payable, though, on all self-contained properties. The local council will advise you of the tax band relevant to that particular property, and you will be liable to pay from the moment your tenancy commences. If you are a single occupier, there is a 25 per cent discount on the full charge.

It is the law that you must obtain a television licence to watch TV. Whatever you may personally think of the pros and cons of the licence fee, you cannot wriggle out of it unless you decide not to have a television. The TV licensing company comes down very hard on non-payers, and it has been estimated that a high proportion of women currently serving prison sentences are there for not having a TV licence.

Sky and satellite television

Nowadays most tenants would like to have Sky or satellite television. In these cases, it is up to the tenant to set it up and pay for it, not the landlord. First of all it is necessary to check whether dishes are allowed on the exterior of the property. In many cases they are not, as they are seen as unsightly. Most modern and newbuild properties will already have connections for satellite television, and where this is the case the tenant has to make arrangements for hire or purchase of the digital box, and pay the monthly rental for the chosen package.

It is the case, for some reason, that around 80 per cent of male tenants do want satellite television, but about nought per cent of female tenants. Even so, provision of Sky or satellite is something landlords should consider when buying a potential rental property.

Once you have moved in you are responsible for paying the rent in full and on time. Most tenancy agreements state that rent is due whether demanded or not, and it must be paid these days by standing order. Few landlords or agents will accept anything else. You should arrange for the funds to leave your account five days before the due date to ensure that they reach the landlord's or agent's account on time. Interest may legally be charged on late payment of rent.

The rent you pay is calculated as follows: monthly rent equals weekly rent times 52, divided by 12. A rent of £200 per week works out thus: £200 times 52 divided by 12 = £866.67. Rents are usually calculated 'pcm' – per calendar month.

While you are in occupation you are responsible for the upkeep and maintenance of the property. This may include replacing broken glass, changing fuses and light bulbs, and repairing any damage to appliances caused by misuse. You will also be responsible for keeping drains and guttering free from obstruction, airing and ventilating the property and taking steps to prevent pipes from freezing should you be absent during winter months. If there is a burglar alarm, it is your responsibility to ensure that it is set when you go out of the place. Should any problems arise, you must report these at once to your landlord or agent, so that they can be dealt with instantly. You are also responsible for the upkeep of the garden, unless the tenancy agreement states the contrary, and could be charged for replacement of neglected plants. Be careful of this one!

If you are sharing, you and the others have 'joint and several' responsibility. This means that should one tenant default, the others become responsible for any unpaid rent or bills. If one tenant causes damage, the other tenants are held jointly responsible. Because of this, any disputes involving sharing tenants must be sorted out by the tenants. It is not the landlord's or agent's responsibility to intervene in these matters.

If your property is managed and you do not have direct contact with the landlord, you should be provided with the name and details of the property manager at the check-in. The managing agent will normally also hold a set of keys. If the landlord is managing the property himself, the agents cannot enter into any communication with the tenant on maintenance issues.

All landlords complain of tenants who ring them up to say a light bulb needs changing. Before contacting the landlord or agent, it may be worth your while to see whether there is a simple solution to the apparent problem. Vacuum cleaners, for instance, should be checked for full bags and blockages. Boilers and heating arrangements should be checked to see whether the timers and thermostats are correctly set. Radiators may need bleeding occasionally. Washing machine filters need to be cleaned, and dishwashers must have salt kept topped up.

If you do need to contact the landlord or managing agent for more serious problems or repairs, necessary works should be carried out instantly. At weekends and holiday times – when most problems seem to occur – there may be some delay. If new parts have to be ordered, machines or appliances may not be working for a few days or a week. You are not allowed to withhold rent because an appliance is temporarily out of action and repairs have been held up because of a hard-to-obtain part or the inability of an engineer to come out immediately.

Landlords or their agents have legal permission to visit and inspect the property from time to time, so long as written notice is given. You do not have to be present at these inspections, which are carried out for the purpose of keeping the landlord up to date with the condition of the property, and noting whether any expenditure seems likely in the near future. Any damage for which you may be responsible will be drawn to your attention and could, in some cases, lead to termination of the tenancy agreement before the due date.

The landlord may or may not be covered by contents insurance but it is possible for you as the tenant to take out insurance to cover your own possessions. Most lettings agents can arrange this for you and it may be a good idea, especially if you have expensive computer equipment, for instance. Nothing of yours that goes missing from the property while you are in occupation is the responsibility of the landlord, nor does the landlord's insurance cover any accidental damage caused by the tenant.

In the case of unfurnished properties, it is up to the tenant to insure furniture and fixtures. Permission *must* be obtained from the landlord or agent before making minor alterations to the property such as putting up picture hooks or installing cable and satellite or shelves. This cannot be stressed too often, as these items are often the main cause of disputes over paying back the deposit.

Moving on

When you wish to terminate the tenancy, everything goes into reverse. You will be advised of a time when the check-out will take place and the meters read. Once the inventory check-out has been completed, you as the tenant are no longer allowed access to the premises, even if the tenancy has not been formally terminated.

As the tenant, it is your job to ensure that everything listed on the inventory is present and in the same condition as when you took the place. Allowances are usually made for reasonable wear and tear, although there may be disputes as to what constitutes 'reasonable'.

Tenants are responsible for cleaning the place and for making sure everything is as impeccable as can be. Some tenants arrange for cleaning companies to come in and clean the place professionally, as if it is not cleaned to the landlord's or agent's satisfaction, the cost of cleaning may be deducted from the deposit.

The cleaner and smarter the place at the end of the tenancy, the more quickly your deposit will be returned to you. If the whole thing has been handled by agents, you will probably not see your deposit for 10 working days after you have vacated the property. If dealing directly with the landlord, you may get your deposit back on handing over the keys, although some landlords still make you wait a week.

Make sure you leave a forwarding address with the agent or incoming tenant, so that post can be sent on to you.

Provided you stick to your side of the bargain and the landlord sticks to his, there should be no problems for either of you with the tenancy arrangement.

The Tenancy Deposit Protection Scheme

Make sure beforehand that you understand all the ramifications of the Tenancy Deposit Protection Scheme. To be on the safe side, sign up with an ARLA-registered agency, as these firms will know all about the scheme (you hope!) and will be able to answer any questions you may have.

If you sign up with a landlord privately, also make sure that your deposit is protected under either the Insurance or the Custodial scheme. Now that the scheme is up and running, the onus will be on tenants to leave the property in absolutely immaculate condition, and for this it is recommended that you use a professional cleaning company used to cleaning rental properties at the end of the tenancy, bearing in mind that by far the most common complaints from landlords concern the level of cleanliness of the place.

Remember that it is not compulsory for landlords to take a deposit, and that it is going to become ever more common for landlords or their agents to insist on having a guarantor, a house owner who will guarantee that the rent is paid on time, in full and that the place is left in good condition. In some cases, the guarantor will be used instead of a cash deposit, and in others, in addition. Some landlords are also now starting to take minimal deposits, of maybe £150, to avoid hassle with returning deposits and arguing over disputed amounts.

The Tenancy Deposit Protection Scheme was designed primarily to benefit tenants, to make sure wily or unscrupulous landlords do not hold deposits unfairly, and that any dispute can be settled quickly by an independent operator.

The TDPS was also designed to prevent tenants from with-holding the last month's rent in case they do not get their deposit back.

Remember also that many landlords and agencies want to see a previous landlord's letter as a reference for future tenancies, and troublesome tenants may find it difficult to rent another place.

For more information on the Tenancy Deposit Protection Scheme, go to: www.direct.gov.uk/en/TenancyDeposit/index.htm OR www.shelter.org.uk

10 Resources

Contacts

ARLA (the Association of Residential Letting Agents)
Maple House
53–55 Woodside Road
Amersham HP6 6AA
Tel: 01923 896555
Website: www.arla.co.uk

Provides details of Buy-to-Let schemes and the nearest ARLA member. ARLA also publishes a yearly Buy-to-Let guide, available free from ARLA agents.

Useful websites:
www.landlordzone.co.uk
www.lettingzone.com
www.studentlandlord.org.uk
www.landlordtenant.co.uk
www.studentaccommodation.com
www.courtservice/gov.uk/mcol (to recover debts online)
www.russwhitney.com (courses for property developers)
www.houseladder.co.uk
www.directgov.org.uk
www.assertahome.com
www.Homes2rent.net (this organization allows you to download an Assured Shorthold Tenancy form)
www.empro.co.uk (puts prospective landlords and developers in London in touch with long-term empty properties: a government initiative)

www.rpts.gov.uk (Residential Property Tribunal Services – again, a government scheme)

The Housing Corporation
www.housingcorp.gov.uk has useful and up-to-date information on social housing and housing associations.

The website of the Royal Institution of Chartered Surveyors (RICS; www.rics.org) has the latest information on average rents and property prices throughout the UK.

The Halifax and Nationwide have useful and interesting material on their websites, including interest rates, statistics and surveys. Put the names in a search engine to find the relevant sites.

Council of Mortgage Lenders (advice on Buy-to-Let mortgages)
Consumer line: 020 7440 2255

Tenancy Deposit Scheme
Information from:
www.communities.gov.uk/housing/renting and letting/private renting/tenancydepositprotection
www.shelter.org.uk
www.TenancyDepositSchemes.net
www.rla.org.uk
www.arla.co.uk/info/deposits_tenants.htm
www.tenantsdepositscheme.co.uk
www.depositprotection.com

Home Information Packs
www.homeinformationpacks.gov.uk
www.hipsdirect.com

Houses in Multiple Occupation
www.communities.gov.uk/hmo
www.landlordzone.co.uk/HMOs

HMO Solutions Ltd
Tel: 0131 622 2213
Website: www.hmosolutions.co.uk
(a commercial organization providing advice, surveys and information on licensing HMOs)

Northern Ireland:
Northern Ireland Housing Executive
Website: www.nihe.gov.uk/hmos

Energy Efficiency:
Energy Saving Trust
Website: www.est.org

Guide to the Housing Health and Safety Rating System (HHSRS)
Obtainable from:
2 The Courtyard
48 New North Road
Exeter EX4 4EP
Tel: 01392 423399

Notting Hill Housing Group (information on leasing to this group)
Landlord line: 0800 074 5999

Paragon Advance (advice on insurance and all aspects of property investment including an advance rental scheme)
4/5 The Briars
Waterberry Drive
Waterlooville
Hampshire PO7 7YH
Tel: 08700 723000
E-mail: mail@paragonadvance.com

Rent Before You Buy
(a scheme which enables tenants to buy their properties by
living in them while saving up the deposit)
Tel: 0845 189 7997
Website: www.rentb4ubuy.net

Property Investment Exchange
(a web-based company specializing in buying and selling
investment properties with the tenant in situ)
www.homeletipex.com

Up-to-date information on buy to let mortgages from:
www.moneyfacts.co.uk

Landlords' Property Insurance Scheme
Alan Boswell Insurance and Financial Services Group
Website: www.alanboswell.com

Property Search Company:
Amax Homes
Tel: 0870 770 8282
Website: www.amaxlettings.com

A Quick Sale
(buys and sells investment properties at below market value)
2 Waverley Street
York YO31 7QZ
Tel: 0800 32 88 239
Website: www.aquicksale.co.uk

Information on short lets from:

Foxtons
1 Camden Walk
London N1 8DY
Tel: 020 7704 5005
Fax: 020 7704 5001
E-mail: isln@foxtons.co.uk

Holiday Cottages:

Mulberry Cottages Ltd
The Granary
Bridge Street,
Wye, Ashford
Kent TN25 5ED
Tel: 01233 813087
Website: www.mulberrycottages.com

Information on rental investment packages from:

Hamptons International
168 Brompton Road
London SW3 1HW
Tel: 020 7589 8844
Fax: 020 7584 4365
E-mail: invlet@hamptons-int.com

Information on Buy-to-Let investment from:

Andrew Reeves
Website: www.andrewreeves.co.uk

General information on letting from:

Leaders
4th floor
Columbia House
Columbia Drive
Worthing BN13 3HD
Tel: 0845 345 4125
Website: www.leaders.co.uk

Information on Landlord Action:
Tel: 020 8906 3838
Website: www.landlordaction.com

Small landlord associations:

If you are new to letting, or just contemplating the possibility, it would certainly be worth getting in touch with your local small landlords' association through this organization. The National Federation has introduced a Certificate of Competence for landlords.

Residential Landlords' Associations
1 Roebuck Lane
Sale
Manchester M33 7SY

National Landlords Association
78 Tachbrook Street
London SW1V 2NA
Tel: 020 7828 2445
Website: www.landlords.org.uk

The National Federation of Residential Landlords
8 Wellington House
Camden Street
Portslade
East Sussex BN41 1DU
Tel: 01273 423295/0845 456 9313
Website: www.nfrl.co.uk

Small landlords associations are run mainly by volunteers, but some, such as the National Federation of Residential Landlords, have a small paid office staff. Most of these organizations now hold courses, meetings and seminars. Most also have a regular newsletter or magazine containing useful – even essential – new information on laws, regulations, government commissions and so on.

Seminars and workshops on property investment:

The London Landlord's Day
A free event held every year in central London, with stands, shows, seminars, workshops. Information: key in 'london-landlord' to download useful information about this event.

National Approved Letting Scheme
Tavistock House
5 Rodney Road
Cheltenham GL50 1HX
Tel: 01242 581712
E-mail: info@nalscheme.co.uk
Website: www.nalscheme.co.uk

Mini-kitchens
Space Savers (London) Ltd
222 Kentish Town Road
London NW5 2AD
Tel: 020 7485 3266
E-mail: enquiries@spacesavers.co.uk
Website: www.spacesavers.co.uk

Elfin Kitchens
Tel: 01376 501333
Website: www.elfinkitchens.co.uk

Furniture Packs for Landlords
Tel: 0845 466 0002
Website: www.niceinterior.co.uk

Oven Valeting Service
Tel: 0870 880 1222
Website: www.ovenu.co.uk

Information and help on landlord, tenant and leasehold disputes (this is a government organization):

Residential Property Tribunal Services
10 Alfred Place
London WC1E 7LR
Tel: 020 7446 7700
Helpline: 0845 600 3178
Website: www.rpts.gov.uk

Note: RPTS can also give help and advice on Housing Act disputes and interpretations.

Information on French property from:
Prettys Solicitors
Elm House
25 Elm Street
Ipswich IP1 2AD
Tel: 01473 232121
Fax: 01473 230002

It is now possible to buy property abroad through the internet:
www.europroperty.com
www.french-property.com
www.spanishproperty.com

Books:
Blake, Fanny (2001) *A Place in the Sun: Buying Your Dream Home Abroad*, Channel Four Books, London
Bray, Roger and Raitz, Vladimir (2001) *Flight to the Sun: The Story of the Holiday Revolution*, Continuum, New York
Church, Adam (2005) *Landlords' Letters – Plugging the Communication Gap Between Landlords and Tenants*, Lawpack Publishing, London
Hampshire, David (2007) *Buying a Home in Italy*, Survival Books, London
Hampshire, David (2007) *Buying a Home in Spain*, Survival Books, London

Hawes, Annie (2001) *Extra Virgin: Amongst the Olive Groves of Liguria*, Penguin, London

Mayle, Peter (1989) *A Year in Provence*, Hamish Hamilton

Mayle, Peter (1991) *Toujours Provence*, Hamish Hamilton

Smith, Stephen and Parkinson, Charles (2002) *Letting French Property Successfully*, Pannell Kerr Forster

St Aubin de Terán, Lisa (1995) *A Valley in Italy*, Penguin, London

Magazines:
French Property News (monthly)
Homes Overseas (monthly)

Exhibitions:
Homes Overseas Exhibitions
Information line: 020 7939 9852

FRANCE
French Property News
Website: www.french-property-news.com

Newbuild Properties
A Place in France
Tel: 023 9283 2949
Website: www.aplaceinfrance.com

Francophiles Ltd (mainly period properties)
Barker Chambers
Barker Road
Maidstone
Kent ME16 8SF
Tel: 01622 688165
E-mail: Fphiles@aol.com
Website: www.francophiles.com

Simmonds En France
PO Box 1737
Fordingbridge
Hants SP6 3NQ
Tel: 01425 653355
E-mail: simmonds@enfrance.co.uk
Website: www.enfrance.co.uk

Paris Property Options (for Paris apartments)
19 Warrior Gardens
St Leonards-on-Sea
East Sussex TN37 6EB
Tel: 01424 717281

SPAIN
Prestige Villas
The Spanish Property Centre
1 The Smithy
Church Road
Rainford
St Helens WA11 8HD
Tel: 01744 886258
Website: www.spainonshow.com

Atlas International
Atlas House
Station Road
Dorking
Surrey RH4 1EB
Tel: 01306 879899

World Class Homes
22 High Street
Wheathampstead
Hertfordshire AL4 8AA
Freefone: 0800 731 4713
Website: www.worldclasshomes.co.uk

One-stopspain
Website: www.one-stopspain.com

ITALY
Tuscany Now
International House
10–18 Vestry Street
London N1 7RE
Tel: 020 7684 8834
Website: www.tuscanynow.com

GREECE
Cybarco
Cybarco House
Dollis Mews, Dollis Park
London N3 1HH
Tel: 020 8371 9700
E-mail: achilleas.l@uk.cybarco.com
Website: www.cybarco.com

CYPRUS
Cybarco
Cybarco House
Dollis Mews, Dollis Park
London N3 1HH
Tel: 020 8371 9700
Website: www.cybarco.com

Cyprus Property Service
Mercia House
3 Brickhill Close
Blunham
Bedfordshire MK44 3NF
Tel: 01767 641564
E-mail: gaubery@lineone.net
Website: www.paphosproperty.com

PORTUGAL
World Class Homes
22 High Street
Wheathampstead
Hertfordshire AL4 8AA
Freefone: 0800 908 984
E-mail: info@worldclasshomes.co.uk
Website: www.worldclasshomes.co.uk

Property Search Portugal
Tel: 0800 052 3948
E-mail: psportugal@aol.com
Website: www.propertysearchportugal.com

UNITED STATES
The World of Florida
St Ethelbert House
Ryelands Street
Hereford HR4 0LA
Tel: 01432 265599
E-mail: homes@worldofflorida.co.uk
Website: www.worldofflorida.co.uk

American First Realty
Tel: 020 7624 8700
E-mail: Bob@a-f-realty.com
Website: www.a-f-realty.com

The Superior Real Estate Group Ltd
The Aztec Centre
Aztec West
Bristol BS32 4TD
Tel: 01454 203450
Website: www.4avilla.com

CANADA
Positive Realty Investments
Tel: 0 01 888 864 6818
Website: www.sellcanadianproperty.com

SOUTH AFRICA
Cluttons UK
Tel: 020 7403 3669 (UK), +27 214 258 989 (South Africa)
E-mail: Cluttons@africa.com

FPDSavills
Tel: 020 7824 9077
Website: www.fpdsavills.co.uk

Pam Golding International
Website: www.pamgolding.co.za

Sotheby's International Realty (UK)
Tel: 020 7598 1600
Website: www.sothebysrealty.com

Capsol for Cape Town Properties
Tel: +27 214 611 083

Rentals:

CROATIA
Information on Croatian Properties
Croatian Embassy
Tel: 020 7387 1790

www.holiday-rentals.com
Tel: 020 8743 5577

Timeshare:
Website: www.timeshare.org.uk/buy_web.html

The Holiday Property Bond
HPB House
Newmarket
Suffolk CB8 8EH
Tel: 01638 660066
Website: www.hpb.co.uk

Useful information on letting matters and other letting sites can be accessed via:

www.fish4homes.co.uk

Students can now find suitable accommodation through the following websites:

www.thelsv.com
www.studentlandlord.org.uk

Referencing agencies:

Taylor Trent Management
Tel: 01476 514695
Fax: 01476 514697

Provides a complete referencing package for landlords and agents, which includes credit referencing, previous landlord's comments, and bank and employer references.

Credit checks online: www.rentchecks.com

Publications

Ahuja, Ajay (2002) *The Buy-to-Let Bible*, Lawpack Publishing, London
Bartholomew, Catherine (2002) *The Fuel Rights Handbook,* Child Poverty Action Group, London

Fullerton, Fiona (2002) *Making Money from Your Property*, Piatkus, London

Henderson, Lesley (1999) *Tenant's Survival Guide*, Robert Hale, London

Randall, G (2004) *Housing Rights Guide*, Shelter, London

Segrave, Carrie (2002) *The London Property Guide 06/07*, Mitchell Beazley, London

Shepperson, Tessa (2002) *Do-it-Yourself: Residential Lettings*, Lawpack Guide, London

Wilde, Peter and Butt, Paul (2002) *The Which? Guide to Renting and Letting*, Consumers' Association, London

Zebedee, J, Ward, M and Lister, S (2007–08) *Guide to Housing Benefit and Council Tax*, Shelter, London – This popular guide has been going since 1982 and is updated yearly.

A useful leaflet on Capital Gains Tax, *CGT1*, is available from your local tax office. Other leaflets and booklets on housing matters are available from Shelter, 88 Old Street, London EC1V 9HU.

Housing: Key Facts
A series of downloadable, free publications on all aspects of housing such as letting rooms in your home, security of tenure, tenancy deposits and guides for landlords and tenants is available from the Departments of Communities and Local Government. Your local library should also have a selection of up-to-date publications from this government department.
Tel: 020 7944 4400
E-mail: contactus@communities.gov.uk
Website: www.communities.gov.uk

Leaflets on assured tenancies and gaining possession, aimed at both landlords and tenants, and produced by the Court Service, are available free from County Courts.

Property Investor News
(this magazine gives advice and information on all aspects of buying to let)
Tel: 020 8906 7772
Website: www.property-investor-news.com

Property Auction News
(this regular newsletter gives advice on buying at auction)
Streetwise Marketing
Riverside House, Claire Court
Rawmarsh Road
Rotherham
South Yorks S60 1RU
Tel: 01709 820033

Residential Property Investor
(a magazine published by the Residential Landlords' Association)
1 Roebuck Lane
Sale
Manchester M33 7SY
Tel: 0161 962 0010
E-mail: info@rla.u-net.com
Website: www.homes2rent.net

The Property Investor Show

Every year in September, a large Property Investor Show is held at ExCel in the London Docklands. Billed as 'the ultimate landlord resource', the show lasts for three days and gives all the latest information on investment opportunities. For more details, log on to: www.propertyinvestor.co.uk.

Index of advertisers